Chelsea School Research Centre Edition
Volume 6

Lincoln Allison (ed.)

Taking Sport Seriously

Meyer & Meyer Sport

Die Deutsche Bibliothek – CIP-Einheitsaufnahme

Taking sport seriously /
Lincoln Allison (ed.).
– Aachen : Meyer und Meyer, 1998
(Chelsea School Research Centre Edition ; Vol. 6)
ISBN 3-89124-479-7

© 1998 by Meyer & Meyer Verlag, Aachen,
Olten (CH), Vienna, Oxford, Québec,
Lansing/ Michigan, Adelaide,
Auckland, Johannesburg
Cover design: Walter J. Neumann, N & N Design-Studio, Aachen
Cover exposure: frw, Reiner Wahlen, Aachen
Typesetting: Myrene L. McFee
Printed by Firma Mennicken, Aachen
Printed in Germany
ISBN 3-89124-479-7

Contents

INTRODUCTION:
BUT DO THEY TAKE IT SERIOUSLY?

Lincoln Allison

Director of the Warwick Centre for the Study of Sport in Society
at Warwick University

It is no longer necessary, at the time of writing, as it was ten years ago, to justify the academic study of sport. Then we had to engage in what became over-familiar protestations about the sheer strength of feeling which sport stimulated, about its economic importance and about its effects and therefore on politics on what came to be known as "the feel good factor". Now, the figures are widely quoted that sport is the 22nd largest industry in the world, ranks 11th in the USA and sixth in the European Union (though all of these particular figures are constructed on different bases). Sport is bigger than steel, bigger than cement. We have an academic body of writing which demonstrates that sport is an important part of the way in which we form identities and allegiances and few people would seek to deny its importance in those respects. Equally, *most* people (though not all) interested in questions of masculinity and femininity in contemporary society would acknowledge sport as an important dimension of their investigation.

However, there are a number of distinct limits to the spread and influence of the serious academic study of sport. In empirical sociology and sociological theory it is given due weight; this is also true of cultural studies and social history. The legal and political aspects of sport are now much more thoroughly researched and theorised than they were a decade ago. But economic analysis of sport remains very limited and superficial. For example, the rapid rise to dominance in contemporary sport of commercial forces previously kept rigorously at bay, which I have described and discussed elsewhere, seems little discussed or understood[1]. Most sport has always been organised on an *amateur* basis; it has, literally, been a labour of love. To turn this labour and its relations

1

into a set of commercial transactions is a revolution with complex consequences. The transition in track and field athletics and Rugby Union has been huge and seems, to this author at least, to have destabilised the system of operation to a much greater degree than is widely realised. Among economists the most telling theory of what he called "the commercialisation effect" is to be found in the work of the late Fred Hirsch[2]. His theory of the advantages of amateurism, which is applied to those important aspects of human life, sex and charity, also applies to sport, though I have yet to see any proper development of it in that context. And it is not just a matter of sports which have made a spectacular transition from one set of norms and practices to another: even association football, described by Dunning later in this volume as "the jewel in the crown" of modern sport, has only recently shifted towards a fully commercial basis, exploiting its media-technical capacities, paying the consequently enormous wages, offering itself publicly to shareholders and so on.

Even the academic writing which does exist on sport seems to have depressingly little influence on that vastly greater body of print, sports journalism. Almost entirely, the revolutionary changes which are taking place are taken for granted and welcomed uncritically (just as the same journalists' predecessors uncritically accepted the often absurd practices of amateurism and limited commercialism which existed even ten years ago, both acceptances being in the name of realism). On the whole, journalistic writing is ignorant even of the (serious, academic) history of the sport it describes and assumes that the more money that is involved, the better off we all are. Perhaps they have inherited that grandly amateur assumption (to paraphrase Richard Holt later in this volume) that sport is too serious to be taken seriously.

What is happening in modern sport is a complex and contradictory syndrome of changes. It is first of all a commercial boom. The roots of this boom lie in the continuing process of economic growth and industrialisation, especially in Asia. The peasant who had little time for frivolous sports is replaced by the urban television viewer, interested in Manchester United and the Chicago Bulls. The full commercial exploitation of technology allows images to become genuinely global. The technology is not brand-new; its exploitation was in fact held back by the remaining bastions of amateurism, so that, in the Olympic movement, 1984 in Los Angeles is universally accepted as the first instance of taking the Olympics seriously in a commercial sense and the breakaway of the 'Premiership' in English football in 1992 is a smaller but parallel step which signals a gloves-off commercial approach by the most powerful clubs in the game. The limits are unknown; the talk (as so often in booms) is of a geometric increase in the game's income, especially from global digital television.

But this boom may collapse and, more interestingly, the collapse may occur because of contradictions at the heart of the system of commercial sport. Hoberman's account of the part played by drugs in modern sport places them clearly as the logical concomitant of a "performance principle" which when taken to extremes may give us a form of gladiator who lacks the heroism or nobility to make sport worthy of admiration (as we have always assumed it to be) or even sufficiently attractive to retain its commercial value. When the runners on the track line up, like so many racing cars, as fast-moving advertisements for the drug companies who engineered them, will we still want to watch? It is an open question. Hoberman is right to point out that it is not so obviously "cheating" to use drugs as it is portrayed in the anglophone press: we accept many similar practices; we accept the use of steroids for many purposes; not all cultures look in the same way upon what we regard as the proper limits of physical improvement. Even so, it is clear that some sports have begun to suffer already from an excess of the performance principle. The declining revenues of athletics have to do with drugs, race and greed, all issues covered in this volume, which culminated in the financial crisis of the British Athletics Federation in October 1997. They are also a little evident in American major sport, especially in baseball and football and even in the "jewel in the crown" it becomes apparent that only about half a dozen of the ninety two professional clubs in England can survive unsupported in a truly commercial world.

In other respects, the boom in sport seems to be out of kilter with important current trends in western society. The dominant masculinity of sport — which is undiminished in its more successful commercial forms like American major league sports, association football and heavyweight boxing — contradicts the more feminised and egalitarian norms which seem to prevail in societies which ironically, but constantly, refer to themselves as "politically correct", as having finally learned to take the values of the Enlightenment straight and undiluted. How do these values relate to watching the brutalities of a Mike Tyson? How do they relate to the misogyny of disappearing in one's leisure time to seek the all-male ambience of the cricket or rugby club? Dunning tackles these issues in a thoughtful essay in this collection — and also confesses, in a footnote, to having given up cricket for these reasons! But is sport, with its masculine vices and virtues, to be like prostitution in Victorian England, a kind of institutionalised hypocrisy, a naughtiness in an otherwise nice world? Or is it our reminder of fundamental truths — about the need for courage and strength and the over-arching importance of differences between men and women — in a world where "politically correct" attitudes are only ever superficial?

These essays are, at the very least, a collection about different aspects of contemporary sport by practitioners of several disciplines. Hoberman, a Germanist scholar, seems central to the changes in modern sport in tackling the concepts of performance and doping. Inglis' cry from the heart about the commercialisation of sport is in the language of cultural studies. One of the most interesting reflections on it is how sympathetic it seems to someone of a much more conservative disposition like this editor: the "left" traditions of which Inglis is so obviously a part are not so far from the traditionalists' suspicion of commercialism. Inglis is close to indicting even the concept of sport in its modern form for covering and distorting our concepts of games, play, joy and fun. Houlihan's piece on the globalisation of sport and on national responses also concerns some issues which are very central to understanding contemporary sport. Holt's description of the development of sports history and my own of the biological concept of race and the part sport has played in civil society (to *very* different degrees in different societies) are only slightly off-centre in terms of the essence of modern sport.

Perhaps the most interesting essay to analyse in terms of a cluster of core sporting issues is that of Roger Philpott on sport in the cinema. This is far from a peripheral subject because when he comes to analyse the values in the (predominantly American) output in what is, arguably, the most important artistic medium in the present age, he finds that personal and national identity are repeated themes, but also that a kind of nostalgia for innocent and amateur sport is at the heart of the way in which sport is presented on screen. Paradoxically, this turns out to be true of *Chariots of Fire*, a film which seems overtly to mock the amateur-elite ethos.

In short, I would claim that these diverse essays are really all about the same things, the meaning and condition of contemporary sport. And that these things cannot possibly be understood except in an inter-disciplinary way. To understand the growing economic importance of sport you must analyse power, nationalism and technology. To understand nationalism (and its opposite and relative, globalisation) you must understand history and culture. To understand culture you must look at books, films and sports clubs. It has been a tactical weakness of the study of sport that it cannot be compartmentalised even to the degree that the study of some economic and political phenomena are confined within a single "discipline" and certainly not within "physical education" or "leisure studies", but it is also a strength. We have acknowledged this in the establishment of the inter-disciplinary Warwick Centre for the Study of Sport in Society, a Centre intended to foster debate among scholars with a serious interest in sport irrespective of whether they were doing sporting "research" or not. I am pleased to say that all of the essays in this volume were first presented at the Centre, whether as lectures, seminar papers or theses.

Notes

1   Lincoln Allison (1993) 'The changing context of sporting life', in Lincoln Allison (ed), *The changing politics of sport*. Manchester: Manchester University Press, p. 1-14.

2   Fred Hirsch (1976) *Social limits to growth*. MA: Harvard University Press, pp. 71-116.

SPORT AND HISTORY:
BRITISH AND EUROPEAN TRADITIONS

Richard Holt

Visiting Professor of History
at the Universities of Leuven in Belgium and De Montfort in England

Sport in Britain, central as it has been to elite and to mass male culture, has not historically been a matter for governments. The very essence of British sport, so long associated with the idea of amateurism, embodied the principle of voluntarism and minimal state interference. The European practice whereby regional or national governments may subsidise not just sporting activity but also inquiry into its origins and development has not been our way. Major historical research into sport has tended to come via personal inclination and enthusiasm, which at first was perceived as marginal or even eccentric in more conventional historical circles. But it is from such individual oddities rather than from big projects sponsored by official bodies that the bulk of research has come. Considering this lack of formal support — there is still no national museum of sport, for example — there has been a remarkable advance. Comparing what little was published twenty or more years ago with the volume and quality of material currently available, a major transformation has taken place in sports history. There has been very ample coverage, too, of the contemporary politics and sociology of sport as well as of the wider field of leisure research past and present, all of which has had a bearing on the concepts employed and topics chosen[1].

Rather disappointingly, despite some excellent early work and prominent individual exceptions, physical education in Britain has not taken much part in sports history. The British approach to 'sport' has been to define it in the narrow sense of modern competitive games rather than general physical culture. This has pushed physical education and sport apart. Sports had higher status than gymnastics in a nation where Waterloo was fondly said to have been won on the

7

playing fields of Eton. We have no equivalent of the founding fathers of European physical culture like 'Turnvater' Jahn in Germany or Ling from Sweden, whose rival gymnastic methods historically dominated the continent. Physical education here developed late and on the fringes of academic life. Oxford and Cambridge, for example, still have no physical education or sports studies despite — or rather because of — the significance attached to playing college sport. The British amateur tradition has worked against the idea of *studying* sport. If 'war was too serious a business to be left to the generals', sport was too important for pedagogues or specialists. Physical culture as a discipline was marginalised in terms of the wider educational and social development of the nation. The British *played*, the Germans drilled; sport was supposed to be moral and spontaneous. To this day the term 'science' seems to strike the wrong note — although, increasingly, physical educators tend to see sport in such terms.

Of course, it is not just British physical education that has gone down the bio-mechanical and institutional path and, to be fair, things are now changing. But there still seems to be more known about athletes' thighs than about athletes, past or present; the imperative of victory has reduced sportsmen and women to bone and muscle with a bit of motivation thrown in for good measure. But there is more to sport than the physical or psychological mechanisms of successful competition or the training of teachers. Living in the tyranny of the immediate future has not been good for the intellectual health of 'sports science'. There has, for example, been little of major significance on the impact of physical culture since the appearance of W. David Smith's solid general survey, *Stretching their Bodies: the history of physical education* (London 1974), which grew out of an M.Phil. dissertation at the University of East Anglia supervised by a distinguished Scottish economic historian; despite excellent work on private education, there is still no proper history of sport in state schools. Bringing 'the professionals' on board is a prime requirement, especially if 'sport' is to be pursued as it should in the wider sense of physical culture, embracing traditional forms and gymnastics — and here the physical educators are ahead of the historians — as well as the team and individual games that Victorian Britain bequeathed to the world.

At least, there is now no lack of good material; and bright ideas abound. There is already a 'critical mass' of research on the sporting past for students to study not just here but throughout the western world; sports history can lay claim to being a sub-discipline — if such a category or status is meaningful. More importantly, problems have been defined and intellectual debate has proceeded, not in a vacuum but drawing on both mainstream social history and on social theory; historically, marxism of an undogmatic and empirical kind has been a presiding influence, although rather surprisingly there is no proper account of the advent of modern sport from this standpoint. Marx, after all, was a German philosopher. He was not culturally that well-attuned to his adopted country and not much interested in sport, despite the triumphal conjuncture of the pure competitive principle in economics and in play. Marxist analysis, it sometimes seems, has been too clever by half. For without seeking to be crudely determinist, it cannot be wholly coincidental that the free market came to capitalist maturity just as the new sports were organised and refined. Industrial capitalism may not have been a sufficient cause for the modernisation of sport, but was it a necessary one? The regulation of modern sports after all followed hard upon the Repeal of the Corn Laws. Or did the origins of modern sports lie elsewhere, as the current orthodoxy suggests, in a potent mixture of educational reform, evangelicalism and Darwinism? Marxism has taken the Gramscian path, concentrating not so much on the genesis of elite culture itself as on the ways 'hegemony' or moral authority was inculcated to the masses. Hence the middle classes remain something of a mystery and neo-Marxist accounts of the rise of sport tend to leave the reader unable to see the wood for the trees. This is intellectually important. For what is at stake here is the ideology and the practice of amateur-ism — a dominant feature not just of British sport but of British society as a whole, and one to which I will return.

The other members of the classic trinity of social theory are present, too, with important 'recent' additions such as Norbert Elias. Max Weber has had an unexpected new lease of life as the prophet of scientific rationality which Guttmann has argued is a key to understanding modern sport; and there is Durkheim whose concern about the tension between individualism and social cohesion has had a bearing on a wide range of work including my own. Sport, perhaps surprisingly, lends itself to serious theoretical analysis; seeming to have an 'essence', it can be neatly linked to one or other of the prevalent 'big ideas' of western society — a seductive approach but one contested by most historians and by other theorists such as Pierre Bourdieu and by postmodernists for whom 'meaning' tends to be in the eye of the beholder, elusive, multifarious and shifting.

For evidence of this intellectual vitality one has only to look at the products of the university presses; not just in the United Kingdom with Manchester,

Leicester, Oxford and Cambridge but in the United States with Illinois, Yale and others, and in France too at Lyon, Bordeaux, Paris and elsewhere. Amongst quality commercial publishers Blackwell, Routledge, Harvester and Cass have been prominent here. The European University at Florence has in recent years bought together historians, sociologists and others to discuss 'sport, culture and nationalism', hoping perhaps to find some basis for the idea of a 'People's Europe' in the legacy of a shared enthusiasm for sports, especially football. In France, despite the *Annales* tradition of economic and social history, there was very little on sport until recently; but now it is positively fashionable as a topic for a 'colloque'; in the last couple of years we have had socio-historical work on winter sports at Grenoble, municipal provision at Lyon, football in Nantes, international relations in Metz, Mediterranean sport in Montpellier, education and youth in Bordeaux and mythologies in Lille. There have been excellent collections of French research papers whilst in Germany the solid tradition of *'sportgeschichte'* — which unlike similar work in the UK has come largely from physical educators themselves — is now beginning to find a serious echo amongst mainstream social historians[2].

The vigour and variety of the European tradition in physical culture exposes some of our ethnocentric limitations; in particular the British have a tendency to see their sports as part of an inevitable evolution of play from lower to higher forms. History is written by the winners and in continental European sport football was the eventual winner. But this happened only after a long struggle unlike anything that happened in the UK. The Scandinavian and German literature has been careful to challenge the hegemony of 'sport' and in particular the work of Hennig Eichberg has been associated with expounding alternative historical uses of the body; looking at North America, the peculiarities of the British are no less striking as the mass of American and Canadian work — some of a very high standard — has revealed[3].

How then do the British stand in comparison? The immediate verdict would be that some good work has been done; the British Society for Sports History was founded a over decade ago and has prospered, publishing the proceedings of its conference annually. The *British Journal for Sports History*, which enlarged its scope to become *The International Journal of the History of Sport* in 1987, provides the main outlet for British material on sport. Physical Education has not had a journal devoted to sport despite there having been a Study Group in the History of Physical Education and Sport formed in 1975 within the History of

Education Society of Great Britain. The British were among the first into the subject, quickly producing some major books, but as the Eighties progressed the cumulative effect of a lack of funding for research students started to be felt. The 'old names' keep publishing but more new and younger ones are needed. Nevertheless, the faith of the founding father of the historical study of sport in Britain, Peter McIntosh, whose training as a classicist and philosopher combined fruitfully with an interest in the history of physical education and modern sports, has been more than amply justified[4]; he was, however, rather a lone figure. Despite a couple of useful masters theses on the rise of sport in Birmingham and Liverpool, little else of consequence was done[5].

Even today the published history of sport in Britain is patchy — a 'curate's egg' of a thing. What, then, are the big gaps? The lack of really good studies of sport in Manchester or Sheffield or other great industrial cities is striking. Where is our counterpart of the American tradition of urban sociology and history, which in the sports area has produced studies such as Steven Reiss's *City Games* on Chicago, Adelman's work on New York or Steven Hardy's *How Boston Played?*[6]. The only published city-based social history of British sport is good but rather special: Bill Murray's *The Old Firm* deals well with the sectarian side of football in Glasgow but makes no claim to give a full picture of sport in the city[7]. The best local work has been on smaller towns such as Stirling in Scotland where a historical demographer, Neil Tranter, applied his skills painstakingly to provide the first detailed account of who played what by comparing lists of teams in the local press with the census records. More of such doctoral level work is desperately needed; and more, too, of the kind of work done by Alan Metcalfe, who has written sensitively on the neglected sports of a specific occupational group — the traditional sports of the south Northumberland coalfield; but the regional capital, Newcastle, and the wider sporting traditions of Tyneside, remain largely unexplored[8].

Most remarkable is the neglect of London whose suburbs bristled with sports clubs, especially in the affluent leafy western parts, Richmond, Twickenham, Wimbledon and Teddington. But until John Lowerson's major survey of *Sport and the English Middle Classes* (1993) the manifest bourgeois enthusiasm for sport *post* public or private school was overlooked and is still not fully understood. Perhaps it is now the turn of the 'humble' accountant to be 'rescued from the enormous condescension of posterity'? For sports history partly grew out of a new social history fed by the boom in sociology, which tended to despise middle class culture in favour of recreating the lost world of the working class. With the exception of public school sport, the aversion of researchers to the bourgeoisie has meant that we have no general history of amateurism — a key and recurring concept. Hence we know rather more about English football than English 'rugger' where young foreign-based researchers seem to have taken the lead of late; more, too, is known about the populist world of Welsh rugby than the patrician traditions of the game in Scotland; tennis and golf as individual middle class sports are very thinly covered as, too, is swimming where the best work on Britain is in French[9].

Neglected too is everything that is not modern. With the exception of Denis Brailsford whose *Sport from Elizabeth to Anne* was published in 1969, there has been relatively little interest in medieval or early modern sport. We have no equivalent, for example, of the detailed reconstruction of renaissance play in France by Jean-Michel Mehl despite recent volumes covering medieval sport by Carter and a survey of pre-industrial sport by Hendricks[10]. The flowering of early modern historiography has not fed our knowledge of play despite interesting work on the place of sports in the theatre; the agenda laid out thirty years ago by Keith Thomas has not been followed through as far as sport is concerned[11]; at present what we know about sports in the seventeenth century is a fraction of what we know about many other social and cultural phenomena. Fashions in early modern history here contrast somewhat with North America where early colonial sports, especially the conflict between the puritan ethic and sports, have been more fully studied But there has been very little on the games and sports of England to match the famous collection of Joseph Strutt that appeared at the beginning of the nineteenth century apart from the work on folk football by Eric Dunning and Norbert Elias[12] which was expanded into a wider discussion of 'the civilising process' in a number of major works, notably *The Quest for Excitement*. Elias's magisterial survey of changing manners in *The Civilising Process* has the great virtue of linking early modern to later work in an apparently seamless pattern of cultural diffusion. However, perhaps too much attention has been paid to the brutal character of earlier sports resulting in what may be a rather simplistic idea of traditional games. From the perspective of 'The Civilising Process' — and I must skip over the theoretical difficulties of the concept — as well as from mainstream social history, what is needed is an historical ethnography of early modern play. Yet here the cupboard is bare and little progress seems to have been made since Malcolmson's *Popular*

Recreations and English Society, 1700—1850, which remains the key text although published in the early Seventies[13]. This was strongly influenced by E. P. Thompson as was Hugh Cunningham's perceptive linking of traditional and modern forms in *Leisure in the Industrial Revolution*; similarly Douglas Reid's important work on the decline of Saint Monday and Peter Bailey's study of *Leisure and Class in Victorian Britain* (using Bolton as a case study) have the Thompson stamp, focusing on the conflict between moral-reform from above and a self-creating popular culture below[14].

British work on sport, then, has tended to concentrate on class as a defining theme or on the development of a single activity at a national level, or on a combination of the two. Academic interest in the history of sport has come from those for whom the economic, social and ideological context of sport has been understandably more important than the nature and evolution of physical activity itself. Unlike in continental Europe, where the physical educationalists have been more active, the history of exercise and movement in Britain has not been taken far except by specialists in the relatively self-contained area of female sport and physical education. Even here the approach has been based upon the history of institutions — women's physical education colleges for Fletcher and private schools for young ladies in McCrone's work. A scholarly and creative article from C. M. Paratt, however, has pointed out possibilities for the use of magazine literature for the study of female sport outside of school[15]. In *Sporting Females*, a new and important synthesis, Jennifer Hargreaves brings together the idea of the construction of a female identity through defining what has been considered 'natural' and 'proper' for women with an awareness of the wider historical context. Female sport has been rather less constrained by national frameworks than other areas and Hargreaves joins the dominant figures in North American women's sport, Roberta Park and Patricia Vertinsky, in drawing freely on transatlantic comparisons. Gender is crucial — male and female — because it highlights the most basic premises. Sport as opposed to physical culture has been a supremely male domain, though this maleness has predictably not been much discussed in itself with the exception of the idea of middle class 'manliness' which fits well into the wider discussion of public school values by Mangan and others[16].

Forms of physical culture other than sport — traditional, gymnastic and recreational — tend to be forgotten as football, for example, has gone from strength to strength. These peculiarities of the British stand out when compared with continental Europe where sport was never as freely or fully accepted and cricket failed completely. Here the 'losers' have been gymnasts, exercise enthusiasts, cyclists, swimmers, skaters, walkers and so on. Sport has been well studied in its narrower sense of high performance male team competition but not in its broader sense of physical culture. Why is Britain out of step with work in Europe — ahead in some respects, such as the study of commercialisation and class structure, but behind in others? This brings us back to the uniqueness of British historical experience. Britain, as an island defended by naval power and without conscription or a large standing army, did not experience the same pressures to promote paramilitary youth training in schools and in the community that were a feature (in different ways) of France and Germany in the nineteenth century. Being a soldier was never part of our ideal of citizenship as it was in republican France. British sport developed separately from 'drill', which was restricted to elementary school children flapping their arms in asphalt play-grounds or in their classrooms — or so we think. Until the potentially rich source of school records has been explored the full story will remain untold. Similarly, the role of war in British sport has tended to be untold with the exception of statistical enthusiasts like Jack Rollin and a useful contribution on the sporting press during the First World War[17].

British sport and its historiography has revolved around the poles of the public school on the one hand and stadium on the other. Although sport in Britain constituted a training for the elite, it was not really considered a question for the state. So much so that when Hitler and Mussolini built up huge political sports systems, the British were bemused, only tentatively recognising sport as a political as well as a social fact. Recent work on sport and appeasement shows the Foreign Office moving slightly but significantly from the dominant ideology of non-interference by the Thirties to prevent a boycott of the Nazi Olympics and to support football matches arranged between England and Germany. There was a powerful public consensus against sport impinging on politics in the Thirties in the sense of avoiding giving offence despite what the Dictators were doing. This persisted into the post-war period despite the Cold War. As often happens, the immediate past can be the most remote, though Allison's recent collections on sport and politics provide a survey of Olympic politics, race and environment setting Britain in a rapidly changing world context; whilst the sheer pace of change makes contemporary sports history a peculiarly difficult business. Tony Mason's short introductory text fills a gap and can be read alongside his larger edited survey of the twentieth century based around essays on individual sports. Insidiously the political climate of sport has changed and what was anathema thirty years ago is now more acceptable. The debate over sporting links with South Africa gradually won round public opinion to the view that sport was not sacrosanct. But the history of this apparent shift in public attitudes remains to be fully explored[18].

Perhaps the most central issue in the contemporary history of British sport has been the crisis and collapse of amateurism. This is the story of the decline and fall of a class of gentleman amateurs who ruled most sporting activities, only reluctantly recognising and emancipating professionals in the 1960s and coming into conflict with the forces of commercialism and television. The defining moment here was surely the 'Packer Revolution' of 1977 followed by the commercialisation of athletics associated with the name of Andy Norman. The full significance of the media is only just emerging. Future historians may see the sale of the rights of live coverage of football to satellite tv as a turning point. There have been several good historically based studies of sport and the media in recent years, notably by Barnett and by Whannel, which fill out the picture first sketched in by Asa Briggs and expanded usefully by Wagg in his contemporary history of football[19]. However, there is still no proper history of either the sporting press or sport in the general press, which has been and remains the main source for most historical research.

It was not until the Physical Recreation Act of 1937 that some government funds started to find their way into what was a vast voluntary enterprise. Hence there are no significant state archives to study. Moreover, clubs and associations have often been careless of or secretive about their records. A statistical history is certainly desirable, but is it feasible? The student of British sport cannot go to departmental archives as in France and order up dossiers kept by the police and prefect on all sorts of local clubs including sport clubs. The 'freeborn Englishman' would not tolerate such interference, but as a consequence we lack data of the kind that has been a cornerstone of much of the best French research in recent years. However, we do now have a splendid bibliography of work on sport since 1800 compiled by Richard Cox, who has done a great service to all of us[20].

Centres for the study of sport should promote transfers of intellectual enthusiasm, temporary or permanent; for sport has the great advantage of being followed avidly by a wide variety of intellectually able people. One historian of football began as a student of strikes and another, Charles Korr, who has written so well on West Ham, started out on Cromwell's navy; and there have been students of Victorian ecclesiastical history like Bill Baker and of demography like Neil Tranter. Welsh rugby has been marvelously evoked jointly by a historian of seventeenth century science and by the biographer of Aneurin Bevan. Wales has its *Fields of Praise* but the border farmers and the Edinburgh bourgeoisie, who made up the strange alliance that was Scottish rugby await their historian[21]. Mandle's work on the Gaelic Athletic Association pointed up the anglocentric nature of much of the work in British sports history — a picture which is now starting to change with Bairner and Sugden's work on sport and nationalism in Northern Ireland and Grant Jarvie and Graham Walker's new collection on *Scottish Sport and the Making of the Nation*[22]. Surprisingly, there has been little regional work on England although a collection on Sport in the North of England edited by Jeff Hill and Jack Williams is in progress, and Geoffrey Moorhouse's *At the George and other essays on Rugby League* (1989) shows what can be done when a talented writer draws on personal memories to evoke a game so deeply identified with the north. A full social history of Rugby League, however, is yet another book waiting to be written.

Regionalism leads two ways: from cultural history on the one hand to historical geography on the other — an area closely linked with the name of John Bale and his pioneering work on regional patterns and sporting migration[23]. The places where we watch sport matter as part of the landscape of our collective affections — what the French like to call 'les lieux de memoire' — and deserve protection as much as other buildings or places. 'Topophilia', or the love of place, has been a further theme in Bale's extensive output. The monstrous sheds and clanking turnstiles that spoke not just of football matches seen and gone but of memories of youth, family, and friendship; and by this route back to social and perhaps to oral history, which is permits the historian to ask all the otherwise elusive questions such as 'What happened before and after a game?', 'Why did you join a certain club?', 'Who were your friends?', ' Did you meet your wife or husband through sport?', and so on. The possibilities of such an approach are just starting to be realised. As yet we have nothing quite like the work that French anthropologist Christian Bromberger has produced on Marseille. Ward and Allistair's study of Barnsley football in the early 1950s was an entrancing reminiscence and recently we have had Andrew Ward's collaboration with Rogan Taylor and John Williams to tell the history of football on *Three Sides of the Mersey* (1993)[24].

This points the way forward, balancing analysis and celebration, but taking care that entertainment value should not overshadow the deeper social purpose; there is always a danger that oral history ends up as nothing more than a few good stories, tales of eccentrics lovingly polished and passed on to the point that they could be studied in their own right as myths. The job of oral history should be to capture vividly material that is otherwise not available: for example, the dense network of contacts and kinship. This is what the French call 'the history of sociability' and poses a particularly difficult and important challenge. Just recently, perhaps partly with the loss of the old standing areas looming as a result of the Taylor Report, football fans have taken to setting down their experience of the terraces. Fanzines have finally given spectators a voice and books about obsessional devotion to a team, such as Nick Hornby's *Fever Pitch*, and other histories of crowd life of varying quality have started to appear[25].

For there is surely a large potential market for the product. Think of the number of clubs of all kinds who want a history. Club histories don't *have* to be bad history. The trouble is that 'writing history', as A. J. P. Taylor once remarked, 'is like W. C. Fields trying to juggle, it looks easy until you try to do it'. Having wrestled recently with the substantial archives of a single suburban golf club, I have some idea of the problems and possibilities of the genre. The influential French sociologist, Pierre Bourdieu, has encouraged his research students to do local empirical work; despite its complexities of expression and some over-theorised passages, this French work does show what can be done on a small canvas and British researchers should take note of it[26].

Critics of academic work on sport often complain that they are watching 'Hamlet without the Prince', that context becomes all and sport is seen only in terms of something outside of itself. This is the other side of the methodological coin whereby for so long sport was seen as something quite separate from society. Looking again at individuals can be illuminating in two related ways that fit particularly well into current trends in thinking in the humanities and social sciences. Firstly, there is the question of approach or method. The postmodernist shifting of interest away from 'big ideas' in favour of looking at images and the messages they carry — surely better use could be made of the visual evidence which abounds for sport. Historians need to take aesthetics and style seriously and try to make connections between the image of a performer and the wider audience. Secondly, the mainstream of current work in social history is moving away from documenting social classes and conflicts to looking at 'invented traditions' and 'imagined communities'. The complexities of culture and a new interest in the power of regional and national affiliations that cut across older ideas of class solidarity seem to be at the heart of new work in modern British social history. All this, of course, must be balanced by solid empirical work — otherwise we get nothing more than a dazzling kaleidoscope of impressions where anything can be construed to mean anything. Getting this balance right is an art not a science. Historians tend to see it in terms of the craft of writing. Put more schematically, it comes down to that interdependency of subject and object which social scientists explain in terms of structure and agency or context and performance. For sport, like dance, involves a fusion of the individual with the activity and frequently with the group. Man, to borrow from Marx, makes his own sports but not in conditions of his own making.

Take a concrete example. That cricket has embodied a certain kind of Englishness, mythologised by Cardus and others, is banal; nor is the importance of county loyalties anything new. Just think of the passionate allegiance to Yorkshire. And yet such feelings do not seem to have figured much in our social histories. What was this county consciousness, which surfaced so fiercely in 'The Roses Match' for instance? What is needed is an exploration of regional and national identity as mythology acknowledging the fact that these sentiments are in a sense culturally 'invented' but nonetheless real. Derek Birley's *The Willow Wand* addressed itself eloquently to this area, demythologising the 'Golden Age' of cricket whilst recognising that the idea itself was a sustaining element in the self-image of the English elite[27]. From the elegance and modesty of Hobbs, the southern craftsman, to the northern grit of his England opening partner, Herbert Sutcliffe, and on to Hutton and Compton, these men were more than cricketers. They groomed their hair and had their 'immaculate' flannels pressed to perfection. Rising from modest beginnings, they set up businesses and bought suburban houses; their accents changed as they ascended the social ladder, respectable 'professional' men in the wider as well as the narrower meaning of the term, models of social mobility for the skilled worker, clerk or shopkeeper[28].

If the full significance of cricketers to the English is not yet clear, how much less is known about footballers? Football as an organised spectacle is well-served with Mason's classic history of the origins of the modern game and Fishwick's useful volume on the period 1910—1950; but what of the players themselves[29]? Research in progress on revising *The Dictionary of National Biography* reveals 153 entries on nineteenth century sportsmen and not a single footballer is among them; the early playing pioneers of the world's largest game are simply not there; no Billy Meredith, for example, the great Welsh winger and star of Manchester City and Manchester United, the subject of a biography by John Harding, who more recently has also turned his attention to that marvelous figure of the Thirties, Alex James of Arsenal and Scotland[30]. We need more biographies informed both by the desire to celebrate a great performer and to understand the deeper social context of the performance. The essay form may be the best way to situate a Steve Bloomer or Dixie Dean, a Raich Carter or Wilf Mannion where a trunk of private papers in the attic is unlikely to be uncovered. Such men deserve historical essays as sensitive as a Tony Mason's recent tribute to Stanley Matthews or Dai Smith's elegy to Welsh boxers[31]. Bobby Charlton, that icon of decent Englishness, has somehow missed out; so, too, has his England partner Bobby Moore whose early death belatedly alerted the press and the public to the quietness, grace and the special ordinariness that has defined the English as opposed to celtic sporting hero. The same could hardly be said of George Best whose wayward brilliance and alcoholism was ideally suited to new reporting forms as written coverage of sport struggled to meet the challenge of television, as Critcher noted in a pioneering sociological essay on 'Football since the War'[32].

Not that the gentleman amateur is much better served. Knowledge of the founding fathers is still sketchy. Despite handsome volumes of memoirs, especially by or about cricketers, the collective biography of those who ran sport is still unclear. Were they gentlemen by birth, education or wealth? How can we hope to understand the full significance of amateurism in British life unless more is known about what happened to the athletic public schoolboys *beyond* the college walls? The Empire is the exception here and proper recognition should be given to Tony Mangan for such extensive scholarship and editing in this area[33]. Trying to get behind the 'ideology of athleticism', that Darwinian trumpet blast to the virtues of the British, to the more mundane realities of Victorian office work and rail commuting is no easy task. Pooter the sportsman is still something of a mystery. Was Victorian sport a middle class innovation reflecting dominant values of competitiveness and rational administration or more concerned with aristocratic notions of honour and chivalry as Mark Girourard suggested in *The Return to Camelot: chivalry and the English gentleman* (Yale, 1981)? Or an intriguing amalgamation of the two? Modern sport arose at precisely the same historical moment as Free Trade and Liberalism and embodied a similar ethic of orderly competitiveness meritocracy. Eisenberg has made a pioneering effort to compare the role of sport among the German and British middle classes and such comparative work is a good way of lifting the film of familiarity and seeing our predecessors afresh[34].

This could be done through a series of biographies. Is it not rather odd that the 'eminence grise' of late Victorian English sport, Charles Alcock, a key figure in the FA, secretary of Surrey CCC, stalwart of Royal Mid-Surrey Golf Club, Old Harrovian and proprietor of a sporting newspaper should be so little known? For those still alive, Michael Marshall has shown what an enthusiast can do in his 'conversations with cricketers' evoking the social conventions of the recent past[35]. In doing so, the nature of the social relationships merge into the qualities of the contest itself to give a glimpse of sport as something not just done but experienced; small moments that stay in the mind, 'spots of time' that give sport its heightened moments of beauty and of loss. Sports are after all aesthetic activities without an aesthetic; forms of movement that create a language of speed, power, precision and grace that approximate to art but which seem so often to defy language despite the best efforts of those in the appealing new area of sports literature emerging in the United States. This is a beauty that all too easily falls into the clichés of reportage, from the older forms with the 'leather spheroid' and 'the hapless custodian', with players 'rising like salmon' and 'turning on a sixpence', to their newer variants. Sportsmen and women themselves notoriously lack words to explain what they do, so getting sportsmen to talk seriously about 'what it was really like' in the way that Eamon Dunphy did for his time at Milwall offers a challenge to all those who care deeply about sports writing[36].

Dunphy wrote about failure and in doing so broke a taboo in a world obsessed with winners. What about the losers? Scottish football is littered with names like Vale of Leven, Cambuslang and Cowlairs (all founder members of the SFA that fell by the wayside). Abercorn, Armadale and Arthurlie begin Bob Crampsey's 'Glossary of Clubs Formerly in Membership of the Scottish Football League', which rolls on through Linthouse and Lochgelly, Mid-Annandale, Nithsdale Wanderers and Renton (the village club which flourished spectacularly in the 1880s to wither only ten years later), St. Bernards and Solway Star, culminating in the Third Lanark Rifle Volunteers, to give them their full name (formerly Cup winners and League champions who disappeared in the mid Sixties only a few years after scoring a hundred goals in a season)[37]. Other sports have other stories of glory and decline. But, to tell them, historians have to cross the line and become writers, perhaps entering into the psyche of the individual and his or her unhappy relationship with their sport: S. F. Barnes, for instance, probably the greatest bowler of all time, but unwilling to take his place in the 'First Class' game.

To conclude this review on the positive side — looking at what has rather than what has not been done — the influence of social and cultural studies as pioneered by Thompson, Williams and Hoggart is striking. Their work flowed into the already strong tradition of social history established by such different figures as Trevelyan, whose *English Social History* was very widely read, and the school of Labour History coming from the Webbs via Tawney and into the Marxist tradition which produced Hill and Hobsbawm, to mention only two of the most influential[38]. 'Social control', though not originally a Marxist concept, became a dominant theme in much of the work in the Seventies on popular culture running from music halls, to working men's clubs to sport. Viewed from the mainstream of the new Victorian social history this was no more than the expression of an emergent culture of 'respectability'; however, 'social control' carried with it from the neo Marxist point of view the idea of a 'hegemonic project'. Was sport part of a wider cultural process by which bourgeois values were spread? Did sport make workers submissive to hierarchy whilst imparting an unthinking acceptance of the competitive principle? Did it divide the skilled worker from his unskilled counterpart whilst at the same time providing a new set of values around which birth and wealth could unite? Such was in essence the view set forth in the first general history of modern British sport written by John Hargreaves[39]. Aside from the manifest dangers inherent in so strongly a theory-led approach, Hargreaves perhaps simply attempted too much, trying to summarise historical developments in one half and current sociology in the other half of a single volume. Sport is not a bloc; it needs to be broken down into different activities that have distinctive social structures: for instance, it is one thing to make out a case for cricket as passing on a 'hegemonic' message about the moral superiority of the 'gentlemen' and quite another to do the same for professional football.

Sport may defy social theory but not social investigation. Some of the most fruitful work has been done by those chafing at the restrictions of studying industrial workers through unions and strikes; sport gave a glimpse of a living culture. Here were new solidarities, new kinds of identities growing up around new kinds of games — team games that balanced group and individual effort, that imposed limits on levels of violence, that fitted new rhythms of work and leisure, time and space. Walvin's *The People's Game* was followed by Mason's authoritative early history of association football which set the standard, and a crop of books followed, most notably the work of Stephen Jones, an assiduous and prolific young researcher, whose central theme was the difficult relationship between organised labour and organised sport between the wars[40]. Jones, interestingly, began from a broadly Gramscian theoretical position but seemed to be retreating from such certainties in favour of a more nuanced quasi-ethnographic approach when his tragic death aged thirty stopped this work in its tracks; no-one as yet seems to have taken his place.

With Mason, Jones and others the social and political context of popular sport was taking shape whilst Wray Vamplew steadily revealed the underlying economic structure, showing that sports were not organised commercially as a kind of leisure business like the music hall. Here was an economic historian who not only explained the fragile career of the professional sportsman but also the less material benefits that accrued to those on county cricket committees and on the boards of professional football clubs in the form of local patronage and prestige[41]. Modern British spectator sport, unlike American baseball, was commercial but not capitalist. This was because the ruling amateur lobby rejected not just payment but the culture of gambling that accompanied it; not merely the reckless gaming of old but the modest betting of the working man, based less on luck than on judgement — first explored by Ross McKibbin and more recently by Mark Clapson[42]. Amateur values not only legislated against gambling but placed professionals in a kind of occupational quarantine, creating two sporting worlds — symbolised by the absolute distinction in cricket between 'gentlemen' and 'players', by the golf club 'pro' and the member, by rugby union and rugby league, and so on.

This idea of the 'two cultures' of British sport emerges clearly from the important research on elite sport from Mangan, Dunning and others which was published at around the same time as the work derived from the labour history tradition. Together these two streams made my own general survey possible and recently Braisford and Birley have added their own important contributions[43]. To this must be added the very substantial work coming from current sociology which has looked not only at gender and the media but most strikingly at violence. The dominant issue of the last decades has been football hooliganism; this social problem provided some funding — an unholy alliance of the Ends and academia — which amongst other things produced an effort to explore violent behaviour in earlier generations. The study of the Leicester local press around the turn of the century showed that there was indeed a good deal of verbal and individual violence at football matches unrecorded in the FA reports but not the collective antecedents of the hooligan sub-culture that has marked youth and football since the Sixties[44].

British sports history has by and large benefited from this diversity of approach. It could also benefit from more comparative work, looking at what has been done elsewhere and the different kinds of questions that can and have been asked of sport. Probably the biggest single failing not just in the study of sport but in social and historical work more generally is the restrictiveness of the national framework. Comparative studies are difficult but they can be very helpful and it is appropriate here to pay tribute to the remarkable efforts of Pierre Lanfranchi in bringing European historians of sport together. There is an urgent need to get those coming from the mainstream 'human sciences' to work with those in the various branches of physical education who at present tend to run along parallel lines with different conferences and journals.

Each nation has its own thematic agenda which in turn calls into question our own. The French have made much of the role of the Church in sport but despite some work on the early 'Muscular Christians' not much more is known about the dense network of Church clubs discovered, for example, in Jack Williams' study of cricket in Bolton[45]. Another dominant French theme has been 'sociability' coming from the work of historians like Agulthon on the spread of democratic ideas through village clubs after the French Revolution. Sociability makes the link between club histories and the major themes of individualism and social cohesion which have been explored in Pierre Arnaud's *Athletes de la Republique* and extensively in the major collections of articles he has edited[46]. We tend not to think this way and the webs of affiliation and friendship — a self-proclaimed feature of rugby union, for example, and more widely embedded in the myriad clubs and teams up and down the country — slip from view. Class solidarity has been our way of handling mass male participation in sports, which call for a closer look at age, masculinity, friendship as well as local and regional pride. Frankenburg's *A Village on the Border* deserves to be re-read as an unusual investigation of sport and community life[47].

Historians notoriously prefer their central ideas to be implicit, buried in the flow of narrative, achieving a kind of 'cumulative plausibility'. The social sciences have differed until very recently, demanding that concepts be made clear at the outset and facts marshalled accordingly. Yet there has been a convergence and this is gathering momentum. We have a social science that does not deny time, that wants to understand both change and the resistance to it. A 'cooler', less dogmatic sociology and political science can work alongside and combine with historians who should neither be afraid to consider social theory nor to criticise it, picking an idea where it seems to fit the evidence and dropping it where it does not. Why should 'eclecticism', providing it is informed and intelligent, be a dirty word?

Sport has come a long way as an academic subject. But the battle has not yet been won. A recent collection on *Myths of the English* did not examine sport despite having a cricket match on the cover, and the History Workshop's recent three-volume collection on British patriotism similarly omits what has been so powerful a vehicle of national identity within the British Isles; and there are other prominent examples of the surprising omission of sport in the latest historical work of the best quality[48]. If research does not keep going and result in high quality published work *both* in the mainstream and the specialist journals and presses the subject will wither and return to its former marginality and insignificance. 'Felicity consisteth in prospering not in having prospered', as Hobbes remarked — Thomas Hobbes, that is, not Jack Hobbs, whose graceful style and long contented life almost spanned the advent of amateurism to its end, and who for so many of the last generation seemed to embody what was best about the English and their sports.

Notes

[1] The main collections on leisure in Britain, often including sporting material, have been J. Walton and J. Walvin, *Leisure in Britain, 1780-1939* (Manchester 1983); R.D. Storch, *Popular Custom and Culture in Nineteenth Century England* (London 1982) and E. And S. Yeo, *Popular Culture and Class Conflict: 1590-1914* (Brighton 1981); this and other work has been usefully examined in P. Bailey, "Leisure and the historian: reviewing the first generation of leisure historiography", *Leisure Studies*, 8, 1989. To compare what was available even ten years ago with what we have now, see W. Baker's valuable bibliographical survey, "The State of British Sport History", *Journal of Sport History (JSH)*, 10, Spring 1983..

2   For an introduction in English to recent French work see R. Holt, "Ideology
    and Sociability: a review of new French research into the history of sport
    (1870-1914)", *International Journal of the History of Sport* (IJHS), 6, 3,
    Dec. 1989; A. Guttmann, "Recent work on European Sport History", *JSH*,
    10,1, Spring 1983 remains valuable, especially in conjunction with Baker on
    Britain; on Germany Guttmann can be supplemented with A. Kruger,
    "Puzzle Solving: German sport historiography of the Eighties", *JSH* 17,2
    Summer 1990; recent social history includes S. Gehrmann, *Fussball,*
    Vereine, Politik: zur sportgeschichte des Reviers 1900-1940 (Essen 1988),
    and a valuable survey of participation from Christiane Eisenberg, "Massen-
    sport in der Weimarer Republik: ein statistische uberblick", *Archiv fur*
    Socialgeschichte, 33, 1993.

3   The most up-to-date statement of Eichberg's critique and analysis of sport
    can be found in his special edition of The *International Review for the*
    Sociology of Sport, 29, 1994 devoted to the 'Narrative Sociology' of
    physical culture; on North America *The Canadian Journal of History of*
    Sport was the first closely followed by the NAASH *Journal of Sport*
    History now past its twentieth year; *Stadion*, the German journal of the
    history of sport and physical education began in 1975 covering classical and
    modern subjects with English and French contributions. In 1984 the
    Australian *Sporting Traditions* appeared as did *The British Journal of Sports*
    History which in 1987 became *The International Journal of the History of*
    Sport (IJHS). In addition, there were several collections of proceedings
    published by HISPA which is now known under the new name of ISHPES
    (International Society for the History of Physical Education and Sport).

4   P.C. McIntosh, *Physical Education in England since 1800* (London 1968
    ed); also *Sport in Society* (London 1963)..

5   D.D. Molyneux, *The Development of Physical Recreation in the Birming-*
    ham District, 1871-1892 (MA Univ. of Birmingham 1957); R. Rees, *The*
    Development of Physical Recreation in Liverpool in C19 (MA Liverpool
    Univ. 1968); more recently P. Bilsborough, *The Development of sport in*
    Glasgow, 1850-1914 (Stirling University; 1983)..

6   S. Reiss, *City Games: the evolution of American urban society and sports*
    (Univ. Illinois 1989); M. Adelman, *A Sporting Time, New York and the rise*
    of modern athletics (Univ. Illinois 1990); S. Hardy, *How Boston Played:*
    sport, recreation and community, 1865-1915 (North Eastern UP 1982) are
    the best examples of this.

7 Bill Murray, *The Old Firm: Sectarianism, Sport and Society in Scotland* (Edinburgh 1984).

8 Tranter's unique research has appeared in article form: see for example *IJHS* 4,3 Dec. 1987 and 6, 1 May 1989; A. Metcalfe's "Organised sport in the mining communities of south Northumberland, 1880-1889", *Victorian Studies*, Summer 1982.

9 The lack of good historical work on English and Scottish rugby is striking with the exception of E. Dunning and K. Sheard, *Barbarians, Gentlemen and Players: a sociological study of the development of Rugby* (Oxford 1979); recent additions, however, have come from a doctoral thesis from Manitoba by J.W. Martens: "To throttle the Hydra: the middle class and rugby's great schism", *Canadian Journal of the History of Sport*, XXII, 1, May 1991; and "They stooped to conquer: rugby union football, 1895-1914", *JSH*, 20,1, Spring 1993; another North American dissertation in article form is D. L. Andrews, "Welsh indigenous! British imperial? Welsh rugby, culture and society, 1890-1914", *JSH*, 18, 3 Winter 1991; finally J. Nauright continues the theme of the anxiety over race deterioration as expressed in Edwardian rugby in "Sport, Manhood and the Empire: British responses to the New Zealand rugby tour of 1905", *IJHS*, 8, 2, Spring 1991, see also note 21; on British swimming, see a recent French doctoral thesis by T. Terret, *Les defis du bain*, Universite de Lyon I, 1992; there are no full academic histories of either tennis or golf in Britain, but John Lowerson, *Sport and the English Middle Classes 1870-1914* (Manchester 1993) is a very significant recent contribution.

10 J-M Mehl, *Les jeux au royaume de France* (PU de Strasbourg 1989), J.M. Carter, *Medieval Games, Sports and Recreations in Feudal Society* (New York 1992); T.S. Hendricks, *Disputed Pleasures: sport and society in preindustrial England* (New York 1991).

11 M.McElroy & K. Cartwright, "Public fencing contests on the Elizabethan stage", *JSH*, 13, 2, Winter 1986; M. McElroy, "Organised sporting contests in the early English professional theatre", *Canadian Journal of the History of Sport*, XXI, 1, May 1990 show what innovative use of the history of drama can do; Keith Thomas, "Work and Leisure in Pre-Industrial Society", *Past and Present*, 29, Dec. 1964.

12 N. Elias and E. Dunning, "Folk football in Medieval and Early Modern Britain", in E. Dunning (ed), *The Sociology of Sport: a selection of readings* (London 1971) — an early collection offering a wide range of interpretations of sport.

13 R.W. Malcolmson, *Popular Recreations in English Society 1700-1850* (Cambridge 1973).

14 H. Cunningham, *Leisure in the Industrial Revolution* (London 1980); R.A. Reid, "The Decline of Saint Monday, 1766-1876", *Past and Present*, 71, May 1976.

15 S. Fletcher, *Women First: The Female Tradition in English Physical Education 1880-1980* (London 1984); K.E. McKrone, *Sport and the Physical Emancipation of English Women* (London 1988); C.M. Parratt, Athletic 'Womanhood': exploring sources for female sport in Victorian and Edwardian England, *JSH*, 16, 2, Spring 1989.

16 J. Hargreaves, *Sporting Females: critical issues in the history and sociology of women's sports* (London 1994); The collection edited by J. A. Mangan and R. J. Park, *From Fair Sex to Feminism: sport and the socialisation of women in industrial and post-industrial eras* (London 1987) has also been influential, and this was usefully followed by J. A. Mangan and J. Walvin, *Manliness and Morality, middle class masculinity in Britain and America, 1800-1940* (Manchester 1989).

17 Jack Rollin, *Soccer at War* (London 1985); J. M. Osborne, "To keep the life of the nation on the right lines, the Athletic News and the First World War", *JSH*, 14, 2, Summer 1987.

18 British involvement in the Nazi Olympics is discussed in Duff Hart Davis, *Hitler's Games: the 1936 Olympics* (London 1986) and in B. Stoddart, "Sport, Cultural Politics and International Relations: England versus Germany 1935", in N. Muller and J. Ruhl, *Proceedings of the Olympic Scientific Congress, 1984* (Niederhausern 1985), and in R. Holt and T. Mason, "Le football, le fascisme et la politique etrangere Brittanique", in *Sports et relations internationales,* rapport final, CNRS 1993 (forthcoming in English in J. Riordan, (ed) *Sport and International Relations between the wars,* (Manchester, forthcoming). On contemporary history see Lincoln Allison (ed), *The Politics of Sport* (Manchester 1986) and *The Changing Politics of Sport* (Manchester 1993); Tony Mason, *Sport in Britain* (Faber London 1988) and Tony Mason, (ed) *Sport in Britain: a social history* (Cambridge 1989) which has some excellent photos; R. Holt, *Sport and the British: a modern history* (Oxford 1989) offers a lengthy postscript on the post war era but is mainly concerned with the late Victorian and Edwardian years.

19 A. Briggs, *A History of Broadcasting*, vols. ii, iv (Oxford 1965, 1979); S. Wagg, *The Football World: a contemporary social history* (Brighton 1984); S. Barnett, *Games and Sets: the changing face of sport on television*

(London 1991); G. Whannel, *Fields of Vision: television, sport and cultural transformation* (London 1992).

20 R. W. Cox, *Sport in Britain: a bibliography of historical publications 1800 — 1988* (Manchester 1991).

21 D. Smith and G. Williams, *Fields of Praise: the official history of the Welsh Rugby Union 1881-1981* (Cardiff 1980).

22 A. Bairner and J. Sugden, *Sport, Sectarianism and Society in a Divided Ireland* (Leicester UP 1993); Grant Jarvie, *Highland Games: the making of a myth* (Edinburgh 1991), and with G. Walker (eds), *Scottish Sport and the Making of the Nation* (Leicester 1994).

23 J. Bale, *Sport and Place: a geography of sport in England, Scotland and Wales* (London 1982) and a wide range of more recent work including "Racing towards Modernity", *IJHS*, 10, 2, Aug. 1993.

24 C. Bromberger, "La passion du football a Marseille et Turin", *Terrain: carnets du patrimoine ethnologique*, no. 8; A. Ward and I. Allister, *Barnsley: a study in football* (Barton-under Needwood, Staffs 1981).

25 N. Hornby, *Fever Pitch, a fan's life* (London 1992); also S. Kelly, *The Kop: the end of an era* (London 1993); for a longer perspective see R. Taylor, *Football and its fans: supporters and their relations with the game 1885-1985* (Leicester 1992).

26 See, for example, *Actes de Recherche en Science Sociales*, 79, Sept. 1989 and 80, Nov. 1989.

27 D. Birley, *The Willow Wand: some cricket myths explored* (London 1989 ed. with 'afterword').

28 R. Mason, *Jack Hobbs, a biography* (London 1960); J. Arlott, *Jack Hobbs: Profile of the Master* (London 1979); G. Howat, *Len Hutton, the biography* (London 1988) has useful social background as does A. Hill, *Herbert Sutcliffe: cricket maestro* (London 1991).

29 Tony Mason, *Association Football and English Society, 1863-1915* (Brighton 1980); N. Fishwick, *Association Football and English Social Life, 1910-1950* (Manchester 1989).

30 J. Harding, *Football Wizard: the story of Billy Meredith* (Derby 1985) and *Alex James: the life of a football legend* (London 1989) 31 See essays by T. Mason, H. F. Moorhouse and D. Smith in R. Holt (ed.) *Sport and the Working Class in Modern Britain* (Manchester 1990).

32 C. Critcher, "Football since the War", in J. Clarke, C. Critcher and R. Johnston (eds), *Working Class Culture: studies in history and theory* (London 1979).

33 J. A. Mangan, *Athleticism in the Victorian and Edwardian Public School* (Cambridge 1981) was followed by his *The Games Ethic and Imperialism* (London 1986); taken together with his work as editor of *Pleasure, Profit and Proselytism: British Culture and Sport at Home and Abroad 1700-1914* (London 1988) and *The Cultural Bond: Sport, Empire and Society* (London 1992) and other collections, the place of sport in imperialism has been more thoroughly explored than for any other nation. This is an impressive achievement.

34 R. Holt, "Amateurism and its interpretation: the social origins of British sport", *Innovation*, 5,4, 1992; C. Eisenberg, "The Middle Class and Competition: some considerations on the beginnings of modern sport in England and Germany", *IJHS*, 7, 2, Sept. 1990.

35 M. Marshall, *Gentlemen and Players: conversations with cricketers* (London 1987).

36 E. Dunphy, *Only a Game? The Diary of a Professional Footballer* (London 1976).

37 Bob Crampsey, *The Scottish Football League: the first 100 years* (Glasgow 1990).

38 See note 1; 'social control' arguments are critically examined in F. M. L Thompson, *The Rise of Respectable Society* (London 1987).

39 J. Hargreaves, *Sport, Power and Culture: a social and historical analysis of popular sports in Britain* (Oxford 1986).

40 S.G. Jones, *Workers at Play: a social and economic history of leisure, 1918-1939* (London 1986); and especially *Sport, politics and the working class: organised labour and sport in interwar Britain* (Manchester 1988); J. Walvin, *The People's Game* (London 1975); Mason, *Association Football*, op. cit.

41 Wray Vamplew, *Pay Up, Pay Up and Play the Game: professional sport in Britain 1875-1914* (Cambridge 1989).

42 R. McKibbin, "Working Class Gambling in Britain, 1880-1939", *Past and Present*, 82, 1979; M. Clapson, *A Bit of a Flutter, popular gambling and English Society, c. 1823-1961* (Manchester 1992).

[43] D. Brailsford, *Sport, Time and Society: the British at Play* (London 1991) and his shorter *British Sport: a social history* (London 1992); D. Birley, *Sport and the Making of Modern Britain* (Manchester 1993) which is largely devoted to the Victorian years, making a particularly useful contribution to the debate over amateurism.

[44] E. Dunning, P. Murphy and J. Williams, *The Roots of Football Hooliganism: an historical and sociological study* (London 1988); for a survey of recent literature see J. Williams and S. Wagg, *British Football and Social Change: getting into Europe* (Leicester 1991).

[45] J. Williams, Recreational cricket in Bolton between the wars, in Holt (ed), *op. cit.*

[46] P. Arnaud, *Le militaire, l'ecolier, le gymnaste: naissance de l'education physique en France 1869-1889* (Lyon UP 1991); also P. Arnaud and J. Camy (eds.), *La naissance du mouvement sportif associatif en France,* (Lyon UP 1986), and P.Arnaud (ed); *Les athletes de la Republique: gymnastique, sport et ideologie republicaine 1870-1914* (Privat, Toulouse 1987); see also note 2.

[47] R. Frankenberg, *A Village on the Border: a study of religion, politics and football in a north Wales community* (London 1957).

[48] R. Porter (ed.), *Myths of the English* (London 1991); R. Samuel (ed.), *Patriotism: the making and unmaking of British national identity,* 3 vols., (London 1989); even Linda Colley's excellent *Britons: forging the nation 1707 — 1837* (Yale 1992) neglects racing, cricket and pugilism as an element in the sporting self-image of the 'bulldog' British; and for all the work on sport in that period, it has no place in Jose Harris's otherwise acute survey of *Public Lives, Private Spirit: a social history of Britain 1870-1914* (London 1992).

THE CONCEPT OF DOPING
AND THE FUTURE OF OLYMPIC SPORT

John Hoberman

Professor of Germanic Languages
at the University of Texas in Austin, Texas

On July 9, 1992, Queen Elizabeth II hosted a garden party on the lawns of Buckingham Palace to honour the outstanding athletes who had brought renown to Britain during her 40-year reign. The London *Times* called it "the greatest gathering of elite sportsmen and women in British history". Among these 1,486 celebrated guests were four men — a weightlifter and three powerlifters — who had been banned for life from their sports for using illicit drugs. When their dubious status was pointed out to the secretary of the Central Council of Physical Recreation who had issued the invitations, he dismissed this oversight as a matter of little consequence. "Everyone who is coming is at the garden party in their own right", he said. "People have qualified by becoming champions. What happened subsequently is a matter of history". The causal illogicality of this statement, which ignored the possibility that drugs might have made these men champions in the first place, appeared to escape him[1].

The presence of these compromised athletes at a royal party, and the social rehabilitation it implies, point to an unacknowledged ambivalence toward performance-enhancing substances that is characteristic of modern civilization as a whole. The origins of this ambivalence are to be found in the fascination with high-level performances of all kinds that is the distinguishing characteristic of a civilization built on the twin ideals of technology and productivity that are so efficiently symbolized by high-performance athletes. The fact that this ambivalence exists has been suppressed in the longstanding public debate about doping because it undermines the moralistic (and only half-sincere) anti-drug position that national and international sports federations have adopted as a public relations strategy vis-à-vis the sporting public. Sports officials around the world, including the leaders of the International Olympic Committee (IOC), have assumed for years that they had no choice but to join multinational campaigns against illicit "drugs" of all kinds. The inevitable result of this policy was to promulgate the (mistaken) idea that, because performance-boosting drugs such as anabolic steroids resemble "recreational" drugs such as LSD and cocaine in being illicit substances, essentially the same reasons would explain why both classes of substances were morally objectionable. Obscured in the artificial fusing of these two categories was the fact that performance-boosters and intoxicants have different functions. For while intoxicants offer tastes of paradise, performance-enhancing drugs make possible a vicarious (and even intoxicating) participation in the ethos of limitless performance most powerfully represented by machines. This crucial difference means that these two types of drugs must be condemned on different grounds if they are to be condemned at all.

The campaign against performance-enhancing drugs in elite sport that has been underway over the past twenty-five years has failed precisely because of their association with the ethos of performance and productivity. This is why modern societies are simply incapable of stigmatizing performance-boosting agents in an unambiguous and decisive way. It should be noted that the stigmatizing of intoxicants is equally half-hearted: cannabis and cocaine are suppressed while alcohol is not. Within the first category, the anabolic steroid possesses an additional appeal in that it is a derivative of the male hormone testosterone and is therefore associated with sexual as well as physical potency. The ambiguous status of performance-boosting drugs, and the consequent refusal of modern societies to subject them to genuinely stringent taboos, make the current anti-drug consensus inherently unstable. Our societal inhibitions about using these drugs clash with our primal fascination with the performances they make possible.

The purpose of this essay is to investigate both the sources and consequences of modern ambivalence toward what we call "doping", with special attention paid to testosterone and other steroids. We must begin by recognizing that the social repression of this ambivalence has become a virtual prerequisite for the continued functioning of certain major sports that are vulnerable to drug abuse. Indeed, how one draws up a list of steroid-dependent sports will indicate to what extent the observer himself is participating in the ongoing cover-up of doping practices. Focusing on sports that do drug testing and thus produce scandals, such as track and field and weightlifting, is profoundly misleading because it contributes to the myth that the steroid epidemic is limited to a few vulnerable sports and that the responsible officials are pursuing a serious anti-doping campaign. This fiction is absolutely indispensable to the Olympic movement and to other international as well as national sports federations that aim at preserving the image of "clean" sport. Precisely how this fiction is maintained is a first-class problem for the sport sociologist or historian.

It is also a problem for the sociologist of knowledge, since it is clear that public information about doping in various sports is handled or "managed" by sports officials and the journalists who are supposed to report on how these bureaucrats behave. The tabloid character of the sporting press can generally accommodate only one scandal — and thus only one set of villains — at a time, and this structural bias tends to suppress the idea that doping is systemic within elite sport to a degree the public does not understand. In addition, the sporting press has a vested interest in preserving rather than destroying the most popular sports on which they report. Thus the use of steroids by professional soccer players in Germany and by both college and professional football players in the United States is either unreported or underreported — "I am firmly convinced", the doping expert Dr. Manfred Donike said in 1992, "that there is doping in the [German] Bundesliga", and this opinion has been seconded by the sports physician Klaus Steinbach, who once served as a professional soccer club's team physician[2]. Yet the issue of doping in soccer and football has never taken on the dimensions of a public scandal because the sporting press has not permitted it to become one. Similarly, the drug-soaked history of the Tour de France and other events on the European professional cyclists' circuit has been effectively managed by the press, which has suppressed not the endless scandals but, rather, the fact that these are quite literally drug-dependent competitions[3]. The logic of dependency is the Tour's "open secret" — a paradoxical expression that captures the ambivalence of a civilization that demands such entertainments but is unwilling to acknowledge their physiological costs. The "open secret" of even greater magnitude is that the logic of drug dependency has become the logic of some elite sports around the world.

Ambivalence toward doping takes a variety of forms in the world of high-performance sport. The sportsmedical establishment that is charged with supervising the health and treatment of athletes includes a significant pro-steroid lobby. Political establishments demand Olympic medals from athletes who are also supposed to test negative for banned drugs. Punitive drug-testing programs are carried out by national and international sports bureaucrats of dubious integrity whose first priority is to preserve their bureaucratic fiefdoms and the all-important cash flow from governmental agencies, corporate sponsors, advertising clients, and paying spectators. The effectiveness of the testing programs is less important than their public relations role vis-à-vis funding sources and the sporting public, whose presumed anti-doping sentiments are seldom in evidence. In fact, the "campaign" against doping itself is inseparable from its function as public relations. For this reason it would be misleading to claim that the conflicts of interest noted above undermine the official anti-doping consensus of the IOC and the federations with which it is affiliated. On the contrary, it would be more accurate to say that these conflicts of interest are *constituent elements* of this consensus. The "consensus" itself exists in the form of official anti-doping rules and the indispensable journalistic condemnations of doping that support IOC policy. Yet both pillars of this consensus, including sports publications, are vulnerable to conflicts of interest. After the Spanish cyclist Pedro Delgado was caught using the steroid-masking drug probenecid during his victorious ride in the 1988 Tour de France, the French newspaper *L'Équipe* — a co-sponsor of the race — announced that he had been "cleared"[4]. In fact, Delgado owed his victory to a pair of technicalities: probenecid was not yet on the banned list, and the presence of steroids could only be inferred from his use of the masking agent. In a similar vein, the American magazine *Sports Illustrated* — a sponsor of the 1994 Winter Olympic Games — has already published a glowing account of the Lillehammer Olympic Organizing Committee[5]. With the exception of the German news weekly *Der Spiegel* and the *Süddeutsche Zeitung* of Munich, the world press has shown little interest in aggressive coverage of doping practices.

The various conflicts of interest that make systemic doping possible deserve a more detailed analysis than they can receive here. Yet even a synoptic presentation of the sociology of doping, describing the motives and stratagems of diverse interest groups, is an indispensable corrective to the widespread impression that doping is essentially a medical or pharmacological issue. Following this abbreviated sociology of doping we will characterize doping as a cultural practice belonging to a larger set of drug dependencies that extend far beyond the domain of sport.

One of the most striking and least publicised aspects of the doping problem is that many physicians provide steroids to athletes for a nontherapeutic purpose — to enhance athletic performance[6]. In 1988 the prominent Swiss sports physician Hans Howald told an interviewer that the most entrenched opponents of doping control were, in fact, sports physicians. (Howald was subsequently forced out of his directorship of the Swiss sports science research center by the Swiss track-and-field federation and the Swiss National Olympic Committee.[7]) In 1989 the German doping expert Manfred Donike stated that it was physicians, in addition to trainers and sports bureaucrats, who were opposed to rigorous testing of elite athletes[8].

Because this voluntary role of the physician in what society defines as steroid abuse would seem to violate the Hippocratic Oath, it is important to try to understand the motives behind these officially illegal and illicit acts. This task is complicated by the fact that public statements by physicians in defence of steroid use have not been common, if only because reputations and medical licenses are at stake. Nevertheless, it is possible to identify or to infer certain views or convictions that enable some medical personnel to reconcile the use of steroids with their own ideas of what sportsmedical practice should be. I believe there are two kinds of motives that correspond to the dual roles of such physicians as both healers and admirers who identify with the ambitions of their patients. Only the healing role, however, is acceptable to society-at-large and the medical boards that are empowered to grant or take away medical licences. The physician's role as an engaged and ambitious participant in the athlete's assault on human limits must remain unacknowledged because it is officially illicit. Small wonder, then, that physicians' infrequent endorsements of steroid use focus on their therapeutic role and do not support the use of steroids to boost performance.

The physician can argue for the "therapeutic" use of steroids to promote recovery from injuries, as was claimed in the case of the Swiss shotputter Werner Günthör, or as a humane therapy for brutal training regimens. The rationale for promoting recovery from training in this manner is commonly referred to as "substitution", implying that the athlete's body is being restored to its normal state. Thus Werner Günthör's physician, Dr. Bernhard Segesser, claimed that he prescribed steroids to promote recovery from a "period of overtraining"[9].In a similar vein, the prominent (and controversial) West German sportsphysician Heinz Liesen said in 1988 that he had prescribed steroids for marathon runners to accelerate their recovery from the stresses of these body-depleting endurance races, and his equally well-known colleague Dr. Armin Klümper has also defended the use of steroids when they are — in his judgment — medically indicated[10]. The same argument has frequently been heard from former East German doping scientists suddenly faced with the challenge of explaining their hormonal manipulation of hundreds of elite athletes. Indeed, Professor Hermann Buhl, former head of the Research Institute for Physical Culture and Sport (FKS) in Leipzig, has accused West German sportsphysicians of having invented the concept of substitution in order to rationalize their own use of steroids. Responding to this claim, Brigitte Berendonk suggested that Buhl was suffering from "postrevolutionary amnesia", since East German sportsmedical documents refer to "hormonal substitution" as early as 1981[11]. This supposedly recuperative procedure played a crucial role as one of several therapeutic strategies euphemistically referred to as "supporting measures" (*unterstützende Mittel*) which also referred to nutrition, vitamin supplements, and fatigue-relieving beverages[12]. After the collapse of the East German state, the former head of its Sportsmedical Service (SMD), Dr. Marc Höppner, offered a ringing defense of "pharmacologically permissible doses" of steroids to promote recovery from the stresses of long training regimens, adding (like Liesen and Klümper) that the medical supervision of steroid use is far preferable to self-administration by the athletes themselves[13]. The Swiss journalist Peter Hartmann has described an international conspiracy of silence among sports physicians who are convinced that many elite athletes in track and field, weightlifting, and long-distance cycling simply cannot endure the physiological stresses of their events without steroids[14].

These proponents claim that prescribing steroids for athletes can be reconciled with the traditional medical interest in healing or preventing harm. Yet behind all the talk about "therapeutic" applications and the "regeneration" of exhausted bodies there is always an interest in boosting performance, and in this sense the divided loyalties of the sportsphysician are clear for all to see. For is it his obligation to serve the human being apart from his or her athletic ambitions, or does he serve the athlete who cannot be separated from the performances for which he or she exists? The answer is that ambitious sportsphysicians East and West focus primarily on the athletic potential of the patient, and any obstacles to boosting performance tend to make them impatient. In 1985 Heinz Liesen expressed precisely this sort of irritability in an interview about steroids: "Why do *[we?]* make such a drama out of this? If a body cannot regenerate itself by producing a sufficient amount of hormone, then it is certainly appropriate to help it out, just as one would give vitamin C, B-1 or B-2 or stimulate its immune system, so that it can recuperate rather than remain sick"[15]. Five years later the idea of medically safe hormonal substitution reappeared in a less inhibited form at a post-Wall conference on "hormonal regulation" held in Leipzig. In their paper on a "medical-bioscientific" view of high-performance sport, two East German scientists assured their audience, including distinguished West German guests like Manfred Donike and Horst de Marées, that their steroid research for the Honnecker regime had been both ethical and productive: "We have thoroughly investigated their effects on the various functional systems [of the body] that are dependent on training regimen while studying problems pertaining to hormonal regulation. The results suggest that high-performance training offers medical opportunities which are scientifically based and that we can prescribe doses without side effects"[16]. Yet today we know that East German athletes suffering from steroid-induced liver damage were pouring into the Charité Hospital in Berlin as early as the 1970s[17].

Ambivalence about the use of steroids extends into the political establishment of any nation that takes responsibility for the development of elite athletes. For the most unscrupulous politicians, of course, ambivalence is not the problem. In the former East Germany, the mass administration of steroids to athletes, including children, was an official (if secret) policy. And today it is widely assumed that the Communist dictatorship in China is pursuing an uninhibited campaign, including doping, to develop high-performance athletes as symbols of national prestige. Federal funding of elite sports programs in Germany and Canada creates analogous, if less severe, pressures to produce medal-winners who will test "clean" for performance-enhancing drugs. In a word, sportive nationalism has made high-performance sports medicine into an applied science that is often vulnerable to political demands even in a democratically governed society, and this can lead to ambivalent policymaking. For example, during his service several years ago as (West) German interior minister, Wolfgang Schäuble — who as a member of the Bundestag actually endorsed the use of steroids in 1977[18] — made a series of statements that revealed a divided mind on the subject of doping. On the one hand, he insisted that "the limits of human performance" be respected; on the other, he defended athletes' use of medications "for the restoration of health" and called for "a new definition of doping"[19] that would, presumably, expand the list of permissible substances. Such ambivalence does not necessarily represent either cynicism or duplicity, but is rather an acknowledgement of the fundamental predicament of high-performance sport, where traditional principles of self-restraint, rooted in medical ethics and the code of sportsmanship, must confront the relentless pressures of the performance principle and its cult of productivity.

This struggle between the cult of performance and traditional restraints in sport is only one part of a much larger cultural process that tends to legitimise pharmacological solutions to human problems. The fragility of the anti-doping consensus as it exists today is, therefore, a direct consequence of the idea that human beings have a fundamental right to improve the quality of their lives by using drugs that do not harm them. This modern belief that human life includes an inherent pharmacological dimension assumes that human beings also have an absolute right to boost a wide range of performances in a variety of ways, prominently including sexual functioning. Understanding the larger cultural context of doping thus helps us to understand why the officially sponsored inhibitions that are supposed to prevent doping cannot do so: they are, in effect, overwhelmed by the broader cultural mandate to boost performances across the board, from increasing gross national products to promoting "world-class" standards in every possible area. The performance principle absorbs other norms by subordinating their purposes to its own. What we call "therapy" is an important example of a cultural practice (and ethos) that can be absorbed and subverted by the charismatic ideal of performance.

Traditional medical pharmacology in the West situates the use of drugs in a "therapeutic" context that makes the legitimacy of such interventions appear self-evident. What is more, these drug therapies have an impressive range of applications that extends far beyond the treatment of organic diseases to include various kinds of "normal" human functioning such as work performance or just coping with the ordinary challenges of living. This elastic concept of therapy easily accommodates the physiological conditions and psychological stresses experienced by high-performance athletes, and the resulting fusion of everyday stress and the realm of extreme athletic exertion already makes it extremely difficult to condemn doping on *a priori* grounds. We simply do not employ a typology of stressful experiences that distinguishes between the pressures of everyday life and sportive stress on a deep enough level. The modern English (and now internationalised) word "stress" homogenises an entire spectrum of experiences and simultaneously implies the need for "therapies" to restore the organism to its original healthy state. By thus making its own contribution to the pharmacologizing of human life, the concept of stress makes it more difficult to sustain the idea that any functional use of drugs can be regarded as illegitimate — or as "doping".

This essay is primarily concerned with important ambiguities inherent in the doping phenomenon in Western societies. At the same time, we should be aware that the doping problem has a cross-cultural dimension that produces ambiguities of its own that show how problematic the doping concept can be. For example, can the use of substances sanctioned by the traditions of a non-western society be classified as doping? The Chinese doping control expert Prof. Yang Tianie claimed in 1992 that many athletes and trainers in his country use traditional Chinese medicines whose precise composition is unknown; and he predicted that their uncontrolled use would cause some athletes to fail drug tests[20]. The astonishing world records set by Chinese women distance runners in August and September 1993, according to their coach, owed something to what The *New York Times* called "an expensive potion made from a rare worm found on China's western high plateau". The coach, Ma Junren, argued in effect that this herbal potion is an integral part of Chinese culture: "This is all natural and Chinese people have been drinking it for hundreds of years"[21]. The magnitude of his athletes' performances created a global controversy about possible doping violations[22]. In a similar vein, officials at the doping-control center in Seoul claimed in July 1992 that four Barcelona-bound athletes had tested positive for banned substances after eating "Kae Soju", a mixture of herbal medicines and hormone-enriched dog meat that many South Korean athletes use as a nutritional supplement[23]. Once again, we see how performance-boosting can inhere in established cultural practices, and thus how difficult it can be to characterize performance-boosting of any kind as an illegitimate strategy that is outside the cultural mainstream.

The modern obsession with performance-enhancement is reflected in the wide range of substances and techniques that are enlisted on behalf of improving the human organism and its capacities. While these methods range in quality from the scientifically proven to sheer quackery, the fundamental point is that all of them benefit from the universal presumption that almost any attempt to expand human capacities is worth trying. Commercial "brain gyms" employ stress-reduction devices such as flotation tanks, biofeedback machines, and somatrons ("devices that enhance the vibrations of music and distribute them through the body, like a massage") in an attempt to affect the brain waves and thereby increase intelligence, boost memory, improve the immune system and combat phobias[24]. So-called "smart drugs", none of which have been proven effective in scientifically valid trials, are sold to bring about "cognitive enhancement"[25].

Beta-blocker drugs, as well as cognitive-behavioural and behaviour rehearsal therapies, are used by orchestral musicians because they are "effective in reducing musical performance anxiety and improving the quality of performance"[26]. Attempts to improve muscle reflexes in athletes have been reported but have not been shown to be scientifically valid. Thus the British track-and-field coach Frank Dick stated in 1988: "We have not yet reached the limits of our knowledge about training methods. Vladimir Kuznetsov, the director of a Moscow research institute who died in 1986, was working on training muscle reflexes in such a way that they could react more quickly, meaning that the person could run faster". In January 1993 a Chinese newspaper attempted to deflect widespread accusations regarding the alleged steroid doping of Chinese swimmers by claiming that their world-class performances had been made possible by a "multifunctional muscle-building machine" that sends electronically controlled bursts of electricity through the muscles[27]. It should be noted that both of these anecdotes are essentially rumours, and that neither source expresses any concern about placing limits on performance-boosting. The Chinese claim is particularly interesting — and, perhaps, naïve — in that the response to an accusation of illicit performance-boosting of one kind is met with earnest assurances that Chinese athletes had succeeded by employing an equally artificial procedure to create their champions. Few anecdotes could better illustrate the fundamental promiscuity of the modern ambition to boost performance.

Doping goes hand in hand with the intensification of the performance principle within certain activities that can be made more competitive. An example of this development is occurring within the "sport" of mountain-climbing, as climbers attempt to make ever more spectacular climbs in "record" time. Because the old-fashioned oxygen bottle has gone out of fashion, climbers are now using cortisone-like medications such as Dexamethason and Prednison to counteract the symptoms of altitude sickness. A German professor of sports medicine who endorses the use of these drugs argues that this is not doping but rather an "emergency treatment" for the climber who must descend quickly. Yet even he concedes that the new dynamic of the sport may cause the use of these drugs to spin out of control[28].

All doping is based on the premise that the human organism is a complex mechanism that is subject to manipulation by certain techniques. A corollary premise is that a wide range of human behaviours or experiences, extending beyond the traditional "aptitudes" such as intelligence or physical ability, can be seen as subject to "therapeutic" intervention or as "performances" that can be managed or improved. One example of this trend is "aroma therapy" — "a type of folk medicine that uses fragrances to alter mood or physical conditions" that has also become a commercial enterprise. The olfactory sense is seen as providing access to the formation of emotions and thus behaviour on the most fundamental level. "Smell", says one researcher in this field, "is our most intimate, individualistic sense. It is primitive, uneducated and therefore vulnerable"[29]. While this human vulnerability to fragrance is exploited by "fragrance engineers" who attempt to seduce retail customers into buying products, its more humane application is "therapeutic" mood altering. But since the idea of therapy has become virtually inseparable from the idea of boosting performance, it is not surprising that a discussion of aroma therapy employs the conceptual vocabulary we associate with doping: "directed behaviour-management", uncertain psychological effects, and "getting more performance out of" people, including students who are exposed to fragrances in the classroom[30].

The modern predisposition to see opportunities for doping has created a limitless interest in substances that might boost performance. The most important of these drugs are testosterone and the many anabolic-androgenic steroids related to it. These compounds enjoy a special status for the excellent reason that there is massive anecdotal evidence that they actually work. The virtual end, over the past five years, of record-setting performances within certain track-and-field events — such as the throwing disciplines and many women's events — suggests that the strengthened doping controls that followed the 1988 Ben Johnson scandal have kept certain performance levels below higher steroid-dependent norms. The most popular nonsteroidal drugs typically acquire potent reputations based on uncontrolled rumors about their efficacy and the ambiguous results of scientific research.

One example of such a drug is the amino acid L-carnitene, which appears on a list of "steroid alternatives" formulated by the Food and Drug Administration (USA)[31]. Like all of the most important doping substances — steroids, human growth hormone, erythropoeitin — carnitene has an inherently ambiguous status in that it has (or may have) legitimate medical applications as well as potential value as a performance-boosting drug for athletes. (The fact that these are, in effect, "dual-use" drugs makes it all the more difficult to argue that they should be banned from sport on the grounds that they are medically hazardous.) Carnitene's pharmacological mystique derives from its energy-releasing role in cell metabolism. Although Swiss researchers have found that additional doses of carnitene can raise the aerobic threshold (V02 max), the scientific evidence about carnitene's effects on muscle metabolism remains inconclusive. Nevertheless, in their typical fashion, many athletes have assumed that additional doses of carnitene will increase muscle endurance, and a flourishing market for carnitene products exists in the United States, France, Italy, and other countries. In Switzerland, carnitene tablets are sold as a "supplementary nutrition for athletes". In France, a combination of carnitene, pollen, and royal jelly is marketed to athletes and other "high-speed" people ("vivre à 100 a l'heure") whose dynamic lifestyle makes them spiritually akin to athletes. This crossover effect that links the general market with the elite athlete is an important characteristic of the modern cult of performance, since the advertising industries in all of the developed countries provide many opportunities for ordinary people to participate in the high-performance ethos. The "normalisation" of carnitene is also promoted by researchers who suggest that carnitene might have a significant role to play in geriatric medicine by preserving mental and physical capacities and by preventing or treating Alzheimer's disease[32] The consequences of making carnitene a standard part of geriatric medicine would certainly promote its legitimacy as a performance-enhancing drug for both athletes and the general public. We will now look at how this process is already well underway in the case of the world's most important performance-boosting drug — testosterone.

The idea that the male hormone is a potential wonder drug was born a century ago. Although the male hormone testosterone was not isolated until 1935, crude testicular extracts (*liquide testiculaire*) pioneered by the distinguished French physiologist Charles Edouard Brown-Séquard were already a medical fad during the 1890s on both sides of the Atlantic. While the chief benefit of this pseudo-therapy was supposedly a general rejuvenation of the aging male, it was given to large numbers of both men and women suffering from a wide variety of disorders[33]. This historical retrospective underscores the fact that the use of testosterone and its steroid derivatives to boost athletic performance is a relatively recent "illicit" application of a substance that had already been legitimized as a standard therapy by the medical establishment even before the turn of the century. What is more, the "rejuvenating" potential of the male hormone, or what Brown-Sequard called its "dynamogenic" effect upon. the human organism, was seen as an entirely legitimate therapy. Inhibitions about the medical use of hormonal products — as distinct from sceptical assessments of their therapeutic value — were unknown. Over the past century our view of hormonal products has changed, and the most important source of their notoriety has been the doping crisis in Olympic sport, which provided an "illegitimate" context in which they could be "abused". It is a curious fact that, compared with the scandalous status of the anabolic steroid, the "legitimate" medical career of artificial testosterone remains virtually unknown to those who have struggled with the doping problem. Indeed, it is interesting to find that much of the debate about the use of testosterone and its derivatives that now pertains to sport was appearing in the medical literature in the early 1940s in connection with clinical trials of hormonal products. Here is more evidence that the sudden notoriety of the anabolic steroid that dates from the 1960s and 1970s was in part an artificial phenomenon that ought to be seen in relation to the contemporary clinical rôles of these drugs. Ambivalence toward steroids now appears as compatible with the ambiguous medical status testosterone has occupied since the market for testosterone products opened up about fifty years ago.

By the early 1940s, or half a century after the testicular extracts boom initiated by Brown-Sequard, methyl testosterone and testosterone propionate were being promoted by pharmaceutical companies[34] and administered to patients as an experimental therapy for several reasons: to treat the "male climacteric" (fatigue, melancholia, and impotence) in older men[35], to deal with impotence in younger men[36], to treat hypogonadism[37], to restore libido in women[38], and to reverse homosexuality — a particularly problematic use of testosterone, as was recognized at the time[39]. While the idea of using testosterone to boost athletic performance does not appear in the medical literature, it was becoming apparent to this generation of scientists that testosterone played a rôle in physical fitness. "There has long been a common belief that male sex hormones are associated with muscular strength and endurance", three American researchers wrote in 1942, and this belief was now confirmed by real scientific evidence. At this point it was time "to inquire whether responses to fatiguing exercise may be altered in normal man by androgen administration". While this experiment found that even fifty milligrams of methyl testosterone did not increase strength in these subjects, the authors had the good judgment to add that "it is not impossible that somewhat different results would be observed with extremely large doses, or with physical exercise which placed more emphasis on endurance"[40]. Fifty years later this premonition of 1942 has become the conventional wisdom among high-performance athletes around the world. But this canny anticipation of anabolic steroid use by elite athletes is not the only sign of things to come in the clinical literature of this period. Of potentially greater importance are the early evaluations of testosterone as a mass therapy for "normal" men both young and old.

The popularisation of testosterone as a rejuvenating wonder drug for millions of aging men dates from the early period of its commercial development. Thus in 1938 a Yale scientist told a meeting of the American Chemical Society that testosterone propionate "rejuvenated" old men by relieving depression[41]. The publication of Paul de Kruif's book *The Male Hormone* (1945) seems to have marked the apex of the promotional campaign to make testosterone a mass therapy for aging males. Two years later *The Negro Digest* announced that: "Today, there are some 10,000,000 men over 45 who are potential users of testosterone. Countless medical case histories point the way to longer mental and physical productivity, escape from the lethargy and fears that haunt so many men in their middle ages"[42]. Pharmaceutical companies advertised testosterone preparations in professional journals throughout the 1940s. And yet, for reasons that are still not clear, testosterone did not become a mass market drug.

A half-century later there are new developments encouraging the widespread use of testosterone. For one thing, the idea of hormone therapy has become a convention even if some applications are still regarded as controversial. In recent years pediatric endocrinologists have faced increasing pressure from the parents of children of subnormal stature to administer artificial human growth hormone (HGH). The dilemmas resulting from the availability of such interventions (whose benefits remain uncertain) today constitute a major issue in the area of medical ethics. These uncertainties notwithstanding, there are reasons to believe that current trends will eventually confer unprecedented social legitimacy on HGH therapy that is intended to increase stature and even athletic potential: "If the benefits of HGH therapy were more reliably documented, or the physical and economic burdens of therapy were lower, or the data showing minimal risks from HGH therapy were firmer, then the arguments against therapy would weaken". Quite apart from these rather technical criteria, it is important to recognise that cultural norms have the power to contest, alter, or even subvert what we think of as the professional judgment of the clinician: "Parental wishes might reflect cultural and ethnic attitudes or sexual stereotypes, as they do now for decisions about other cosmetic interventions". Such pressures will inevitably create a policy vacuum that will be filled by the most aggressive interest groups. As these authors point out, nonmedical "decision makers, whose decisions may reflect political, social, or market forces", will determine the fate of HGH therapy in the absence of an organised effort by pediatricians to determine therapeutic criteria[43]. (This is exactly what has happened in the case of anabolic steroid use by athletes and bodybuilders.) The recent decision by the U.S. National Institute of Health to recruit healthy children to test the efficacy of biosynthetic HGH is yet another sign that social barriers to hormonal treatments are now facing unprecedented challenges. According to the NIH panel that approved this clinical trial: "There is substantial evidence that extreme short stature carries distinct disadvantages, including functional impairment and psychological stigma-tization"[44]. This rationale makes it clear that the concept of therapy itself is itself a cultural construct and therefore inherently responsive to social pressures. Indeed, a formula as open as "functional impairment and psychological-stigmatization" reminds us that it is a short step from prescribing increased stature to prescribing athletic proficiency for the purpose of promoting the emotional well-being of a child.

The growing legitimacy of hormonal manipulation is further evident in a recent proposal by the proponents of "evolutionary medicine" to use exogenous hormonal therapy for the purpose of redressing an alleged hormonal imbalance that has caused a range of medical disorders. These theorists argue that, while the human genome has scarcely changed over the past 10,000 years, "our genetically determined physiology and biochemistry now contend with circumstances vastly different from those for which they were selected by evolution. The resulting imbalance fosters afflictions of affluence ranging from heart disease and hypertension to many of our commonest cancers". The immediate target of such hormonal therapy would be cancers of the female reproductive organs, and the promise of success would undoubtedly affect general attitudes toward hormonal therapies: "the evolutionary inference, that current mortality from women's cancers far exceeds the hypothetical or 'natural' basal rate, could influence public and scientific interest regarding further development and possible clinical application of this approach"[45].

Testosterone therapy for hypogonadal males has been practiced since the early 1940s and is today a standard treatment for a condition that "is now recognised as a common occurrence in older males"[46]. The resulting demand has stimulated a growing market for testosterone patches[47], a development that has been presented in a German tabloid as a rejuvenation therapy for the menopausal male[48]. But once again the significance of hormonal therapy extends far beyond the clinic and into the public sphere in which medical "disorders" and "crises" are defined in accordance with social (and commercial) demands. Thus in 1992 the National Institutes of Health requested research proposals to test whether testosterone therapy can prevent physical ailments and depression in older males, thereby raising the question of whether the aging process itself is about to be officially recognised as a treatable deficiency disease. "I don't believe in the male midlife crisis", commented Dr. John B. McKinlay, an epidemiologist at Boston University who is a specialist on aging. "But even though in my perspective there is no epidemiological, physiological or clinical evidence for such a syndrome, I think by the year 2000 the syndrome will exist. There's a very strong interest in treating aging men for a profit, just as there is for menopausal women"[49]. The emergence (or creation) of such a syndrome would signify new (social) definitions of physiological normality and of maleness itself. In addition, this new standard of health would help to legitimise the sheer ambition to "boost" the human organism in a variety of ways.

Routine testosterone therapy for millions of "menopausal" and elderly males would transform the "climate of opinion" in which athletes and bodybuilders use anabolic steroids. The certification of low testosterone doses (10-20 mg.) as medically safe would do much to remove the stigma attached to steroids; indeed, the fact that many athletes use megadoses rather than clinical doses would in all likelihood be lost on a lay public that has shown little concern about doping in the first place. The new medical status of hormonal manipulation would present the International Olympic Committee (IOC) and its Medical Commission with an unprecedented opportunity to demonstrate the pragmatic amorality that underlies all of their rituals and statements of principle. Faced with the continuing demoralising effects of its uncontrollable doping crisis, the IOC might announce that, after careful consultations with a panel of experts, its Medical Commission had decided to recognise testosterone as a natural substance in (male) athletes and remove the current 6:1 (testosterone:epitestosterone) ratio as the official threshold at which "doping" begins. This liberalisation, which has already been proposed by prominent figures in the world of German sport[50], might be accompanied by an inspiring reaffirmation of the Olympic motto of *citius, altius, fortius* emphasising the innate human need to transcend human limits and reach new levels of performance. The inability of today's elite athletes to reach, let alone surpass, the steroid-assisted records set over the past two decades in track and field and weightlifting might play a rôle in opening the door to uncontrolled (but "medically supervised") hormonal manipulation endorsed by prominent sports physicians and officially sanctioned by the IOC.

The scenario described above assumes a mutually reinforcing relationship between unprecedented (officially sponsored) hormone use in the respective worlds of elite sport and society as a whole. While the evidence to date suggests that large-scale societal trends are doing much more to determine the eventual status of the male hormone than anything that is happening in the world of sport, it is entirely possible that popular steroid-enhanced athletes — sponsored, perhaps, by pharmaceutical companies making the conventional payments to the IOC — could promote testosterone and its "safe" derivatives to a mass audience. (The current black market in steroids is simply an illegal version of the hypothetical situation I am describing, the advertising models being popular bodybuilders, professional wrestlers, and pumped-up film stars.) Such a development would undoubtedly create a crisis of conscience for many physicians and public health officials. "Steroids", the doping expert Manfred Donike urged in 1989, "must not be promoted as a kind of popular nutritional supplement *(Volksnahrungsmittel)*"[51]. While it is easy to endorse the medical wisdom of this warning, the history of doping in this century shows that it has been very difficult to draw a firm line between (legitimate) nutrients and (illegitimate) stimulants that are meant to boost performance[52]. Along with the other factors described above, this definitional ambiguity will tend to legitimise hormonal manipulation as a mass therapy of the future[53].

Notes

1   "Banned champions join elite for garden party at palace", *Times* [London] July 9, 1992. See also "Star gazing at the royal sports party", *Times* [London] July 10, 1992.

2   "Stuttgarter Bargeplauder, das zum brisanten Vorstoss wird", *Süddeutsche Zeitung* September 1, 1992.

3   'Freunde quer durch alle Rennställe", *Süddeutsche Zeitung*, December 31, 1992/January 1, 1993.

4   *ibid.*

5   William Oscar Johnson, "The LOOC of Success", *Sports Illustrated* March 29, 1993. It is also worth noting that *Sports Illustrated* has shown little interest in investigating steroid use in the National Football League.

6   "[M]any physicians collaborate in steroid abuse through the inappropriate

supplying of steroid prescriptions to athletes". See Jonathan P. Jarow, MD and Larry I. Lipschultz, MD, "Anabolic steroid-induced hypogonadotropic hypogonadism", *American Journal of Sports Medicine* 18 (1990): 429.

7 Urs Paul Engeler, "Magglingen oder Der heile Körper am Ende der Welt", *Die Weltwoche* (June 29, 1989): 33.

8 "DSB-Dopingtests schmalbrüstig", *Süddeutsche Zeitung* November 29, 1989.

9 Brigitte Berendonk, *Doping Dokumente: Von der Forschung zum Betrug* (Berlin: Springer Verlag, 1991): 7. This episode is also referred to in "Früher herrschte dunkle Doping-Zeit — auch bei Günthör", *Die Weltwoche* August 6, 1992.

10 "Frontmann, Guru, Zielscheibe: Klümper öffnet die Tür", *Süddeutsche Zeitung*, July 19, 1988; "Stuttgarter Bargeplauder", *op. cit.*

11 Berendonk, *Doping Dokumente* 287.

12 "Umfangreiche Sachen, die nicht korrekt waren", *Süddeutsche Zeitung* November 9/10, 1991.

13 "Bonn fordert schnelle Untersuchung", *Süddeutsche Zeitung*, November 30, 1990.

14 Peter Hartmann, "Wie schwanger ist Herr Günthör?" *Die Weltwoche*, May 10, 1991.

15 "Zuviel Theater um Anabolika", *Süddeutsche Zeitung*. January 23, 1985.

16 R. Hücker and A. Lehnert, "Sportliche Höchstleistung aus medizinischbiowissenschaftlicher Sicht", R. Häcker and H. de Marées, (eds.) *Hormonelle Regulation und psychophysische Belastung im Leistungssport* (Cologne: Deutscher Ärzte-Verlag, 1991 (p. 17-18).

17 "Interview der Woche: Else Ackermann (59) CDU-Abgeordnete und Pharmakologin", *Süddeutsche Zeitung*, January 30131, 1993.

18 Berendonk, *Doping Dokumente* 21.

19 "Minister Schäuble warnt vor einer 'Doping-Hysterie'", *Frankfurter Allgemeine Zeitung* October 21, 1989.

20 "Doping in Barcelona — schlecht für Peking 2000", *Süddeutsche Zeitung* January 23, 1992.

21 "'Ma's Army' Runs on Worm Elixirs and Turtle Soup", *New York Times*. September 12, 1993.

22 See also "Scientists defend success of Chinese sportsmen", *The Times* (London), September 6, 1993; "Wang pulveriserte Ingrids W-rekord", *Aften-*

posten (Oslo), September 9, 1993.

23 "Kurz & olympisch", *Süddeutsche Zeitung*, July 14, 1992.

24 "Riding the Waves", *New York Times* August 16, 1992.

25 "Ultra Think Fast", *Time*. June 8, 1992.

26 Mary L. Wolfe, "Correlates of Adaptive and Maladaptive Musical Performance Anxiety", *Medical Problems Of Performing Artists* (March 1989): 50. "Some degree of stress and tension is necessary for effective musical performance. Intervention for musicians should, ideally, maintain concentration, intensity, and arousal while it decreases feelings of inadequacy and the threat of impending disaster. Bayer suggested that the imaginal and meditative techniques used with professional athletes, which promote relaxation yet permit concentration and intensity, could be adapted for use with musicians (p. 55).

27 "Die Deutschen haben aufgehört zu glauben", *Der Spiegel* (August 15, 1988): 142.

28 "Wunderkasten statt Doping", *Süddeutsche Zeitung*. January 21, 1993.

29 Walter Aeschimann, "Reich mir die Pille gegen den Gipfelrausch", *Die Weltwoche* (October 8, 1992): 63.

30 "Taming the Frontier of the Senses: Using Aroma to Manipulate Moods", *New York Times* November 27, 1991. See also "Fragrance Engineers Say They Can Bottle The Smell of Success", *New York Times*, October 26, 1992.

31 "Direkt ins Hirn", *Der Spiegel* (November 2, 1992): 142-145.

32 I am indebted to Dr. Jean L. Fourcroy of the FDA for providing me with a copy of this list of "alternative doping methods".

33 Charles Inwyler, "Ein Stoff aus Muskelfleisch geht um bei den Muskelprotzen", *Die Weltwoche* (June 6, 1991): 29.

34 See Merriley Borell, "Brown-Séquard's Organotherapy and its Appearance in America at the End of the Nineteenth Century", *Bulletin of the History of Medicine* 50 (1976): 314. An Austrian scientist estimated in 1896 that no fewer than 2,000 "therapeutic experiments" using testicular extracts had been carried out by physicians by that year. See Oskar Zoth, "Zwei ergographische Versuchsreihen über die Wirkung orchitischen Extraktes, "*Pflüger's Arkiv* 62 (1896): 337. On Brown-Séquard's research on testicular extracts and its relationship to the anabolic steroid, see John Hoberman, *Mortal Engines: The Science of Performance and the Dehumanization of Sport* (New York: The Free Press, 1992): 72-76.

35 "At the present time, however, with pharmaceutical concerns widely advertising androgens for gynecic disorders in this and other journals, conscientious and scientific clinicians cannot continue to dismiss placidly the victimization of women as being the result of natural 'growing pains' of a new science". See E.C. Hamblen, "Androgen Therapy in Women", *Journal of Clinical Endocrinology* 2 (1942): 575.

36 See, for example, H.B. Thomas and R.T. Hill, "Testosterone Propionate and the Male Climacteric", *Endocrinology* 26 (January-June, 1940): 953-954; Stanley F. Goldman and Mark J. Markham, "Clinical Use of Testosterone in the Male Climacteric", *Journal of Clinical Endocrinology* 2 (1942): 237-242; Allan T. Kenyon *et al.*, "Metabolic Response of Aged Men to Testosterone Propionate", *Journal of Clinical Endocrinology* 2 (1942): 690-695; Ernest Simonson, Walter M. Kearns, and Norbert Enzer, "Effect of Methyl Testosterone Treatment on Muscular Performance and the Central Nervous System of Older Men", *Journal of Clinical Endocrinology* 4 (1944): 528-534.

37 C.D. Creevy and C.E. Rea, "The Treatment of Impotence by Male Sex Hormone", *Endocrinology* 27 (July-December 1940): 392-394.

38 H.S. Rubinstein, "Combined Use of Testosterone Propionate and Psychotherapy in Treatment of Hypogonadal Behavior-Problem Boys", *Journal of Clinical Endocrinology* 2 (1942): 519-526.

39 Hamblen, "Androgen Therapy in Women", *op. cit.*; Robert B. Greenblatt, "Androgen Therapy in Women", *Journal of Clinical Endocrinology* 2 (1942): 665-666; Udall J. Salmon and Samuel H. Geist, "Effect of Androgens upon Libido in Women" *Journal of Clinical Endocrinology* 3 (1943): 235-238; R.B.G., 306; Harold D. Palmer and Margaret de Ronde, "Reversible Testosterone-Induced Virilism", *Journal of Clinical Endocrinology* 3 (1943): 428.

40 S.J. Glass, H.J. Deuel and C.A. Wright, "Sex Hormone Studies in Male Homosexuality", *Endocrinology* 26 (January June 1940). 590-594, S.J. Glass and Roswell H. Johnson, "Limitations and Complications of Organotherapy in Male Homosexuality", *Journal of Clinical Endocrinology* 4 (1944). 540-544

41 Leo T. Samuels, Austin F. Henschel and Ancel Keys, "Influence of Methyl Testosterone on Muscular Work and Creatine Metabolism in Normal Young Men, *Journal of Clinical Endocrinology* 2 (1942). 649, 649, 653.

42 "Minds Rejuvenated by Sex Hormone", *Scientific American* (November

1938): 250. "The group included, in addition to the case of old men being rejuvenated, a number who were suffering from various types of glandular deficiency. Improvement was greatest when the deficiency had been greatest. Rational aggressiveness took the place of irrational irritability, for some patients. Nervousness and emotional instability were decreased. Muscle tone, energy, and stamina returned. Emotionally and sexually the patients were in better condition".

43 William Goode, "For men only: a new miracle drug", *Negro Digest* (January 1947): 37-39. The interest of this publication in testosterone derived in part from the important role of a black scientist in its production: "Foremost among the present day researchers in mass production of the male hormone is the topflight Negro chemist, Dr. Percy L. Julian".

44 John Lantos, Mark Siegler, and Leona Cutter, "Ethical Issues in Growth Hormone Therapy", *Journal of the American Medical Association* 261 (February 17, 1989): 1023-1024.

45 "Medical ethicists ask, Is shortness a disease?" *Austin American-Statesman* July 2, 1993.

46 "Ancestors May Provide Clinical Answers, Say 'Darwinian' Medical Evolutionists", *Journal of the American Medical Association* 269 (March 24/31, 1993): 1477.

47 John B. Morley et al., "Effects of Testosterone Replacement Therapy in Old Hypogonadal Males: A preliminary Study", *Journal of the American Geriatrics Society* 41(1993): 149.

48 See, for example, Norman A. Mazer et al., "Enhanced transdermal delivery of testosterone: a new physiological approach for androgen replacement in hypogonadal men", *Journal of Controlled Release* 19 (1992): 347-362. The author wishes to thank Norman A. Mazer, M.D., for providing this and related publications.

49 "Neu: das Pflaster, das den Mann jung erhält", *Bild am Sonntag* (October 4, 1992): 68.

50 "Midlife Myths: What About Men?: Studies Show Testosterone Drops, But Supplements Are Controversial", *International Herald Tribune*, July 21, 1992.

51 For example, the prominent sports physician, Wilfried Kindermann; the Olympic speedskating champion (1968 and 1972), Erhard Keller; the former West German recordholder in the shotput, Ralf Reichenbach, the chairman of the FC Homburg soccer team, Manfred Ommer, the former

president of the German Swimming Federation, Harm Beyer; the Olympic champion biathlete (1984) Peter Angerer. See "Kontrollen in den Trainingsphasen, *Süddeutsche Zeitung*, August 8, 1988; "Erhard Keller befürwortet maßvolle Anabolika — Freigabe", *Süddeutsche Zeitung*, November 18, 1989; "Heuchelei um Anabolika", *Süddeutsche Zeitung* January 5/6, 1989; "Stuttgarter Bargeplauder, das zum brisanten Vorstoß wird", *Süddeutsche Zeitung*, September 2, 1992; "Legalität und Popularität", *Süddeutsche Zeitung*, September 2, 1992; "Angerer für Freigabe", *Süddeutsche Zeitung* February 18, 1993. For the anti-liberalization statement of the anti-doping commissioner of the German Track-and-Field Federation (DLV), Rüdiger Nickel, see "Doping-Freigabe — Todesstoß für den Sport", *Süddeutsche Zeitung*, August 13, 1992.

[52] "Hohe Dunkelziffer beim Doping", *Süddeutsche Zeitung*. February 10, 1989.

[53] See, for example, Hoberman, *Mortal Engines*: 27, 140-141.

[54] The German historian Wolfgang Schivelbusch has pointed out that the cultural status of drugs can undergo a fundamental change over time: "All the exotic spices, stimulants, and intoxicants introduced to European civilization in modern times have gone through this [demystifying] process, becoming habitual or domesticated. The fantastic expectations and fears with which seventeenth-century Europeans greeted coffee, tobacco, and the other exotic substances are gone today, as much as the spirit of Dionysus from a modern middle-class wine-party. The stimulants which by their very novelty once shook mankind to the core have become ordinary everyday rites". Of particular interest for a comparison with steroids is the status of coffee, which two centuries ago was regarded as "a first-rate efficiency factor", as "a powerful force for change, helping to forge a new reality", and associated with both productivity and progress. See Wolfgang Schivelbusch, *Tastes of Paradise: A Social History of Spices. Stimulants, and Intoxicants* (New York: Pantheon Books, 1992): 223-224, 39, 63, 43, 39. To use Brown-Séquard's term from the year 1889, the nineteenth century made coffee into a "dynamogenic" drug that evoked fantasies of untested human powers.

SPORT AND CIVIL SOCIETY

Lincoln Allison

Director of the Warwick Centre for the Study of Sport in Society
at Warwick University

Political science and sport: the story so far

Over the twenty years to the time of writing, the study of sport in United
Kingdom universities has advanced from an obscure and rather technical
territory within physical education to a clear place of its own in several centres
and courses and a foothold in a wide variety of social studies departments. The
idea that an academic career might be founded in the study of sport is no longer
so surprising or amusing as it once was. Before I proceed to the main objective
of this essay, which is to attempt to advance the political understanding of sport
through a consideration of the concept of civil society, it would be useful to
sketch out the context of the change in status of academic sports studies. Why
has it happened and what does it amount to?

I have argued before that what kept sport off the academic agenda was a
'myth of autonomy', a belief that the causes and effects of sporting events were
confined to sport itself[1]. The myth did not necessarily imply, of course, that
sporting events were thereby uninteresting, but the unstated assumptions of the
study of society were that physical production and the system of class based on
the organisation of production were the important and determinant areas of social
life. Under these assumptions, sport wasn't of much importance, but when that
paradigm broke down and culture, meaning and leisure came to be seen as
important in themselves, sport could be seen as more relevant to the central
concerns of the study of society.

The autonomy of sport was always a pretty thin piece of ideology. The
development of modern sport in the nineteenth century had overtly moral and
undeniably social purposes and nobody could study (say) the life and thought of

53

Baron de Coubertin without accepting that there were moral and social purposes to the establishment of the modern Olympics. Yet it has taken some fairly crude changes to ram home the 'relevance' of sport: it is now, broadly defined, the sixth most important industry in Europe; it was an important bargaining chip in South African political change; football 'hooliganism' on several occasions during the 1980s forced its way into the headlines and to the top of the government's agenda. One would like to think that it was heroic academic figures like my colleague Tony Mason with his history of football who, without much immediate prospect of reward or esteem, insisted that sport was worthy of study[2]. They did, but the effort was much assisted by Nike and by the hooligans; that is the way life works.

It is less easy to see what outside recognition of the importance of sport amounts to or even what significance its practitioners think it has. Both often start with a banality, that 'sport reflects society'. How odd, even inconceivably odd, if it didn't and nobody would have bothered to assert this were it not for the existence of an elite myth that playing games was about getting away from the problems of 'society' and that it gave you, temporarily at least, more in common with the ancient Greeks than with non-sportsmen in your own society. But the claim that sport reflects society often assumes that it *only* reflects society, that it cannot actually be causal or important in itself. Thus academic analysis often looks to the ways in which ideological, class, ethnic or gender relations in society as a whole are exemplified by sport. The stronger and more interesting claims, that sport creates interests, principles and meanings which do not exist if there is no sport and which have an effect on other aspects of society, are less frequently asserted or accepted. It is these claims which amount to saying that sport is really interesting and important and which are the basis of the belief in the academic study of sport which I am attempting to develop.

Although there are now scholars from law, economics, politics and several other disciplines who have turned their main attention to sport, the two disciplines of social history and sociological theory have dominated the study of sport. In each case the time has already arrived that a textbook can be written which draws on and surveys a large established literature: thus Holt's *Sport and the British* and Jarvie and Maguire's *Sport and Leisure in Social Thought*[3]. Yet the two disciplines are, in important respects, opposites. The social historians are rooted in a very British, archive-oriented empiricism which regards theory and methodology with suspicion. On the whole, they regard detail as the key to a high level of understanding and admire the writer who can tell a detailed story well. Sociological theory, by contrast, is concerned from first to last with the argument between different whole approaches to the interpretation of human action, with 'methodology' which is also 'theory'. It is, therefore, highly sectarian and consists of arguments between figurationalists (key concept: the civilising process) and feminists (patriarchy) as well as Marxists, neo-Marxists, functionalists, Weberian neo-empiricists and so on. Its advantages, to an outsider, appear to be that it sees things as a whole and debates them vigorously. Its disadvantages are that it hides and confuses evaluation in its interpretative explanations and it seems difficult to see how the exponents of each watertight 'ism' can ever persuade those of another once their minds are made up.

What then is, and can be, the contribution of politics? The subject as a whole (I hesitate to say discipline) is eclectic rather than sectarian. That is, it draws on a wide variety of theories and methodologies in a kind of 'horses for courses' way without any of them making much attempt (or having much chance) to establish a hegemony over the subject as a whole. Thus forms of rational choice theory may play an important part in, say, theories of international relations or of committee behaviour and have tended to expand their territory, while a statistical positivism descended from behaviourism still dominates electoral studies. When we talk of states or systems as a whole we tend to be functionalists and to consider the needs and responses of the 'body politic' in a holistic way which descends from Bagehot and even Plato.

One way of putting this is that 'political scientists' casually assume socio-logical theories without clarifying them or bothering very much to dispute them. Perhaps the normal range of such theory is Weberian, insisting on an ultimate reduction of explanations to real states of mind which are converted into a 'plausible story' and 'checked with the facts'. But it reads more commonly as a bit of this and a bit of that, with the respective emphasis on insight, fact and hypothesis being a matter of the researcher's taste.

So far the specific contribution of academic political science to the under-standing of sport falls into this general pattern. Earlier attempts to describe the politics of sport were fairly heavy on narrative, whereas the books which I have edited on the subject tell a series of stories (Communist sport, Irish sport, South Africa, etc.) with the general theme of a contest over the values implicit in sport, especially between an amateur-elite ethos and the forces of commercial pro-fessionalism. Barrie Houlihan[4] has successfully used the idea of a 'policy community' to account for the state's approach to sport.

The question, then, concerns what might be the contribution of politics to an area of study dominated by sociology when there is a complex relationship between the two approaches. In their assumptions about the importance of theory and methodology they tend to be very different, whereas the theories and methodologies overlap, though can be treated in a wide variety of ways. Political scientists tend to be more tightly positivist in their use of concepts than are sociologists. This is particularly true, for example, of their handling of the concept of power. In debates about power, political scientists have, on the whole, insisted on the identification of power-holders, who are able to exercise control in social situations, if power analyses are to work. Thus the great power debate in political science ended with a schism between sceptics who thought that the identification of power-holders in modern societies was not possible with any satisfactory precision and therefore recommended a de-emphasising of the concept of power, and 'radical' or 'sociological' theorists who argued that this lack of precise locatability captured the very essence of power[5]. Thus sociology accepts a broad explanatory concept of cultural power which inheres in structures and transcends particular situations while political science now assumes that the question of how we are governed and by whom has to be treated more particularly, carefully and sceptically. This is the context in which the political concept of civil society must be examined: like power and nationality it is a concept which is used in both the sociological and political traditions in ways which partly overlap, partly diverge and partly conflict.

What is Civil Society?

The meaning of 'civil society' is immensely complex. We might start an investigation in two ways. First, what definitions exist of the concept? Second, what is the point of the concept? That is, what do people use it for? This second approach is the more important and potentially fruitful; the purposes for which the concept is used have far more power to explain the range of definitions than is the case *vice versa*.

The general context of these purposes is that civil society is a revived concept. During the 1970s and even for much of the 1980s it was not in common currency in discussions of social theory and was absent from many textbooks and works of reference. It was, as Gordon White put it, in "its coffin in the crypt of the great church of political theory"[6]. Even as recently as 1986 David Robertson could describe it as a term which "is seldom employed today"[7]. Thus, in trying to outline the purposes writers have had in using and developing the concept of civil society recently, we must start with the observation that they have revived the concept, much as 'corporatism' was revived in political science to explain the 'political economy' (itself something of a revival) of such countries as Sweden and Austria.

Although one might say that there was a vague general purpose to the revival and as many precise purposes as there are authors, there are also three general categories of purpose. First, there are Marxists for whom the categories of class and state had ceased to work in a deterministic way, but who were not prepared to see political development as mere local contingency. John Urry, for instance, attacking Nicos Poulantzas' rejection of the concept of civil society, insists that the concept is necessary if Marxism is to escape the "dichotomy between reductionism/functionalism and autonomism"[8]. Then there are, in some respects at an ideologically opposite pole, the market liberals who, in the context of collapsing communism, want to speculate about the existence or non-existence of social structures independent of the state which will provide conditions for the development and stabilisation of democracy and capitalism. Thus Earnest Gellner's definition of civil society as "that set of diverse non-governmental institutions, which is strong enough to counterbalance the state, and whilst not preventing the state from fulfilling its rôle of keeper of the peace and arbitrator between major interests, can nevertheless prevent the state from dominating and atomising the rest of society"[9]. Civil society, in this rôle, tends to include in its definition strong property institutions *per se*, including a general understanding of and respect for the institution of private property and particular institutions for resolving disputes about ownership. Thirdly, there are political scientists who are looking to create a more neutral category of political structures which are 'above' the basic institutions of society and 'below' the state.

Naturally these latter two — the market liberal and political science versions — tend to overlap and shade into one another, even though their extreme versions are quite different. There is a tendency even in supposedly neutral political science to treat civil society as if it meant *respectable* civil society. In effect, this means recognising institutions as part of civil society only if they support norms which the author respects or which he thinks are generally accepted. Generally, civil society is subject to the criteria of democratic functionalism, the assumption that for a practice to be part of civil society it must help in the achieving or maintaining of democratic practices. Larry Diamond lists the democratic functions of civil society: checking government power, developing participatory skills and practices as well as democratic values, recruiting and training leaders, disseminating information and providing channels for the expression of interests. He also adds functions which might be said to further capitalist values more easily than those of democracy as such: civil society mitigates and complicates class struggles, legitimises the state by engaging with it and (in post-communist societies) helps create the consensus for economic reform[10]. I would add that there are often important international features of civil society institutions: they can transmit ideas across frontiers more effectively than governments despite governments' attempt to stop them and they can develop international associations and as part of an international civil society.

The variety of purposes for which civil society has been re-developed generates a wide variety of definitions. For Robertson, civil society is "the organised society over which the state rules"[11]. For Roberts and Edwards, it consists of "those relations which are a part neither purely of the private sphere of the family, nor purely of the public sphere of the state"[12]. Roger Scruton typifies it as forms of association which are "spontaneous, customary and in general not dependent on law"[13]. John Urry has it as "the individualising sphere of the circuit of capital's path to expanded reproduction"[14]. At an even higher level of abstraction, Keith Tester defines civil society as "an imagination which attempted to identify, represent and legislate some basic unity in the experience of being human"[15].

In other words, in a familiar way in social theory, we are dealing with a concept which is interesting, which promises to help us understand some important aspects of reality, yet which is vague, stretched and contested. For some civil society may be strong in a place where there is great diffusion and little civility, but strong representation through 'pressure groups' and 'non-governmental organisations', whereas for others it is more important to have civility and 'gemeinschaft' associations which work by habit and assumption. (Compare most of urban California with a variety of rural European contexts.) For many like Gellner, civil society can only function *against* communism, but is more positively related to liberal capitalism, while for Chris Hann, Hungary had a much more effective civil society under communism than after the breakdown of the system[16]. These ambiguities and contradictions must be borne in mind when we consider the relation of sport to civil society.

Sport and civil society

It follows necessarily from what has been said that sport *could* be an important component of civil society. If we take Diamond's list of the (democratic) functions of civil society, then sports clubs can perform most of them. In a club people can develop democratic skills, practices and values by making collective decisions and running committees. Sport organisations certainly recruit and train leaders and disseminate information, though usually all of this happens within a sporting context. The sheer scale of sport in some countries is an important consideration in this respect: in the UK there are a little more than 1,500 amenity societies concerning themselves with planning and it would be universally acknowledged that they are an important part of civil society, but there are more than 40,000 football clubs and 7,000 cricket clubs.

This is to suggest the contribution that organised sport may make to civil society on account of its being organised. In this respect, sport is no different from the arts or from women's organisations and its distinctive features are its large scale and its capacity to activate people who could not be activated in any other way. But we can also construct a claim (as we might a parallel claim for the arts or women's organisations) that there is a distinctively sporting contribution to civil society, based on sporting values. These values would include the importance of competing while retaining respect for opponents; the ability to express and suppress individual talents and ambitions within a team; the acknowledgement that there is something — the good of the game — beyond our immediate ambitions; and an ultimate willingness to accept authority, however harsh its judgements (whether those of selectors or those of referees) may seem at the time. "All that I know most surely in the long run about morality and the obligations of men, I owe to football" is one of Albert Camus' most often quoted remarks[17]; it is curiously reminiscent of the reasons for Thomas Arnold's reluctant acceptance of the value of organised games as of the more enthusiastic commitments of later 'Muscular Christians'. In 1995 a 'Sportsmen's Party' contested the Georgian general election[18] and the Sports Organisation for Collective Contributions and Equal Rights (SOCCER) the South African Election. Such stories are relatively rare, but sport is often taken to stand for values. Those values are espoused by both the 'right', such as the "old farts"[19] who tried to maintain Rugby Union's amateurism up to its 1995 demise, and elements of the 'left', such as Camus and Fred Inglis[20]. They are, if not opposed, then treated as much less significant by the market-liberals who see sports as merely a set of leisure tastes with differing degrees of commercial potential.

It may seem odd that sports organisations could effectively check government power, but it is not so unusual. Later in this essay I will discuss the South African case, but Britain has provided examples of this almost as striking. With the exception of three sports with strong military connections — shooting, yachting and equestrianism — British sports organisations vigorously resisted government attempts to organise a boycott of the Moscow Olympics in 1980 and government proved completely ineffective in its attempts to control them. The comparison with the United States is instructive because there the boycott was entirely enforced. There is, of course, an ideological difference between the fervour, or the transcendence, with which people on the two sides of the Atlantic held anti-communist beliefs. It may well have been that Margaret Thatcher played her cards badly and hopelessly underestimated the depth of conviction with which even people who supported her in other respects would defend the autonomy of sports organisations[21]. But there is also a difference in the structure of sport in the two countries.

British sports of all kinds have been dominated by their grass roots, the private amateur clubs. These often own their own grounds and almost invariably live mainly on the income from their members' subscriptions. They thrive on an atmosphere of British political agnosticism: no flags, anthems or pledges and a cultural tradition which demands that 'politics' is treated as dirty and peripheral in comparison with the interests of the club and the sport. There is a very basic historical reason for this: British sport grew up in the Victorian and Edwardian periods as part of an a-political realm of sportsmen which had nothing to do with the state. American sport, by contrast, seems more corporatist, more caught up in a state-supported milieu, despite the generally acceptable orthodoxy that the US in general has fewer corporatist tendencies than most western countries. But the dominant agencies in American sport are the major leagues, with their constituent clubs and the colleges. To greater or lesser extent these agencies are all dependent on relationships with levels of the state: cities own many of the stadia in which professional clubs play and most of the university sector is state financed. It was this sector which was dominant in the Olympic sports in 1980. American sport was not in a position to defy government even if it wanted to.

Perhaps, too, the Moscow example exaggerates the independence of British sport. That was a case of many fairly conservative sports administrators refusing to use sport as a political sanction and defying a Conservative government. Defiance of the Gleneagles Agreement of 1977, which prohibited sporting contacts with South Africa, proved more difficult, though not impossible, since local authorities largely sympathetic to the ban owned some of the grounds and employed some of the personnel involved. For that matter, British sporting organisations might prove far less capable of independent action now: as commercialisation and dependence on government money (especially since the institution of a National Lottery in 1994) has increased, it has become less easy to flout or ignore government policy.

The same ambiguities about the purposes and effects of organisations exists in sport as exist in the rest of civil society. Is all organisation to be counted or only that which functions to maintain certain respectable norms? Australian soccer provides a real example of this ambiguity. From the 1950s onwards it came to be dominated by groups of immigrants, mainly from southern Europe, so much so that the name 'wogball' for the game can be found in the *Macquarie Dictionary*. According to Wray Vamplew, "the soccer field offered European migrants ... a slice of their own community, a link with their homeland and a base for the socialisation of their Australian-born offspring"[22]. Philip Mosely says that soccer and social clubs "provided a means of communal networking centred on material support; they served as emotional bulwarks against an often hostile host society; they helped preserve cultural identity"[23].

The problem has been that these cultural identities are predominantly Balkan and, even before Marshall Tito's death in 1981, the whole range of Balkan ethnic conflict came to be duplicated in Australian stadia by such clubs as Melbourne Croatia, Preston Makedonia, Yugal and Heidelberg Alexander. Australian sporting authorities have made attempts to ban overt ethnic identification as a result, but there is for some a more tacit desire to eradicate organisations which serve to 'preserve cultural identity' in the interests of a more integrated Australia. Thus, as in many other contexts, one can argue, from different perspectives, that these particular sporting organisations add in some senses to Australian civil society, but that they undermine it in others. There has certainly been little that was civil in the mini Balkan wars which have afflicted Australian soccer, even though their horrors may have been exaggerated by 'Anglo-Celtic' Australians.

Three case studies

I want now to consider sport in relation to civil society in the context of three diverse examples, all of which have experienced some form of 'democratisation' in the 1990s. They are the Republic of Georgia, the Kingdom of Thailand and the Republic of South Africa. Although these three countries are very disparate, they also have important similarities: in all three democracy is recently acquired and in doubt, a government elected by universal suffrage in the 1990s having been preceded by, in the South African case, a government based on a narrow racial electorate, in the Georgian by a communist government and in the Thai case by a military regime. However, the orthodox accounts of civil society mark them out very sharply from one another: South African civil society has been said to be strong, Thai civil society to be weak and embryonic and Georgian almost minimal. Thus, the comparison between them might be expected to throw light, at least, on any hypothesis about the relationship between civil society and democratization, though it is only fair to tell the reader that the selection of these three countries was dependent on the contingency of the author having been professionally involved in all of them. I will offer a brief profile of the historical and geographical background of Georgia and Thailand, and an even briefer one of South Africa before discussing civil society and the part played by sport in it.

Georgia is usually described as being in the Caucasus. This is true, but it is much more informative to say that Georgia is in the Trans-Caucasus, divided from the Caucasian republics in the Russian Federation by high mountains, with only a small Russian population and a vigorously independent national culture. Approximately, the country is the size and has the population of Scotland. Its history is extremely violent: twenty seven Islamic invasions followed by Russian protection in 1783 and complete incorporation into the Russian Empire in 1800. Georgia was an independent state from 1917 to 1921 before being conquered by the Soviet Army. However, it prospered in many ways during the Soviet period, helped by the prominence of Georgians (including Stalin, née Dugashvili) in the Soviet establishment. It was, among other things, the wine and tourist capital of the Soviet Union. Since the disintegration of the Soviet Union, Georgia has experienced as complete a collapse as any country in the world: in purely economic terms the GDP for 1995 was 17% of that in 1989, the world's worst score[24]. One aspect of Georgian culture is that Georgians have a strong image of themselves as 'Christians' and 'Europeans', though many outside observers have concluded that the country is very far removed, culturally, from Western

Europe. Given my reference to the strength of the national culture, one of Georgia's problems is that only 73% of the population are Georgian, the largest minorities being Azeri, Abkhazian, Armenian and Ossetian.

Thailand is the size and has the population of France. It is the only country in South East Asia to have avoided the experience of imperialism. Since the metamorphosis of the monarchy into a constitutional form in 1932, the country has experienced nineteen elections and seventeen military *coups d'etat*. In 1992 a series of popular demonstrations brought about the re-institution of elected government, an event which was nicknamed "the revolution of the mobile 'phones". I have commented elsewhere that apparently dramatic events in Thai political history are not so dramatic as they appear since Buddhism, the monarchy and economic growth have emerged virtually untouched from them[25]. Indeed, Thailand's 'double digit' economic growth and 'tiger' status dominates the academic literature on the country: even books on Thai politics turn out to be largely about the success of Thai business, and analyses of Thai society are largely concerned with what has been called the 'sleeping giant' of the new Thai middle classes[26].

Since South Africa's recent history has been played out on the world stage, it requires far less comment. It is worth noting, though, that the current proportion of the population of forty five million which is black African is 78%, rather higher than the proportion of Georgians in Georgia. However, I do not wish to imply that in every respect, or even in important respects, South African blacks constitute a single ethnic group.

Sport and civil society in Georgia

In nearly every respect, civil society in Georgia is weak and undeveloped. There is an almost complete lack of local, workers', charitable and religious organisations, for example. Political parties have so far proved to be weak, naïve and schismatic. It is in this context that one must understand how Georgians came to elect Zviad Gamsakhurdia as their leader in 1990 by an overwhelming majority. This was a man who was immensely sophisticated in some respects — he had taught English literature in an English university, for instance — but with a 'spiritual' vision of politics and almost no understanding of economics combined with a petty and vindictive attitude to his enemies, including his academic enemies[27]. In respect of the rôle of "recruiting and training leaders", Georgian civil society had nothing to offer and after a short war in early 1992 the supposedly hated former communist leader, Eduard Shevardnadze, returned to the country. His tenure of power, despite appalling circumstances, has proved more durable and he has been the effective victor in elections in 1992 and 1995.

East Germany had its Protestant churches, the Czech republic its intellectual associations and traditions with strong western contacts; Poland had the rapidly developing civic rôle of its catholic church and trade unions. All of these have provided a wide spectrum of leadership in the post-Communist period. But Georgia has had none of these: even its religion, Georgian orthodoxy, has been traditionally quietist and apolitical. In developmental terms it can be argued that Georgia's civil society lags behind that of Russia because modern institutions have been placed on Georgia from the outside, during the Soviet period.

However, I did say that Georgia's society was obviously weak in 'nearly' every respect. There are some respects in which Georgia is strong, including the sense of nationality and national tradition, the strength of the family and, at least in some rural cases, the community. Georgian society is strong at the level of what Edward Banfield called "amoral familism"[28] and it has bred a correspondingly strong range of Mafia-like organisations, including the Mkhedrioni, an 'order' of 'horsemen', which has been influential in government and in organised crime, though its influence was almost entirely destroyed in the aftermath of the failed attempt to assassinate Eduard Shevardnadze in 1995. These traditions and institutions have helped Georgia through some difficult times though they have also helped cause the difficulties. On the whole they have not made it easier to govern the country nor to move towards a mature party system.

Georgian sport does reflect Georgian society insofar as civil society seems pathetically weak. Georgia has produced great sportsmen, especially in football, but also in tennis, wrestling and weightlifting, but Georgian sport has always been entirely co-opted and controlled by the state in the typical Soviet manner[29]. In fact, Georgia might be said to be worse off in this respect than Russia and several other Eastern European countries since it was Sovietised at a level of development which preceded any modern sport. Paradoxically, sport in Georgia has also had quite a nationalist dimension: although the World Cup and the Olympic Games required Georgians to support the 'Soviet Motherland', internal Soviet football competitions allowed Georgians to cheer for Dinamo Tbilisi against Russian and Ukrainian teams, much as F.C. Barcelona have been a focus for Catalan nationalism in games against 'Spanish' teams.

Therefore since the 1980s sport has been in serious decline in Georgia, though the decline of football has in some respects now begun to reverse, largely due to the relatively vast amounts of money that can be made by talented Georgian clubs and individuals in the European context[30]. Even so, the reality of grass roots Georgian sport in the 1990s is a picture of overgrown football pitches and broken basketball hoops. In November 1995 I watched Dinamo Tbilisi, the former (1981) winners of the European Cup-Winners Cup, play Durugi in the Georgian League. There were 200 spectators in a stadium which can seat 80,000. I left when the score was 8-0 to Dinamo. It is a similar picture to provincial Hungary where Hann comments that, "Sports life is still moribund..." Not only does sport appear to be an irrelevance to the harsh conditions of life in Georgia, but it is also associated with the Soviet period and still conceived and understood in a Soviet context. It is a source of bafflement to Georgian friends and colleagues that I can turn down opportunities to make money in order to play cricket, and peasants in Megrelia could not understand why I climbed their mountains — an activity which wasted energy and shoe leather, both precious. It seems uncertain whether mass sport will revive in Georgia or how it could do so.

Sport and civil society in Thailand

It is more difficult to summarise the condition of civil society in Thailand. To an outsider, the essence of understanding how the country works is that its population of sixty million is dominated in every way by Bangkok, population ten million and rising. And Bangkok is dominated by a royal/business/military elite of about a quarter of a million people. Thus political struggles are in many ways only significant when they are intra-elite: it is intriguing that in talking of what seem to an outsider to be normal and natural political phenomena, such as peasant protests about dams and produce prices, Bangkokers seek explanations as to who (in the elite) 'lies behind' them. Moreover, the circulation within the elite is such that generals who had been prominent in military governments later turn up as party politicians. For example, General Chavalit Yongchaiyudh who became the Prime Minister of a coalition government in late 1996 had in 1990 described party politics as "a system of administration by money, power and lies"[31].

Much academic writing, including that by Thais, about contemporary Thailand starts with the record of Thai economic achievement and suggests that the institutions which compose civil society may be strengthening[32].

The professional and commercial middle class is growing and sensing its own strength. A wide variety of 'non-governmental organisations' are developing. Even the most excluded and peripheral class in society, the peasants, are beginning to organise themselves in protest against deforestation and golf course development, for example, sometimes with the aid of Buddhist monks. Without denying the general tendency in this direction, I would incline to scepticism about the extent of change. The 'sleeping giant' of the middle class is not much interested in politics and the main political change since 1992 seems to be the penetration of a group of forty-something professionals into the existing elite. 'Forest priests' and 'NGOs' are small phenomena with relatively ephemeral effects on the policy process, though academic attention is keen to highlight their importance as signs of change. In short, it is more difficult to say that civil society is weak in Thailand than it is in Georgia, because the strength of the elite structure makes the concept less relevant. Yet in most senses it is weak because many of the basic concepts and relations of a strong civil society seem to be western imports which are not yet well rooted. What is debatable is the extent to which this situation is changing.

In some respects the sports scene in Thailand seems to be thriving; certainly, it is not moribund and declining as is sport in Georgia. There are large followings for football and for Thai boxing, and badminton is widely played. The ancient sport of *seepak-pakraw*, a S.E. Asian game played with the feet using a wicker ball, is widely played in several forms, including a modernised version based on volleyball. Elaborate 'King's Cup' football tournaments involving visiting teams are played in Bangkok. Yet this range of activity masks what is largely seen as malaise and failure in Thai sport. Thais would dearly love to 'win' the Asian games, a feat which they last achieved in 1966; they are extremely unlikely to do so again since the arrival of China in world class sport. But in 1996 there was some considerable consolation when the boxer Somluck Khamsing became the first Thai to win an Olympic gold medal at the Atlanta games. He was rewarded with $1.5 million in cash, a B.M.W. car and a Ph.D. (in physical education). This was by far the most substantial package given by any government to an Olympic champion.

But Thai sport has failed to develop anything like the kind of grass roots which can be found in western countries. In football, there are immensely skilled individuals, but an inadequate structure of coaching and of amateur clubs. There is no established professional league and Thai fans pay more attention to English football than to their own game. In reality, the sporting organisations of Thailand are all under the complete control of the ruling elite which controls the state: for them the central question about sport is, 'What might be the roles of the government and business in producing Thai champions?'. Even the four billion baht (about £100 million) which the Thai state claims to spend on sport each year can do little to substitute for a lack of spontaneous grass roots tradition or to ameliorate the immense congestion which is urban Thailand, which leaves little time or space for sport[33].

The lack of grass roots organisation is not because the state or the ruling elite has seized control, as in Georgia, but it may have occurred for more fundamental reasons. Organised modern sport in Thailand, as in other Asian countries, is an imported, imposed institution. There may be spontaneous enthusiasm for it, but it does not have the same sort of place in the values and practices of popular culture that it does in Western societies. Thus for ambitious urban Thais there is little room for playing and organising sport; this situation mirrors that in Asian communities in Britain and their otherwise baffling failure to produce players who progress into professional football. An extreme example of this effect was the 'white elephant' system of scholarships which was intended to link the most promising sportsmen with the best university coaches ('white elephant' denoting an elite in Thailand, rather than something irrelevant and useless). The problem with the scheme was that the endowed scholars spent too much time in the library and not enough on the playing field. Thus, although Thai sport looks very different from Georgian sport from some angles, they have it in common that sporting organisation has been co-opted by a ruling elite and has not developed at the level of civil society.

Sport and civil society in South Africa

It has become orthodox to say that South Africa has a strong civil society. Almost more than any other it is the republic of the acronym: there are a wide range of trade unions, party and church organisations. Black Africans, without being formally represented in the state, have been represented in some sense by the African National Congress since 1910. Local, township, society has had its non-violent direct action organisations (generally known as the 'civics')[34]. On several occasions the actions of (white) non governmental organisations has been crucial to the changing of government policy: sport apart, perhaps the most famous example is the change of heart by the Dutch Reformed Church in 1986 which removed the theological underpinnings of *apartheid*. It is the strength of civil society, many people believe, which enabled the *apartheid* state to change so surprisingly smoothly into a republic based on 'one person, one vote'.

But such are the ambiguities of the concept of civil society that it is proper to express considerable scepticism about South African civil society. In many respects the place is outstandingly uncivil: for all the 'smooth transition', it has a murder rate some two and a half times that of Georgia, despite Georgia's extreme level of civil disorder, and the Georgian rate is, in turn, some twenty times that of the UK. According to many accounts of the concept, a strong and working civil society generates authority and helps resolve conflicts; if so, it must be failing in some respects in South Africa, given the endemic violence of that society. It is doubtful whether most black South Africans are actually connected to organisations which form part of a civil society. In any case, one of the paradoxes of civil society is that when an organisation which has been a bastion of a supposedly civil society becomes part of government, civil society may well be weakened: Solidarity in Poland and the ANC seem to be the two principal examples of this. Even so, there is no doubt that in some senses and respects South African civil society is much stronger than that in the two other examples.

Nor can there be any doubt that South Africa is a phenomenal sporting country which in 1995 was able to put on a Rugby Union World Cup, an African Nations Association Football Cup and a test match cricket series against England and win them all. South African sport has been strong off the field as well as on: a powerful range of sports organisations grew up under *apartheid* which were able to influence South African society and to challenge government. These included general sports organisations such as the South African Council on Sport (SACOS) and the South African Non-Racial Olympic Committee (SANROC) as well as both white and non-white organisations in general sports. There is no room here for the whole story, which can be read elsewhere[35]. But what happened essentially is that powerful private sports organisations were able to respond more positively and flexibly than the government to the institution of sporting sanctions. Two examples stand out. First the formation of the South African Cricket Union (SACU) in 1977 as (in principle) an integrated, non-racial organising body for cricket, contrary to government policies and the laws of 'petty *apartheid*'. This was not successful in its aim of re-admitting South Africa into international cricket, and the anti-*apartheid* movement led by bodies such as SACOS responded with the slogan that there should be 'no normal sport in an abnormal society'. It did not even persuade the (non-white) South African Cricket Board to affiliate. But it was instrumental in causing the nationalist government to allow sports federations a free reign on questions of integration from 1979 and to begin the demolition of petty apartheid. The ideological stance of the government shifted from 'racial discrimination is a legal requirement' to 'it is not our policy to enforce or ban racial discrimination by private organisations' and this change had been forced, in effect, by private sports organisations.

A second major example was the 'Safari in Harare' in which Dr. Louis Luyt of the Transvaal Rugby Football Union, acting as envoy for Dr. Danie Craven of the South African Rugby Board, negotiated directly with the ANC and the (non-racial) South African Rugby Union in Zimbabwe in October 1988. Many agents of South African civil society had had dealings with exiled officials of the ANC, but these, after all, represented a core Afrikaaner organisation, hitherto thought of as conservative, negotiating with people the Nationalist Party insisted on describing as totally unacceptable terrorists. The ANC's strategy, according to Steven Gruzd, was specifically couched in terms of civil society: it was a strategy of "putting out feelers into civil society, in order to understand it and to know with whom it was dealing before formal talks began with the government"[36]. This strategy, and the negotiations, were successful, arguably, for all parties: the ANC was to allow South African rugby back into international competition much earlier than expected and before 'one man one vote' elections while South African rugby was able to lend its weight to the case for the necessity of reform. The (white) "image of the ANC was transformed from that of the terrorist to that of the negotiator who had the best interests of South African sport at heart"[37]. In few countries could institutions of civil society outflank and manipulate what appeared to be a powerful state in this manner; in no other country, perhaps, could sporting institutions have played so large a part in forming the direction the state would take.

Conclusion

In stating the purpose of this essay, I suggested that the way of dealing with concepts in the study of society varies between disciplines. Economics has tended to develop relatively technical terms with fully agreed definitions; the advantages of such an achievement are considerable, but the disadvantage is that the flavour of the discourse sometimes seems far removed from the flavour of reality. In sociology, terms often seem absorbed into bodies of theory to which you must adhere as a whole or not at all: thus 'civil society' has its meaning and role within functionalism or figurationalism or one of a variety of forms of marxism, and it is a necessary and sufficient condition of the acceptance of a particular meaning that one accepts the system of theory as a whole.

But in political theory, there has been less progress in establishing or agreeing meanings. According to one influential account, originated by W.B. Gallie and developed by a number of writers, most notably William Connolly, we 'contest' meanings[38]. The "essential contested concepts" which are at the core of our interest do have a glimmer of agreed application (including, according to Gallie, an "original exemplar"), but will never have a fully agreed definition which allows us to say what is or is not a case of 'x' or, even in principle, to measure the extent to which a real circumstance is a case of 'x'. What legitimises debate on such an apparently sloppy basis and allows concepts to be 'essentially contested' rather than 'radically confused' is that 'progress' is made intellectually. But we must at least entertain the case for astringent scepticism; it is possible that the debate about civil society is radically confused, that it is a case of a lot of people talking at cross-purposes, using different senses of a term which they define 'persuasively' in C.L. Stevenson's sense and re-define stipulatively, but unsuccessfully (in that their definitions do not become widely accepted)[39]. There is a strong case for conceptual scepticism about civil society on these grounds as there is about power and about democracy.

On the other hand, there have been times when researching sport when I have felt that a strong sense of the reality of civil society is the key to understanding how countries differ. In 1995, Georgia began to turn a corner: after the unsuccessful assassination attempt on Eduard Shevardnadze in August and his re-election as president in November, many criminal elements were incarcerated. For the first time in six years Georgia was at peace with a fair degree of law and order and a stable currency (the lari); international confidence in the country began to revive as did substantial parts of the small business sector of the economy, though large-scale industry had been wiped out and a real revival of the state service sector seemed far off. In these circumstances I was interested in detecting signs of a revival of sport. Were people founding their own football and basketball clubs? Were they beginning to organise volunteer coaching schemes for children at school? In many cases my questions fell on uncomprehending ears. How could they compete internationally, my respondents demanded, when there was no money available for travel? How could schoolchildren be coached when there was no money to pay coaches? In vain I insisted that I wasn't talking about international sport, but about the grass roots level and not about paid coaches but about the kind of enthusiastic volunteers who run most of western sport. The assumption of almost all my informants was that sport must be organised from the top down and that Georgian sport could only be revived when the economy revived and major new companies were established who could sponsor clubs. It was all very different from talking to South African rugby players and cricketers who saw themselves as having a duty to society to spread and organise their own sports in the townships: the two assumptions, that the activity must be spontaneous and voluntary and that it was for the ultimate benefit of society as such, were entirely absent in Georgia.

Georgians seemed often, in this respect, to have no concept of society. It did not occur to them to 'volunteer' any more than it occurred to them to remove a rock or a dead animal off the road once they had driven past it. People who will risk life, or give their last penny to help family or friends, had no notion of acting privately to benefit a 'community' or a 'public'. Sporting institutions remained largely in the control of the remnants of powerful interests. Dinamo Tbilisi was, for the first half of the 1990s, entirely controlled by the para-military, political-criminal organisation the Mkhedrioni. The second most successful football team, Dinamo Batumi, was part of the fiefdom of the long-established Adjarian party boss, Aslan Abashidze. Given Georgia's 'failure' at the Atlanta Olympics of 1996, the Minister of Sport, Kakhi Asatiani, instinctively called for more state involvement and control over sport.

There were exceptions: student unions proved capable of establishing their own competitions, starting with a national student basketball league founded in 1994. Wrestling, too, showed a capacity for spontaneous grass roots organisation, but it is one of the few sports with genuine roots in Georgian rural society, maintained since pre-Soviet times. It is also, of course, a particularly cheap and easy sport to organise. The Georgian Rugby Union also organised itself on an independent basis with a full range of officials, including junior and veterans sections, in 1995[40].

In these cases, apart from wrestling, the really influential phenomenon has been the international links which Georgian organisations have been able to cultivate. In the case of rugby, the whole effort is aimed at the World Cup in 1999 and the Olympics in 2000 and there is awareness of the importance of working with the major rugby-playing countries. (There is an element of irony about this since the Georgian Rugby Union presents itself as the inheritors of an ancient, partly Georgian, game called Lelo which was modernised rather than created in England.) Sir Sridath Ramphal has suggested that international civil society is vastly important, but underestimated and little understood[41]. The study of sport tends to confirm this strongly: if Georgian football and rugby are successfully reorganised, the efforts of FIFA and the International Rugby Board will be important. The status and financial benefits which come with international links are attracting and motivating Georgians in a process which is parallel to that which helped destroy *apartheid* in South Africa. But it is not only in sport that this happens: the Bristol-Tbilisi Association, the Byron Society and the vast range of university contacts and links between Georgian and western institutions which have come into being during the 1990s are just some examples of contacts which simultaneously link Georgians to an international civil society and help form a civil society within Georgia. The International Society for Fair Elections based in Tbilisi has been assiduous in cultivating contacts in many countries and has extended its brief to a concept of civil society, organising meetings, for instance, between local politicians and their electors, a procedure which both sides seemed to find rather baffling at first.

Scepticism about civil society must be muted by the perception that, however vague and contested the concept, it does help illustrate the differences between societies and the directions of social change in ways which cannot be achieved by more particular or more precise concepts. There is perhaps an ambiguity in the criterion that 'progress' must occur for concepts to be contested rather than confused. I remain sceptical that this condition is met if the criterion is interpreted to mean progress towards a clearer and less contested *concept*, but I would argue that debating the broad concept does help us progress towards a deeper and more complex understanding of how particular societies work.

According to this criterion the concept of civil society offers insight into the workings of sporting institutions and sport is an informative dimension of civil society. To some degree we must accept the banality that sport *tends* to reflect the rest of civil society, but that reflection is not necessarily that seen in a plain mirror. It may be the sort of exaggerated reflection seen in a convex mirror. Thus Georgian sport has collapsed to an even greater extent than other aspects of Georgian society, Thai sport is even more dominated by a royal/military/business elite than other aspects of Thai life and sporting civil society is relatively even stronger than South African civil society. This latter case shows how important sport can be, the other two how much less important it often is.

Notes

1 L. Allison, 'Sport and Politics' in Lincoln Allison (ed.), *The Politics of Sport*, (Manchester, Manchester University Press, 1986), pp. 1-26.

2 Tony Mason, *Association Football and English Society 1863-1915*, (London, Harvester, 1980).

3 R. Holt, *Sport and the British, a modern history*, (Oxford, Oxford University Press, 1989), Grant Jarvie and Joseph Maguire, *Sport and Leisure in Social Thought*, (London, Routledge, 1994).

4 B. Houlihan, *The Government and Politics of Sport*, (London, Routledge, 1991).

5 For the first see, for instance, W.J.M. Mackenzie, *Politics and Social Science*, Penguin, 1967 and for the second Steven Lukes, *Power: a radical view*, (London, Macmillan, 1975).

6 G. White, 'Civil Society, Democratization and Development (1): Clearing the Analytical Ground', *Democratization*, vol. 1, no. 3, (Warwick, 1994), p. 378.

7 D. Robertson, *The Penguin Dictionary of Politics*, (London, Penguin, 1986), pp. 44-45.

8 J. Urry, *The Anatomy of Capitalist Societies, The Economy, Civil Society and the State*, (London, Macmillan, 1981), p. 12.

9 E. Gellner, 'The Importance of Being Modular' in John A. Hall (Ed.), *Civil Society: Theory, History, Comparison*, Polity 1995, (London) p. 32.

10 L. Diamond, 'Toward Democratic Consolidation', *Journal of Democracy*, vol. 5, no. 3, 1994. Reprinted as 'Third World Civil Society Can Promote Democracy' in Jonathan S. Petrikin (Ed.), *The Third World*, Opposing Viewpoints, (San Diego, Greenhaven, 1995), pp. 151-159.

11 Robertson, *op. cit.*, p. 44.

12 G. Roberts and A. Edwards (eds.), *A New Dictionary of Political Analysis*, E. Arnold, (London 1991), p. 133.

13 R. Scruton, *A Dictionary of Political Thought*, (London, Pan, 1982), p. 66.

14 Urry, *op. cit.*, p. 12.

15 K. Tester, *Civil Society*, (London, Routledge, 1992), p. 124.

16 C. Hann, 'Philosophers' Models on the Carpathian Lowlands", in J. A. Hall (ed.), *Civil Society. Theory, History, Comparison. Polity, 1995*, p. 178.

17 Quoted, for example, in S. Redhead, 'Sporting Culture, Post-Fandom and Hyperlegality', in L. Allison (ed.), *Warwick Working Papers in Sport and Society*, vol. 4, (Warwick, 1995-96), yet, despite a reasonably comprehensive reading of Camus, I cannot find anywhere Camus actually published this remark.

18 See L. Allison, A. Kukhianidze and M. Matsaberidze, 'The Georgian Election of 1995', *Electoral Studies*, vol. 15, no. 2 (Warwick, 1996).

19 The phrase refers to a description of the committee of the Rugby Union by Will Carling, the England captain.

20 F. Inglis, 'The State of Play: Sport, Capital and Happiness' in Allison (ed.) *Warwick Working Papers in Sport and Society*, vol. 4, 1995-96 and *Popular Culture and Political Power*, (London, Harvester, 1988).

21 See T. Monnington, 'Politicians and Sport: uses and abuses', in L. Allison (ed.) *The Changing Politics of Sport*, (Manchester, Manchester University Press, 1993). I am grateful to T. Monnington for further comments on the case.

22 W. Vamplew, 'Soccer in Australia: a lost cause?' in L. Allison (ed.), *Warwick Working Papers in Sport and Society*, vol. 4, (Warwick, 1995-96), p.4.

23 P. Mosely, 'Balkan Politics in Australian Soccer', in J. O'Hara (ed.), *Ethnicity and Soccer in Australia*, (Sydney, 1994), p. 33.

24 European Bank for Reconstruction and Development Transition, 1995 Report. See K. Drone and A. Robinson, 'Strong growth forecast for Eastern Europe', *Financial Times*, Thursday November 2nd 1995, p. 12.

25 L. Allison, 'The Concept of Civil Society in Georgia, Thailand and South Africa', in *South African Journal of International Affairs* Vol. 4, No. 2, 1997, pp. 18-38..

26 See, for instance, A. Laothamatas, 'Sleeping Giant Awakens: the Middle Class in Thai Politics' in C. Phuangkasem, S. Sornsri, C. Songsamphan and S. Wajjwalku (eds.), *Democratic Experiences in South East Asian Countries*, Thammasat University Press 1993, pp. 80-98 and Kevin Hewison, *Power and Politics in Thailand: Essays in Political Economy*, Journal of Contemporary Asia Publishers, (Manila and Wollongong, 1989).

27 For the first hand account of Gamsakhurdia's (incredible) world view, see Z. Gamsakhurdia, *The Spiritual Mission of Georgia*, (Tbilisi, Ganatleba), 1981. Other published work by the author on Georgia includes L. Allison, 'The Other Georgia On My Mind, Hopes and Fears for an Ancient Land',

The World & I, vol. 8, no. 7, 1993, L. Allison, A. Kukhianidze and M. Matsaberidze, 'The Georgian Election of 1992', *Electoral Studies*, vol. 12, no. 2, 1993, L. Allison, 'The Georgian General Election of 1995', *Electoral Studies*, vol., 15, no. 2, 1996, and L. Allison and N. Kukhianidze, 'An Everyday Story of Ethnic Cleansing', *New Statesman and Society*, 27 January 1995.

28 In E. Banfield, *The Moral Basis of a Backward Society*, (Glencoe, Free Press, 1958).

29 See James Riordan, *Sport, Politics and Communism*, (Manchester, Manchester University Press, 1991).

30 I would like to thank the following staff of the *Georgian Times* for talking to me about contemporary Georgian sport: Alexander Breyadze, Slava Sologhashvili, Akami Grimradze and Sandro Bregadze. Also Zviad Kozidze (editor) and Bidzina Makashvili of *7 Days* magazine.

31 Hann, *op. cit.*, p. 166.

32 E. Bardecke, 'Six-party coalition set to rule in Thailand', *Financial Times*, 19.11.96, 8.4.

33 See P.G. Warr (ed.), *The Thai Economy in Transition*, (Cambridge, Cambridge University Press, 1993) and P. Jumbala, *Nation-building and Democratization in Thailand: a Political History*, (Bangkok Chulalongkorn University Press, 1992). I would like to thank Prudhisan Jumbala, my host in Thailand, for many helpful comments and much assistance.

34 On February 23rd 1995 I was the opening speaker (apart from an introduction by the Minister of Sport) at what was said to be the first academic conference held in Thailand on the subject of sport, and this analysis reflects the discussion at that conference. I would like to thank, among others, Dr. Nat Indrapana, Deputy Governor of the Sports Authorities of Thailand and member of the International Olympic Committee, Thavatchai Sajakul, Chairman of the Technical Committee of the Football Association of Thailand, Prof. Chargen Wattanasin, Vice President of the International Badminton Federation and Mr. Edward Thangarajah, Senior Sports Editor of the Bangkok Post for talking to me. See *Bangkok Post*, February 22nd 1995, *Sunday Post* February 26th 1995.

35 For an early account of the civics under apartheid, see J. Seekings, 'Trailing behind the masses: The United Democratic Front and Township, Politics in the Pretoria — Witwatersrand — Vaal Region, 1983-84', *Journal of Southern African Studies*, vol. 18, no. 1, 1992. Their current dilemmas are

covered by J. Cherry, 'The Politics of Hegemony and the Politics of Development: the 1994 Elections in South Africa's Eastern Cape', *Democratization*, vol. 1, no. 3, 1994.

36 See A. Guelke, 'The Politicisation of South African Sport' in L. Allison (Ed.) *The Politics of Sport*, (Manchester, Manchester University Press 1986) and A. Guelke 'Sport and the end of *apartheid*' in Lincoln Allison (Ed.) *The Changing Politics of Sport*, (Manchester, Manchester University Press 1995).

37 S. Lee Gruzd, *Back on the Field: the Changing Political Rôle of Sport in South Africa*, 1988-95, thesis, Witwatersrand University, 1995, p. 21.

38 Ibid., p. 53.

39 See W.B. Gallie, 'Essentially Contested Concepts', *Proceedings of the Aristotelian Society*, vol. LVI, 1955-56 and W. Connolly, *The Terms of Political Discourse*, D.C. Heath, 1974.

40 C.L. Stevenson, *Ethics and Language*, (New Haven, Yale University Press, 1944).

41 See *Georgia's Rugby Union*, pamphlet produced by the Georgian R.F.U., 1996.

42 In remarks in his preliminary address to the conference on Civil Society held by the Centre for the Study of Democratization at the University of Warwick, 17 February 1996.

NATIONAL RESPONSES TO GLOBAL SPORTS

Barrie Houlihan

Professor of International Relations and Politics
at Staffordshire University

Introduction

Almost without exception, industrialised and many developing states have, over the last thirty years, increased their funding for sport at a pace greater than that for most other services. It is well recognised that part of the explanation for the steady increase in public funding lies in an instrumental perception of sport. In other words, sport is rarely valued for its intrinsic qualities but rather for its capacity to ameliorate or camouflage problems ranging from poor cardiovascular health and juvenile delinquency to low tourist volume. Recently, a broad range of states have been giving greater prominence to the capacity of sport to promote a sense of national identity and then to project that identity abroad. This shift in policy has been due in large part to two factors: first, an increasing awareness and suspicion of cultural globalisation, and second, the dramatic shifts in global politics, especially the ending of the Cold War and the fragmentation of the Soviet Union.

There is already a vast literature on globalisation both generally and, more specifically, on the globalisation of sport[1].The evolution of the debate over the nature and form of cultural globalisation has resulted in the emergence of two fairly distinct characterisations of the process. The first emphasises the imperialist rationale of globalisation which stresses the grossly unequal relationship between the culturally dominant capitalist and predominantly Western economies, and the developing economies of the southern hemisphere. The development of the relationship is motivated by a desire to extend the market for capitalist cultural products (film, television programmes and sports) and also to foster the emergence of a consumerist culture. According to this view, cultural imperialism is "the sum of the processes by which a society is brought into the

77

modern world system and how its dominating stratum is attracted, pressured, forced and sometimes bribed into shaping social institutions to correspond to, or even promote, the values and structures of the dominating centre of the system"[2]. The relationship is one that leaves the peripheral nations as "more the taker than the giver of meaning and meaningful form"[3].

The way in which talented athletes from poorer countries are exported to richer clubs in track and field, soccer, baseball, cricket and basketball provides evidence in support of this view. Similarly, the energetic global promotion of Anglo-European sports through the media, the Olympic movement and the Commonwealth Games, and the undermining of local sporting traditions, could also constitute evidence of an imperialistic and highly exploitative relationship. The relationship displays the power and cultural confidence of the industrialised West and the vulnerability of the cultural colony. Attractive though this conceptualisation of the relationship is, there has been considerable dissatisfaction with the underlying assumptions of the cultural imperialism thesis, especially the unidirectional flow of culture and the coercive nature of the relationship. This criticism has encouraged the formulation of an alternative theorisation of globalisation which suggests an "interconnection and interdependency of all global areas which happens in a far less purposeful way"[4]. According to this conceptualisation the net effect is the weakening of the cultural coherence of individual states including those among the major capitalist economies and the former imperial powers. Thus the assumption of cultural dominance and confidence among the major capitalist states is replaced by the assertion that they too are subject to a growing sense of cultural insecurity. Globalisation is therefore a process which results in the production of a 'third' culture which has also been described as transcultural and a-national[5]. The conclusion is that despite the significance of the advanced industrial states in the production of a putative global culture they have not been able to insulate their own cultures from the unsettling effects of the phenomenon. Hannerz sums up this position as a loss of the pre-twentieth-century world which was essentially a cultural mosaic "of separate pieces with hard edges" and its replacement by "a global ecumene of persistent interaction and exchange"[6]. Although the impact of globalisation is much greater for the weaker developing nations, both powerful and weak states face the problem of greater cultural insecurity.

At worst, states see themselves tackling problems of social cohesion and international prestige against the background of a global culture which is not only ahistorical and rootless but which makes a virtue of its lack of roots and historical association. This global culture is not self-referential and deliberately eschews any historical or temporal context; it is determinedly eclectic and is manifest within a persistent present which denies any assumption of progress. Most modern international sporting events possess many of these characteristics, mixing classical allusions, militaristic triumphalism, fashion show glamour and a degree of national sentimentality that would have embarrassed Walt Disney. Although a caricature, this is a far more plausible view of cultural globalisation and explains the enthusiasm of most Western states for heritage politics and, with regard to sport, the desire to protect 'traditional' national sports even when that tradition is short-lived, fabricated and forced to operate within an international framework which is a primary vehicle for globalisation.

The concern shown by many states for the politics of identity has also been sharpened by major developments in the international system, especially the ending of the Cold War and the re-emergence of ethnic nationalist politics in post-communist Europe. Although the development and maintenance of national identity has been a constant concern for the modern state the collapse of communism in Europe has given the concern a new momentum. Cable argues that the ending of the Cold War has meant the decline of the left-right dialectic as the primary global fault line, but "as the old division between left and right fades a new one is appearing, centred on different ways in which people define their identity"[7]. Parekh has traced the contours of the current debate on national identity in a variety of countries. In Britain, for example, he suggests that the problem has been defined by the New Right as one of erosion of identity, particularly by imported ideas, and also from the supranational aspirations of the post-Maastricht European Union: the solution lies, for the Conservative Party, in a confirmation of traditional values (and traditional sports). In Canada, by contrast, the problem is one of confusion of identity, and centres on whether the country is homogeneous and singular or bi-national, tri-national or even multiethnic. Parekh also charts the identity crises in Germany, Algeria and India and suggests that while each of the five countries experiences the crisis in a distinctive fashion the sources of the crisis are similar to those identified by Cable[8]. In essence the threats to identity are twofold: on the one hand the development of a global economy and media is perceived as delocalising values and practices, while on the other there is, for many states, the increasing assertiveness of ethnic minorities.

The debates that have developed around cultural globalisation, national and ethnic identity and the role of the state have struck a rich vein among scholars interested in the relationship between politics and sport. Recent contributions include the examination of the attempts to use sport, and particularly elite sporting success, to achieve a greater degree of national unity or to develop a sharper sense of national identity. Other studies have used sport to track the disintegration of states and the fragmentation of identity (USSR), the re-establishment of national identity (Germany) or to plot the ambiguities of identity such as those found in Ireland, Scotland and Northern Ireland. The significance of these studies is reinforced by the continuing salience of sport specifically and cultural politics generally to governments. This is certainly true of the three countries examined in detail in this chapter. In Canada there was a threefold increase in federal government annual funding for sport between 1978 and 1987 to a total of Can $60m designed to "Fund sport in keeping with its contribution to our culture, national heritage and economy"[9]. In Britain an important policy paper on sport referred to sport as a "central part of Britain's national heritage" and as "one of the defining characteristics of nationhood"[10] and looked forward to the improvement in sporting achievement that the estimated £300m annual investment in sport from the National Lottery will bring. Finally, in Ireland, government funding for sport has risen from IR£3m in 1986 to IR£17m in 1994 enabling, inter alia, 'elite sport', in the words of the minister, to play "a major role in enhancing the profile of our nation abroad"[11].

The relationship between sport and culture

Given the recent policy statements and public expenditure decisions of many governments, particularly in industrialised states, the cultural centrality of sport would seem to be clearly established. Among social scientists there are those who argue that sport is an integral and even defining element of the culture of a community. Geertz, for example, argues that sport, as a collectively sustained symbolic structure, is a powerful metaphor which reveals the most deep seated values of a culture[12]. In a similar vein, Morton has argued that an analysis of a nation at play "reveals the stuff of its social fabric and value system and tells us much about other facets of political and economic life, particularly in modern industrial society"[13]. Yet the opinions of Geertz and Morton are based on a view of culture which characterises it as essentially indivisible and where a rough equality of significance of cultural elements is assumed. Little attention is paid to the need to distinguish between elements that are core, deeply embedded and

slow to change and those that are more superficial and transitory. Few attempts
at a disaggregation of culture have moved beyond the crude neo-Marxist
formulations which see culture as a reflection of economic relations.

One of the more sophisticated attempts to disaggregate culture comes from
Ulf Hannerz, who, using the notion of "cultural flows", distinguishes three key
flows, the first of which concerns cultural commodities that circulate within the
marketplace and which would include sports goods and fashion wear as well as
televised sport. The second flow is located in the political sphere and is centred
on the actions of the state as an organisational form, but also as a manager of
meaning. Hannerz's final cultural flow is the "form of life" which he uses to refer
to the "habitual perspectives and dispositions" that define everyday life and
which would include such elements as religious beliefs and practices as well as
gender, family and intergenerational relations[14]. This cultural flow is relatively
insulated from other cultures and cultural flows.

Undoubtedly, Hannerz's typology can be challenged, particularly with regard
to the boundaries between cultural flows. What is significant about Hannerz's
work is the questions it raises about the relative significance of particular cultural
elements and the implications that this has for the engagement of local cultures
with global culture and also for the capacity of the state to manipulate meaning.
In essence the problem is one of being able to specify the core elements of a local
culture. For example, is the recent popularity of American football or martial arts
in Britain an invasion of, and challenge to, the nation's core identity or merely
an example of cultural ephemera confined to the marketplace and the cultural
periphery? A similar problem arises when sport in Ireland is considered. Is the
apparent decline in the popularity of traditional Irish sports, which were so
important in defining Irish national identity during the anti-colonial struggle, and
the rising popularity of (the English game of) soccer, evidence of successful
penetration by global culture? Finally, how does one assess the relative significance of particular sports as opposed to the pattern of sports organisation found
in local cultures? In other words, is the success of globalisation to be measured
in terms of the spread of leagues, functional specialism among players, complex
rules and other features of organisational rationality or in terms of the global
adoption of particular sports? Correspondingly, is the integrity of national
identity to be assessed by the distinctiveness of the pattern of sports and their
organisation, and by the capacity of a nation to insulate its core values and
practices from the global culture?

Part of the value of Hannerz's argument is that it draws attention to the rôle of the state as a manager of meaning, but avoids the sweeping assumptions of hegemonic capacity made by, among others, neo-Marxist structuralists. Rather, the state is seen as operating in a more pluralist arena and in competition with other sources of cultural change such as religious organisations and media institutions. In addition, the notion of cultural flows suggests that there are elements of culture which are partially insulated from the economic and political sphere and where change is more effectively contested. The idea of communities possessing a cultural core (form of life) parallels the broader study of the roots of national identity which trace the relationship between the modern nation and the pre-modern, looser collective cultural groups which are referred to as ethnic communities or ethnies. Ethnic communities are defined by Smith as "named units of population with common ancestry myths and historical memories, elements of shared culture [such as religion, customs, language or institutions], some link with a historic territory and some measure of solidarity, at least among elites"[15].

The link between the modern nation-state and ethnic communities is strong if not always authentic. Clearly most of the longest-established nations were formed on the basis of pre-modern ethnic communities and consequently have acquired the status of models of nation formation for subsequent aspirants. More importantly, where aspirant nations had no, or only weak, recognisable ethnic antecedents they frequently felt obliged to manufacture "a coherent mythology and symbolism of a community of history and culture"[16]. But here it is important to bear in mind that even where there is a strong continuity between the ethnic communities and modern nation-states the two phenomena face different problems in ensuring their persistence. While the ethnic community may thrive on the basis of the maintenance of ancestry myths and shared history through ritual, the state faces a very different set of problems. The state, operating within a political community, has, among its varied responsibilities, the protection of territorial boundaries, the management of an economy, and the administration of a political/legal system.

Wherever possible, political leaders will attempt to adapt the mythology and symbolism of the ethnic community to help achieve their objectives. For those who see the culture of the ethnic community as fixed, the problem facing the state is simply to identify and then cloak itself in the mantle of ethnic identity. Scruton, for example, suggests that British national identity is historically determined, like an archaeological treasure, and an unalterable fact of life which one can seek to understand and come to terms with but not change[17]. There have been numerous attempts to capture the essentials of English (and possibly British) identity. One of the most resonant descriptions was by T. S. Eliot who argued that British culture encompassed "all the characteristic activities of a people. Derby Day, Henley Regatta, Cowes, the twelfth of August, a cup final, the dog races, the pin table, the dartboard, Wensleydale cheese, boiled cabbage ... beetroot in vinegar, nineteenth-century Gothic churches, and the music of Elgar"[18]. John Major's more recent version talked of "the country of long shadows on county [cricket] grounds, warm beer, invincible green suburbs, dog lovers and pool fillers" as constituting the essence of Englishness[19]. In both these attempts to encapsulate the essential ingredients of English/British cultural identity sporting images plays a central role.

But for some the essence of Englishness can only be captured through the imagery of sport. On the death of Bobby Moore, the captain of the 1966 World Cup winning side, *The Independent* newspaper (26 Feb. 1993) spoke of, "The death of Bobby Moore, England's hero. Golden-haired, a gentle giant, a great Englishman. Sport, where Britain supports different national teams, has become one of the few areas where an uncomplicated celebration of Englishness is permissible. It is only a mild exaggeration to call England the submerged nation... So England becomes a country that exists on the sports field, but not elsewhere". So closely intertwined are the notions of Englishness and sport that sporting behaviour has become almost synonymous with the virtues of the English way of life. As Clarke and Clarke suggest, such moral tales incorporate within the notion of 'sporting', "such themes as the sense of fair play, a proper respect for authority and the rules, the importance of self-control and self-discipline. These virtues help us to distinguish ourselves from others"[20].

The vision of an unchanging and unchangeable culture, which Robertson aptly refers to as "wilful nostalgia", in which sport figures so prominently, is as much a myth as the images it contains[21]. A contrary, and more plausible, view is that national identity is the product of negotiation and is constantly being refined, and occasionally redefined. One might note the way in which the German gymnastic Jahre movement was of central symbolic importance in a variety of conceptualisations of German identity. According to Hobsbawm "the mass movement of German gymnasts [was] liberal and Great German until the 1860s, Bismarkian after 1866 and eventually pan-German and anti-semitic"[22].

National identity, and the sporting elements of it, is more likely to be founded on historical invention and reinvention than fact. As Gellner noted, "Nationalism is not what it seems ... The cultural shreds and patches used by nationalism are often arbitrary historical inventions"[23] and therefore closer to the model of a "narrative strategy" noted by Bhabha[24] than the revealed truth of Scruton.

If the maintenance of identity is problematic for the relatively long-established nation-states then it is often far more so for the aspirant which has no dominant ethnic mythology or ethnic community around which to coalesce. Where this is the case, the state is faced with the challenge of manufacturing a coherent mythology and history which can anchor the character and form of the nation and provide a basis for national unity.

The use of sport to manage identity

With very few exceptions, all states are faced with the problem of reconciling a paradox when it comes to the management of identity. At the heart of the paradox is the pressure to establish and project a sense of national unity on the world stage, but through means of a limited and increasingly uniform set of strategies, including, for example, the adoption of national anthems and flags, the issuing of national currency, the formation of armed forces, the design of tourism products, membership of major international organisations such as the United Nations, Council of Europe, and the International Olympic Committee, and participation in major international sports events. As Wallerstein observed: "It is almost as though the more intense the nationalist fervour in the world, the more identical seem the expressions of this nationalism"[25].

Part of the explanation for the similarity in strategy adopted by states lies in the enlargement of the frame of reference of states from one which is dominated by their immediate neighbours or (ex)imperial power to one which is regional and frequently global. Part of the explanation also lies in the increasingly common aspiration to a model of political identity based on Western European experience. Smith summarises the defining characteristics of the Western model of nationalism as incorporating the following elements: first, territorialism, by which is meant a commitment to place rather than genealogy; second, the active participation of the people in the nation, commonly through political party organisations; third, citizenship, which is seen as a bond between the individual and the state which is intended to weaken other bonds, such as to the ethnic group; and finally, civic education, which is designed to impart a sense of common cultural inheritance as well as inculcate dominant political values.

There are many ways in which modern sport can and does contribute to the achievement and refinement of the characteristics of the Western model. For example, as regards "territorialism", national teams participating in competitions are an embodiment of the territorial basis of the state. Interestingly, this can be achieved even when the members of the national team could claim association with other nation-states. The fact that the English cricket team regularly contains players born in Zimbabwe, South Africa and Wales does not seem to dilute the nationalist impact of the (occasional) victory or, more commonly, heroic defeat. Even where international club soccer is concerned' the fact that key players might be nationals of other countries does not seem to detract from the nationalist significance of the victory. For example, the achievements of AC Milan in soccer in the early 1990s were hailed as major Italian victories despite relying on three Dutch players in key roles. Even the hosting of sports events can help to assert, both internally and externally, the territorial dimension of the state. The hosting of the Olympic Games by Seoul reinforced the territorial integrity of South Korea particularly in relation to its hostile northern neighbour, and the marathon held in Berlin in 1990 which followed a route which deliberately criss-crossed the line of the wall was a poignant symbol of the new territorial boundaries of the German state.

However, sport is also capable of reflecting the ambiguities of the territorial basis of the nation. The overlap between British and English identity is clearly evident in sport. While there is only an English soccer team at international level, track and field athletes will compete for England in the Commonwealth Games, but for Britain in the Olympics. In Ireland the tension between Irish, Northern Irish and UK identity is also reflected in the definition of 'national' teams. In soccer the Irish Republic and Northern Ireland have separate teams, but in hockey and rugby union the teams are drawn from all thirty-two counties.

The second feature of the Western model of nationalism is its emphasis on citizen participation. Where the state is democratic, voting is one obvious demonstration of involvement and commitment to the nation-state. Where democracy is constrained, the opportunities for voluntary participation in the 'life of the nation' will obviously be limited but, in most countries, whether democratic or not, the opportunities for personal participation in national political events will be rare. As a result, opportunities for symbolic association with the state will be created to act as surrogates for participation as citizens. Almost without exception countries will have public holidays or celebrations linked to events (such as Independence Day, Bastille Day, or Remembrance Sunday) or people (St Patrick's Day, Washington's birthday) which have a nationalist resonance. Sport, however, provides a number of emotionally charged occasions for citizens to be made aware of and express their common identity within the nation. The participation in major sports events as spectators has the element of ritual and emotional appeal capable of sustaining the 'imagined community' of the nation. Following the fortunes of individual athletes, clubs or national teams provides a common reference point within a nationalist context for a large proportion of the population in many countries.

In many ways sport is an ideal context within which to explore and debate the basis of citizenship. Citizenship defines not only membership of the nation-state (and thereby access to its services and benefits), but also seeks to override other claims on allegiance such as family, religion and ethnicity. Eligibility rules for membership of national squads frequently reinforces and mirrors debates about criteria for citizenship. For example, the courting of foreign-born cricketers such as Alan Lamb, Robin Smith and Graham Hick to establish their eligibility to play for England provoked the reaction that questioned the commitment of players who were not English born. Similar debates have been provoked by the sight of the boxer Lennox Lewis and tennis player Greg Rusedski, both Canadian born, competing for England and, most memorably (notoriously), by the speed with which the white South African athlete Zola Budd was able to gain British citizenship and compete in international competition. In contrast, the British-born long-jumper Fiona May was subject to charges of disloyalty for moving to Italy and subsequently winning a World Championship gold medal for her adopted country.

The spate of defections from communist to capitalist countries in the 1960s and 1970s provided opportunities for Western politicians and the media to highlight the rejection of Soviet or East German communist identity. Sport has also been used to question the depth of commitment to British identity by citizens from ethnic backgrounds. For example, Britons of Indian ethnic background who support the visiting Indian cricket team in test matches are deemed to have failed the 'Tebbit test' of citizenship. The linking of cultural traits and patterns of behaviour to citizenship is part of the process by which identities are provided "which legitimize claims to rights ... [and are used as] strategies or weapons in competition over scarce social goods"[26]. More recently, a fierce debate was prompted in the British press by an article in a cricketing magazine which questioned the capacity of foreign-born players to play for England with sufficient commitment[27]. These debates keep the questions of citizenship and national identity at the forefront of public debate and provide a surrogate for debates about immigration policy and the granting or refusal of refugee status. Finally, the national *team* is a valuable metaphor for the nation. In soccer, cricket and rugby union, club loyalty and partiality is pushed (albeit temporarily) into the background in preference to loyalty to the nation. However, the relationship between local and national loyalty is occasionally problematic. For example, the deep animosity between Glasgow Celtic and Glasgow Rangers complicates Scottish support for the national side. While the depth of animosity between the two Glasgow clubs is not totally subsumed when Scotland play the Irish Republic or when Scotland temporarily played their home matches at Ibrox (Glasgow Rangers home ground) in the early 1990s, it does not dilute support for the Scottish national team when playing international matches against England. However, at best the sectarian divisions are simply suspended for the duration of the match. Jim Sillars, previously a Scottish National Party MP, reflecting on the variability in the intensity of Scottish nationalist feeling, observed, with obvious despair, that "Scotland has too many ninety minute patriots whose nationalist outpourings are expressed only at major sporting events"[28].

Fourthly, for most states, mass public education (along with the mass media) makes an important contribution to cultural homogenisation. Sport and Physical Education are frequently seen as complementing the impact of classes in history and literature in the process of homogenisation and are particularly valued for their contribution to the moral development of the young and the transmission of the sporting heritage of the nation. This is most clearly evident in the former Soviet Union and East Germany where a hierarchy of multi-sport qualifications was available through the school which developed physical fitness and expertise in a range of sports within a highly patriotic context.

Progress towards the Western model of nationalism is easier for some states than for others. With a relatively limited range of strategies available, states have to attempt to manage both a cultural and a political identity, or put another way, to balance an ethnic definition of identity with a territorial definition. For many nations the consolidation of identity is a bottom-up process and is the product of an extension of ethnic identity to incorporate a political and territorial dimension.

For other nations the process relies more on the active promotion of territorial and political nationalism by the state: a top-down model. A simple linking by the state of its objectives to the promotion of ethnic identity is rarely possible as few countries are ethnically homogeneous. A more common situation is where a state has within its boundaries a majority ethnic group and one or more significant minorities. In this situation states may use the identity of the majority ethnic groups as the basis for national identity (as in Spain, Canada, Britain, Kenya and Australia). Normally, the aim is to incorporate the minority within the dominant ethnic identity and redefine the latter as the national identity. The goal in this case is not so much the invention of identity as its reconstruction or reconfiguration. While this is frequently successful, it is, by definition, likely to create disaffected minorities. This is particularly the case in the twentieth century where the urgency of the task of establishing nation-states (in the era of post-colonialism) has been far greater than in the past.

However, there are some countries, such as Nigeria, India, Zaire, Syria, Czechoslovakia and Yugoslavia, where the state faces or, as in the case of the last two examples, faced, the problem of attempting to unite a diverse and often historically hostile range of ethnic communities. Confronted with this challenge, states will frequently seek to construct a substantially original overarching national identity which attempts to avoid marginalising significant minorities.

Whatever the precise challenge facing governments, history (and frequently religion), are less fertile sources of defining moments and cultural myths even in the relatively homogeneous states. Too many historical events are divisive, such as the Battles of the Boyne, Culloden or Bannockburn, and there are too few historical events such as the battles of Agincourt and Trafalgar and Rourke's Drift, which are sufficiently ancient, obscure or ambivalent not to offend major current allies or contiguous ethnic groups. Modern Germany, particularly since reunification, has faced distinct problems in finding nationalist symbols which are not tainted by Nazism or which do not celebrate comparatively recent victories over current allies (especially France) or powerful neighbours (such as Russia). In the absence of convenient historical symbols Germany has enthusiastically embraced its sports stars, such as Boris Becker, Katrin Krabbe (until she failed a drugs test), Jurgen Klinsman and especially Michael Schumacher, as symbolic of the country's new identity. Consequently sport, and particularly elite sport, is used to provide the focus for the definition of national identity, which, once successfully established, is often projected back to foster the impression of cultural continuity. Not only is elite sport more malleable but it can also be more effectively insulated from particular ethnic cultures.

In a minority of countries the attempts by the government to manage meaning and identity will not lead to any conflict with the 'form of life' which equates to ethnic identity. However, there are many more examples where state intervention in matters of identity is problematic and results in tension between cultural flows. To complicate matters further, the state is not only concerned with the development of national identity for purposes of maintaining social cohesion, it is also concerned to differentiate the nation-state from its immediate neighbours and within the wider international system. Yet, it is here that a clear paradox emerges. The state's concern with maintaining its distinctiveness would, one assumes, lead to a preoccupation with fostering traditional sports and pastimes or the deliberate invention of a unique sporting tradition. Intercultural borrowing would be discouraged while cultural idiosyncrasy would be fostered. Yet, the actual behaviour of states bears little relationship to this model as differentiation between nation-states is increasingly at the margin. For example, an increasingly similar range of sports is used to assert cultural distinctiveness. Consequently, if national identity and sport is to be fully explored the analysis needs to be set within the context of the emergence of global culture.

In each country the relationship between state managed identity and ethnic identity will vary and produce a distinct cultural mix. In general, the state is concerned with the establishment and maintenance of the unity of the country, its own legitimacy and the formal inclusion of all people as citizens. The state is also concerned to achieve external recognition and status. The consequences for sport are normally an emphasis, in public policy outputs, on elite development, the hosting of international events, formal organisation and the participation in global (particularly Olympic) sports. By contrast, the maintenance of ethnic identity requires the confirmation of the membership and nature of the ethnic group through ritual and the constant reinvention of community. Here sport is likely to stress mass involvement (spectating and/or participating), traditional and idiosyncratic sports, and local organisation. Admittedly, in some countries state and ethnic conceptions of identity will prove complementary, however, for the majority, there will be some degree of tension. The emergence of a global culture raises a number of questions about the impact that this development will have for state and ethnic culture and the capacity of each to sustain its particular cultural priorities. The following section discusses the tensions arising from the attempts by governments in Canada, Ireland and Britain to further state interests in the face of challenges from globalisation and from ethnic communities.

Sport and the politics of identity

Canada faces the problem of a confusion of identity which goes beyond the well-publicised friction between the francophone Canadians of Quebec and the Anglo-Canadian majority. Additional tensions arise from an ambiguous relationship between native Canadians and the European colonists, the cultural and economic dominance of the United States, and from the pattern of recent immigration and the growing ethnic diversity in some of the country's major cities. The government continues to be concerned to establish a commitment to Canadian territory as a whole rather than simply to specific regions, to define the bond of citizenship in federal rather than provincial terms, and to lay the foundations for a common heritage. From the late 1960s, sport has been an important part of government strategy for achieving these objectives and for symbolising an independent and inclusive Canadian identity. Two examples will provide ample illustration of the relationship between state policy, globalisation and national identity. The first concerns the place of ice hockey as an element in national identity and the second concerns the relationship between the Euro-Canadian identity and the identity of native Canadians.

In their study of ice hockey in Canada, Gruneau and Whitson paint a picture of a Canada in the early postwar period united across class, language, region and age (but not sex) in its enthusiasm for ice hockey. Although the centrality of hockey within Canada's cultural self-perception has waned with growing ethnic diversity and the rise of alternative sports, it still "continues to have a powerful grip on the imaginations and collective memories of Canadians"[29]. What is particularly interesting in Gruneau and Whitson's study is the attempt by the state to create a role for international ice hockey in fostering a sense of national identity (and distinctiveness from America) in addition to the sense of locality (place) that was a more common by-product. In the 1950s and 1960s ice hockey fulfilled an important rôle in confirming a common popular cultural identity among immigrant Canadians. It was seen as the game Canada invented and, for a time at least, distracted attention from the deeper divisions between English and French Canadians. At the level of popular culture, ice hockey was less important in confirming the abstract notion of national identity than in confirming ideas about a national character which was "tough, hard, passionate yet determined, individualistic"[30].

Success in pre-war international club matches had created a comfortable confirmation of status and achievement. Given this context, ice hockey presented itself as a prime opportunity for the government to seek to enhance the state's territorial integrity and national identity, especially under Pierre Trudeau's government which, more than any previous government, promoted ice hockey as 'our national sport'. The government's promotion of ice hockey, as epitomising the Canadian personality, achieved its greatest success during the series of passionately nationalistic matches between Canada and the Soviet Union in 1972, and on the return of the ice hockey team to Olympic competition in 1980. Even the acrimony surrounding the move by the star player Wayne Gretzky to the Los Angeles Kings in the late 1980s, a furious debate about loyalty and defection, served to emphasise Canadian identity problems. The Gretzky debate also took place at the same time as a bitter dispute over the refusal of a young Canadian player to accept the draft to a Quebec club. Both episodes prompted indirect debates about the nature and obligations of Canadian citizenship.

The complementary relationship between the national popular culture as reflected in sport in general, and ice hockey in particular, and the state definition of national identity, had an important role to play in the government's attempts to "promote unity and a unique Canadian identity"[31]. Unfortunately this state strategy for the promotion and defence of national identity conflicted with the direction of globalisation. Although the general inability of the state to persuade (mainly American) commercial interests to put country before club and release elite players for international matches limited the opportunity to maximise the prestige value of international sporting success, it had the effect of emphasising in a particularly public and painful way the nature of Canada's relationship with the United States.

The use of sport by the state to develop and project a sense of national identity also affected government policy towards native Canadians. Paraschak examines the tensions arising from an attempt by native northern Canadians to preserve their sporting traditions in the face of pressure from the Eurocanadian 'power-bloc'. In the example she outlines there are clear pressures from the government to make the sporting contests conform to Western conceptions of organisation and structure, in much the same way that lacrosse, originally a native game, was codified and renamed to suit a European heritage. The Arctic Winter Games established in 1970 are sponsored by the state and comprise a diet of sports selected predominantly from a European heritage. The Northern Games were organised in reaction to the Arctic Winter Games and include traditional sports. Paraschak shows clearly that both these Games have been the focus of tension between, on the one hand, Eurocanadian sports and organisational expectations and, on the other, ethnic sports, games and forms of organisation. Over the twenty or so years that the two sets of Games have been held there has been a degree of compromise, with more native sports being included in the Arctic Winter Games while the Northern Games have moved closer to a "Eurocanadian, meritocratic model of sport"[32]. In her conclusion Paraschak notes that the greatest degree of change has been to the Northern Games yet nonetheless suggests that the changes in both Games reflect the "ongoing ability of native people to shape their own future"[33]. However, this may be an unduly optimistic conclusion, for it is also clear that the motive of the Canadian government is "modernisation" as a form of cultural incorporation and that to a considerable extent they have been successful. The nature of the incorporation is not necessarily into a culture exemplified by the participation in Eurocanadian sports, but rather the incorporation into the deeper values reflected in a bureaucratic form of social organisation.

These two examples of Canadian cultural politics illustrate the complex interweaving of global commercial interests with state priorities, and national and ethnic identity. In the first example the central issue was in part the ownership of the symbolism of ice hockey and in part the relative priority of club/locality over country/nation. The organisational basis of sport and the role of ice hockey as Canada's most popular sport were both accepted. What was in dispute was the capacity (or right) of the state to redefine ice hockey and imbue it with a symbolism of Canadianness. While it was relatively straightforward to incorporate popular nationalism into the state's strategy, the stumbling block proved to be the inability of the state to overcome commercial interests in ice hockey. Whether those interests are defined as global or, due to the peculiarities of the Canadian case, American is of less importance than the acknowledgement of the constraints external to the country that limited the scope for state activity. On the one hand, it is possible to argue that the increasing commercialisation of sport will lead to a decline in the utility of major sports to state strategies of nation-building. On the other hand, the Canadian example also shows that the conflicts between foreign commercial interests and nationalism can aid the nation-building objectives of the state by highlighting the power of the external cultural and economic threat. In other words the symbolism of heroic defeats, such as the evacuation from Dunkirk, the charge of the Light Brigade in the Crimean War, Henry Cooper's defeat by Cassius Clay, or England's defeat by Germany in the 1990 World Cup semi-final (and Gascoigne's tears) can be every bit as powerful and evocative as glorious victories.

The second example illustrated the role of the state in acting as the conduit through which elements of the global culture are transmitted. The concern of the Canadian state to bring native Canadians into the 'modern world' made sport an attractive policy tool. Of far less importance was the range of sports played. While an enthusiasm for ice hockey would doubtless have been welcomed, an engagement with Euro-Canadian organisational processes was a priority.

Over the last hundred years or so, key phases in Ireland's history have been interwoven with sports politics and sport remains a powerful metaphor of contemporary Irish politics and an effective state resource. However, the relationship between support and Irish identity is not without tensions and ambiguities which were amply highlighted during the 1994 soccer World Cup finals held in the USA. While none of the four countries of the United Kingdom qualified for the World Cup finals, the Irish Republic was successful and progressed to the second stage of the competition. Ireland's progress generated huge interest in America's Irish community, the nationalist community in Northern Ireland, and also in Ireland itself. Yet Ireland was achieving success at an English sport, with a team managed by an Englishman, and with a number of team members born outside the Republic of Ireland. This enthusiastic acceptance of English sports-culture seems paradoxical when the recent history of sport in Ireland is examined.

The intertwining of cultural/sporting, military and political opposition to English rule in Ireland has been intense for well over 100 years. Sport is not only significant as a symbol of resistance in Anglo-Irish relations; it has also been a locus for the organisation of political opposition and, at least in the early part of this century, a source of para-military recruits. The focus for Irish opposition to the English sporting tradition was the Gaelic Athletic Association (GAA), established in 1884 with the express aim of rescuing traditional Gaelic sports such as hurling and Gaelic football from obscurity, and actively resisting English sports such as rugby, soccer and cricket. An aggressive campaign, closely linked with the militantly nationalist Irish Republican Brotherhood, resulted in a revival of the moribund sport of hurling and was instrumental in defining Gaelic football and distinguishing it from English rugby. The revival of Gaelic sports was partly the recovery of lost traditions, partly a recognition of the consequences of the unchallenged attraction of 'Anglo' sports, and partly a process of cultural invention and mythologising. Whatever the motives behind the Gaelic sports revival, the success of the GAA in orchestrating Irish cultural resistance is impressive. Success was largely based on the strong emotional appeal to nationalism and the strict enforcement of rules of eligibility that restricted members to playing Irish/Gaelic sports, and which also prohibited contact with clubs subscribing to English sports. Consequently, during the first half of this century sport was both a potent symbol of resistance to English rule and a key element in the definition of identity in the early years of the Irish state. During this period the GAA, due to its use of the parish as the basic administrative unit and the prohibition on player transfer, contributed strongly to the development of a powerful sense of loyalty to place. The overt political and social function of the GAA club provided a focus for active participation in the aspiring Irish state and a source of civic education. Following the creation of the independent Irish state, the government was content to support the GAA and the place of Gaelic sport in schools.

In Northern Ireland the GAA and Gaelic sports continue to fulfil these functions; they remain central to the definition and promotion of Irish nationalism and are symbolic of the continuing challenge to 'British' identity. However, while Gaelic sports continue to be the major spectator and participation sports in the Republic their popularity may well have peaked and the last ten years has witnessed a rapid increase in the popularity of soccer, helped by strong performances by the Irish national team in the 1990 and 1994 World Cup competitions. The growing popularity of soccer might be interpreted as successful penetration by a global sport or as a concession to British identity. A more plausible interpretation lies in the growing confidence of the Irish state, a growing appreciation of the value of a global stage on which to display its contemporary national identity, and, not least, the repeated failure of the GAA to export Gaelic sports. While the symbolism of Gaelic sport is still acknowledged, particularly within the Ministry of Education, as a powerful demonstration of the particularity of the Irish nation, soccer is now able to project the national cultural identity before a global audience, much to the satisfaction of both the foreign ministry and the tourist board. Thus, sportive nationalism remains important but the form of its articulation has been adapted to the contemporary objectives of the Irish state and built upon a secure basis of popular support.

The embracing of soccer as an additional symbol of national identity reflects not only the declining significance of the relationship with Britain, but also reflects an acknowledgement of the effect of the Irish diaspora on identity. Soccer effectively encapsulates this redefinition of identity. Not only does soccer provide a global arena for the expression of Irish identity, but the make up of the Irish team reflects the strength of links between Ireland and the 'Irish abroad', who, in the words of the playwright Dermot Bolger, "would grow with foreign accents and Irish faces"[34]. The broadening of the basis of Irish sportive nationalism has been reflected and encouraged by public policy. While the GAA is still the major recipient of public money, an increasing sum is being directed to the preparation of elite athletes in soccer and especially Olympic sports. Although Gaelic sports still remain a key symbol of an independent Irish identity, global sports, even if they are British, are increasingly recognised as more valuable vehicles for projecting that identity abroad.

Superficially, at least, Britain provides a marked contrast to both Canada and Ireland. The integrity of its territorial boundaries has long been acknowledged; the institutions of civil society are deeply rooted; the concept of citizenship is as firmly embedded as in almost any other country; and the institutions of civic education, such as the church, mass public education and the media, are also long established. Britain was at the height of its power in the eighteenth and nineteenth centuries when the modern world was being shaped and remains a significant military and diplomatic power today. Such a history should have relegated concerns over identity, and the role of sport in its management, to the margin of political debate. Indeed, for much of Britain's recent history, that was clearly the case. The source and intensity of British identity lay primarily in English imperialist history. As Anderson observes "the organising definition was inescapably imperial — the 'British' people, strictly speaking emerging as an artefact of the empire-state, from the various island nationalities"[35]. If a British identity was largely refined and promoted by nineteenth-century imperialism, it was also shaped by the more pragmatic forces arising from the longer established fear of invasion, particularly by Catholic France, which, with occasional exceptions, forged a common cause between Wales, Scotland and England. As Colley remarks, "They defined themselves against the French as they imagined them to be, superstitious, militant, decadent and unfree"[36]. The conceptualisation of the British nation was an English elitist construct designed to rationalise direct rule over the Scots, Welsh and Irish and also to provide a cultural *cordon sanitaire* to protect the English upper class's notion of its social and cultural superiority and exclusivity from being tainted through direct association with the colonies and dominions. Thus, while "English and Welsh law, the English language, the Anglican church, English sporting traditions and Westminster-style political institutions either became paramount or were accorded high status"[37], these cultural products were defined as British rather than English. The deliberate cultivation of ambiguity of identity signalled both a disdain for identity politics and an underlying cultural self-confidence. For example, and in marked contrast to the Scots and the Welsh, there is still little evidence of resentment among the English when they find their identity subsumed under that of Britain at major sporting events such as the Olympic Games.

However, any examination of the roots of the cultural self-confidence of the English finds sport playing a central part. Sport was not simply a source of moral values (as suggested in Hughes's novel *Tom Brown's Schooldays*) but was also "inseparably associated with down-to-earth, assertive and patriotic English-ness"[38]. Government involvement in sport for most of this century has reflected a confidence in the capacity of the upper class and aristocratic leadership of voluntary sports organisations to foster a distinctive English sportive nationalism. Only from the mid-1960s did the government accept sport as part of its broad welfare state responsibilities and, while there was some concern to defend British sporting prestige in the face of East German Olympic achievements and Hungarian soccer superiority, the main policy objectives of the new Sports Council were domestic and welfare oriented. However, more recently, from the mid-1980s, there has been an increasing concern within the Conservative government to address the issue of national identity and to use sport for nationalistic purposes.

In part the government's concern grew out of a painful recognition of the negative impact on England's international image of repeated incidents of soccer hooliganism at international matches and the association of the Union Jack with violent behaviour and neo-Nazi groups. However, episodes of hooliganism were only one element in the emerging debate which had its primary origins in the political agenda of the radical right of the Conservative Party which saw the erosion of national identity as one among a number of issues to be addressed as part of a broad programme for national regeneration. For the radical right the erosion of identity was partly responsible for the steady decline of Britain's economic and diplomatic status. In Parekh's words, Britain was "losing touch with its great past and becoming devoid of the qualities of character that had made that past possible. As a result, Britain was beginning to drift and [fall] prey to the fashionable but highly dubious ideas and practices imported from abroad"[39]. The favoured policy response was to reawaken the forgotten familiarity with the national heritage and characteristics. The 'heritage' content of the history and English literature national curriculum was the focus of some fierce debate, but sport was also subject to a redefinition of curriculum objectives. In general, the social welfare focus of sport policy was gradually augmented by an emphasis on sport as an element of the national heritage and as a contributor to the development and projection of national identity.

For Mrs Thatcher, British national identity was renewed through the Falklands military adventure and through her robust defence of national interests within the European Community: for her, sport was peripheral or indeed a source of embarrassment through the damage to Britain's image due to the persistence of soccer hooliganism abroad. In contrast, for John Major, sport was an integral part of his conception of English national identity and was reflected in a number of policy developments including the redesign of the physical education curriculum to put a greater emphasis on traditional team sports in school, the proposed establishment of a British Academy of Sport, the creation of the Department of National Heritage and the restructuring of the Sports Councils.

During the debate over the content of the Physical Education national curriculum both the prime minister and the then education secretary, Kenneth Clarke, intervened vigorously to ensure that the playing of sport (rather than sports history, biomechanics and psychology) was at the heart of the curriculum. The rationale for emphasising participation in sport was that it developed positive moral values and that it maintained continuity with the past and that "our great traditional sports — cricket, hockey, swimming, athletics, football, netball, rugby, tennis and the like — are put firmly at the centre of the stage" (*Guardian* 6 June 1995). These sentiments were later incorporated into the government's policy paper on sport, *Sport: Raising the Game*, which also contained the proposal to establish, with the use of funds from the National Lottery, a British Academy of Sport with the aim of producing a new generation of world class sportsmen and women. Modelled on the highly successful Australian Institute of Sport, the Academy would concentrate on Olympic sports and traditional team sports. In the words of a leading article in *The Times*, the proposals in the policy paper "constitute[d] proof that national decline does not have to be accepted" (14 July 1995).

For those who recognise the intrinsic benefits of sport there is much in recent government policy to be welcomed, certainly when compared with the Thatcher years when sport was either an irritation or at best a photo opportunity. However, there is an unresolved tension running through current policy between a distribution of resources which enables the local and the idiosyncratic to flourish, and a desire to restrain innovation and eccentricity because it conflicts with a model of the traditional, national sporting heritage. The policy ambiguity was reflected in the clumsily named Department of National Heritage which was replaced by a Department of Culture, Media and Sport after the Labour election victory of May 1997.

Conclusion

Among the questions that arise from the discussion of the triangular relationship between ethnic identity, state managed national identity and globalisation is whether states still retain the capacity to exploit sport as a significant element in a strategy of national identity management. Canadian experience would suggest that at best the value of sport is short lived and probably only effective where the cultural aspect being exploited by the state is reasonably deeply embedded at the popular or ethnic level. For the Canadian state three problems arose: first, that the associations generated by ice hockey were as much a confirmation of place and locality as they were of national community. Even when the association was with a national community, as during the Canada-Soviet series of matches, the impact seemed short-lived. The second problem was that the conjunction of the centrality of ice hockey in the popular cultural imagination and the priority of unity to the government was relatively short-lived. By the 1980s other dimensions of the problem of national identity were beginning to emerge, such as an increasingly politicised native Canadian community and a growing cosmopolitanism in many larger cities due to immigration. The third problem concerned the unwillingness of commercial interests to co-operate with the nationalist strategy of the state. Although the intense public debate stimulated by the reluctance of American commercial interests to support Canadian national sporting goals had the effect of fuelling Canadian nationalism, the prospect of an increasing number of sports achieving financial independence through commercialism and also becoming locked into commercial values and processes indicates that state capacity to manipulate sport will weaken, and not just in Canada. The recent speculation about assembling a Canadian Olympic ice hockey 'dream team' will only come to fruition if it makes good marketing sense to the commercial clubs.

Ireland's experience of the politics of culture is very different from that of Canada. In the late nineteenth and for much of the twentieth centuries, the state was an English one, consequently putting Irish people in a similar position to the native Canadians. Both groups adopted similar strategies for preserving their ethnic identity in sport although for the native Canadians the core values of their culture were more deeply embedded in the form of play than in the sports played. For the Irish the particular sports took on the symbolism of nation, resistance and liberation. This contrast highlights the malleability of sport's symbolic value and the problem of assuming that it is the form of sport rather than particular sports that are more likely to constitute a community's core values.

The early Irish state reinforced the cultural politics of the GAA, and to a large extent still does. But the political objectives of the modern Irish state are different and, aided by a similar complementary evolution of Irish ethnic identity, it has successfully adapted sports symbolism to the current demands for a role on the world stage. Should Ireland move to union with the North the rôle of sport in the new united Ireland would surely change again. Ireland is also interesting because there is little evidence, until recently, of the state focusing primarily on elite development. During the period of colonial resistance and in the early phase of independence, reinforcing popular Gaelic culture was a logical state policy. With the passing of that phase of Irish history and the country's greater engagement with the international system, one would expect the state to become more actively involved in the promotion and development of elite sport. The high profile political support for the national soccer team and the increasing use of public (lottery) funds to support potential Olympic/world championship medalists is indicative of policy change. As yet there is little tension between the government's support, on the one hand, for Gaelic sports and its powerful capacity to confirm and reinforce national identity and, on the other hand, the government's growing support for international sport and its capacity to project Irish national identity globally.

Britain provides a contrast with both Canada and Ireland. It is only comparatively recently that the nature of identity has become a political issue. The policy response of defining and protecting a sporting heritage is obviously attractive given Britain's central rôle in developing and spreading major sports throughout the world. The challenges to this strategy come, externally, from global media interests and, internally, from the capacity of traditional sports to provide an inclusive modern British identity. The speed with which rugby union altered its policy on payment of players in the face of pressure from the foreign media entrepreneurs, Rupert Murdoch and Kerry Packer, does not indicate a marked capacity to preserve the distinctively British/English features of particular sports. More importantly, there is a danger in attempting to define a contemporary sporting identity based on early-twentieth-century traditions. The persistent failure to establish cricket leagues which are open equally to Asian, Afro-Caribbean and white cricketers is still a matter of great concern, as is the slow pace at which governing bodies in cricket, soccer and rugby union are supporting women's participation in their sports. More worrying still is the failure of people of Afro-Caribbean ethnic background to be a welcomed part of that imagined community of the district, city and nation that watches soccer and watches a large number of black soccer players in Premier League and national teams. The greatest danger is that the identity fails to match the pattern of gender relations and the ethnic mix of modern Britain, and that an identity is defined which is exclusive rather than inclusive, and nostalgic rather than contemporary.

Britain is also interesting because it sounds a cautionary note in assuming too readily that there exists within the modern state an agreed conception of national identity. The current round of policy debate has exposed a number of tensions within the British state: for example, between the UK Sports Council, which favours support of a broad range of sports and the Department which favours a more concentrated focus; between the local authorities, who generally favour mass participation in sport and the Department which favours elite development; and between schools, which favour physical education, and the governing bodies of sport and the Sports Councils which favour the practice of sport. Similar tensions within the Irish state are also evident between the greater concern of the Education Ministry with Gaelic sport and the more international concerns of the tourist board and their interest in promoting golf, motor racing and world championship boxing.

A second question concerns the impact of globalisation on ethnic or local cultures. With regard to the relationship between the Canadian state and the native Canadians, the growing intrusion of global culture should strengthen the state in its strategy of modernisation and cultural assimilation. However, it is undoubtedly the case that in Canada, as in many other countries, assimilation is a far less explicit objective and accommodation is probably a better description. More importantly, the seemingly insatiable appetite of the global media for sports to broadcast may create opportunities for ethnic sports to receive funding and encouragement to preserve and develop their sports, even if it is only as a media curiosity. However, the paucity of media coverage of hurling and Gaelic football by comparison with soccer has contributed to the stagnation in participation in Gaelic sports and the burgeoning participation rates in soccer. Finally, the slow loss of television coverage of cricket to the pay-to-view channels may have the effect of undermining attempts to enthuse a new generation of players.

In conclusion, the picture painted of sport and its relationship with global culture and with ethnic and state notions of identity creates an impression of a highly malleable source of cultural symbolism. It is also, at times, a powerful signifier of identity. Yet it is also an extremely unstable cultural source. In many cultures the symbolism of a sport, but particularly a sports event, may be intense but it is also often very brief. However, it is not just the symbolism of military events, such as the 1916 Easter Rising, the battle of Waterloo and D-Day, that have a much longer shelf life. Even other cultural products have a capacity to sustain meaning for far longer than sport: the paintings of Turner and Constable, the music of Elgar and Vaughan Williams, and the books of Austen and Dickens for example. In soccer, the English World Cup victory of 1966 lasted, at most, until the 'failure' in 1970. By way of contrast, the humiliation of losing the Ashes series in the fifth test against Australia in the summer of 1997 only seemed to last until the heroic victory in the sixth! It would seem therefore that for the state the manipulation of sport for purposes associated with national identity poses few problems (as exemplified by the GDR and the Soviet Union), but sustaining that effect so that the symbolism becomes rooted (and unambiguously so) in the personal mythology of the people is a rare feat indeed.

Notes

1 See A.D. King, "Introduction: spaces of culture, spaces of knowledge in A.D. King (Ed.), *Culture, Globalization and the World System*, G. Jarvie and J. Maguire, *Sport and Leisure in Social Thought*, Routledge, 1994, L. Sklair, *The Sociology of the Global System*, Harvester-Wheatsheaf, 1991.

2 H.I. Schiller, *Communication and Cultural Domination*, Sharpe (New York), 1976, p. 90.

3   U. Hannerze, "Cosmopolitans and Locals in World Culture", in H. Feather-
    stone (Ed.), *Global Culture: Nationalism, Globaization and Modernity*,
    Sage, 1990, p. 107.

4   J. Tomlinson, *Cultural Imperialism: A Critical Introduction*, Pinter, 1991, p.
    175.

5   See Featherstone, *op. cit.*, p. 9.

6   Hannerz, *op. cit.*, p. 107.

7   V. Cable, *The World's New Fissures: Identities in Crisis*, Demos (London),
    1994, p. 5.

8   B. Parekh, "Discourses on National Identity", *Political Studies*, Vol. 42, No.
    3.

9   Canadian Ministry of Sport, *Sport: The Way Ahead*, Ottawa, 1992.

10 Department of national Heritage, *Sport: Raising the Game*, HMSO, 1995, p.
    2.

11 Department of Education, *National Sports Council, Annual Report, 1994*,
    Dublin, 1995, p. 1.

12 C. Geertz, "Deep Play", *Daedalus*, Winter 1972.

13 H.W. Morton, *Soviet Sport*, Collier, 1963.

14 Hannerz, *op. cit.*, p. 114.

15 A.D. Smith, *Nations and Nationalism in a Global Era*, Cambridge Univer-
    sity Press, 1995, p. 57.

16 A.D. Smith, *National Identity*, Penguin, 1991, p. 42.

17 See R. Scruton, *The Philosopher on Dover Beach*, Carcanet (London),
    1990.

18 T.S. Eliot, *Notes Toward the Definition of Culture*, Faber, 1948, p. 30.

19 Reported in *The Guardian*. 23.4.93.

20 A. Clarke and J. Clarke, "'Highlights and Action Replays' — ideology,
    sport and the media" in J. Hargreaves (Ed.), *Sport, Culture and Ideology*,
    Routledge, 1982, p. 81.

21 R. Robertson, "Mapping the global condition: globalisation as the central
    concept" in Featherstone, *op. cit.*

22 E. Hobsbawm, "Mass-producing tradition: Europe 1870-1914" in E.
    Hobsbawm and T. Ranger (Eds.) *The Invention of Tradition*, Cambridge
    University Press, 1983, p. 273.

23 E. Gellner, *Nations and Nationalism*, Blackwell, 1983, p. 56.

24 H.K. Bhabha, *The Location of Culture*, Routledge, 1994.

25 I. Wallerstein, "The National and the Universal: Can there be such a thing as world culture?" in King, *op. cit.*

26 P. Worsley, *The Three Worlds: Culture and World Development*, Weidenfeld & Nicholson, 1984, p. 249.

27 See R. Henderson, "Is it in the blood?", *Wisden Cricket Monthly*, July, 1995.

28 Quoted in G. Jarvie and G. Walker (Eds.), *Scottish Sport in the Making of the Nation: Ninety Minute Patriots*, Leicester University Press, 1994, p. 1.

29 R. Gruneau and P. Whitson, *Hockey Night in Canada: Sport, Identities and Cultural Politics*, Garamond (Toronto), 1993, p. 3.

30 Ibid., p. 267.

31 D. Macintosh et. al., *Sport and Politics in Canada*, McGill-Queens University Press, 1987, p. 186.

32 V. Paraschak, "Sports festivals and race relations in the northwest territories of Canada" in G. Jarvie (Ed.), *Sport, Racialism and Ethnicity*, Falmer (London), 1991, p. 16.

33 Ibid., p. 16.

34 D. Bolger, *In High Germany: a Dublin Quartet*, Penguin, 1990, p. 107.

35 P. Anderson, *English Questions*, Verso (London), 1992, p. 10.

36 L. Colley, *Britons: Forging the Nation*, Yale University Press, 1992, p. 6.

37 R. Cohen, *Frontiers of Identity: the British and the Others*, Longman, 1994, p. 16.

38 R. Holt, *Sport and the British: a Modern History*, Oxford University press, 1989, p. 263.

39 Parekh, *op. cit.*, pp. 493-4.

SPORT, GENDER AND PATRIARCHY
IN THE WESTERN CIVILISING PROCESS

Eric Dunning

Director of the Centre for Research into Sport and Society
at the University of Leicester

Introduction

This essay grows out of my earlier work on the development of sport and leisure, sport as a male preserve, and football hooliganism[1]. However, while in that work one of the principal issues that concerned me more or less directly was sport and sports-related contexts as sites — to whatever degree they were/are socially approved — for the inculcation, expression and perpetuation of masculine habituses, behaviour and ideals, in the present paper I want to extend my focus and look in a preliminary way, not simply at sport and masculinity but at aspects of sport and femininity as well.

This broadening of focus does not represent a sudden switch to the area of gender relations. It may not have been widely perceived as such, but, as a figurational ("process") sociologist who employs a fundamentally dynamic and relational perspective that is concerned with studying social processes over time and tracing the emergence, maintenance and breakdown of chains and networks of interdependence ("figurations")[2], that has been one of the central foci of my and my colleagues' work since the 1970s. This was recognised in 1988 by Susan J. Birrell when she wrote that:

> Kenneth Sheard and Eric Dunning's 1973 article, "The Rugby Club as a Type of Male Preserve", gained respect as a subcultural study, but because it focused so clearly on males, it was not fully recognised for its importance to feminist scholarship until gender relations was recognised as the proper focus of the field.[3]

My previous work thus focused primarily on aspects of male habitus, behaviour and ideology in changing contexts of gender power relations. In the present paper I shall seek to extend this field of vision to incorporate more aspects of the female as well as the male sides of the equation: more specifically, those connected with the direct involvement of females in sport. Let me elaborate on my reasons for wanting to write a paper of this kind[4].

The sociological marginalisation of sport and the study of gender

Probably in large part as a consequence of its marginalisation generally as a subject of sociological theorising and research, sport does not figure centrally in many of the recently published mainstream texts that deal with gender[5]. Even where it is mentioned, sport is usually only considered peripherally and in passing rather than as a site which is of importance in the construction of gender identities. Since sport remains to this day a largely male-dominated affair, this may not be particularly surprising in female-orientated texts on gender. It is, however, rather more surprising in the growing number of books and articles which have the social construction of masculinity as their principal focus.

Clues as to why sport may have been marginalised in attempts to come to grips with the social construction of masculinity may be provided by the way in which Arthur Brittan approaches the subject. In his *Masculinity and Power*, he writes:

> Perhaps the most popular image of masculinity in everyday conscious-
> ness is that of man-the-hero, the hunter, the competitor, the conqueror.
> Certainly it is the image celebrated in Western literature, art and in the
> media ...
>
> In a sense, the belief in man-the-hunter, or hero, would seem to have
> no foundation in the everyday world that most men inhabit. There are
> very few occasions available for men to be heroes, except as a hobby or
> for sport. Man-the-hunter has been transformed into man-the-bread-
> winner. Opportunities for heroism only arise in the sporting field, not in
> the forest in hot pursuit of food for the tribe.[6]

Brittan here correctly identifies sport as a source of the "hero image" for men. However, by bracketing it with "hobbies" and conceptualising it as separate from the everyday world, he relegates it to a peripheral status compared with what he regards as the principal locus for experiencing "masculinity" in present-day societies: the role of "man-the-breadwinner". As a result, he is prevented from exploring in depth what is arguably one of the most important sites in modern societies for the expression and preservation of masculinity in its more traditional forms. Brittan, of course, is by no means alone in tracing contemporary masculinity principally to the world of work. 'Economistic' thinking of this kind appears to enjoy something approaching hegemonic status in contemporary sociological studies in this and other areas. It is, that is to say, widely taken for granted, enjoying a status close to that of a sociological orthodoxy.

It is not my intention in saying this to deny the *importance* of work, the economy and the sexual division of labour as sites for the inculcation, expression and perpetuation of patriarchal — or perhaps more properly "andrarchal"[7] — habit, practices and values. It is simply that I question the assertion that economic processes are the *only* ones *centrally* involved in these regards. I think, moreover, that the marginalisation of sport as a subject of sociological enquiry may have unnecessarily restricted the range of research as far as issues of sex and gender are concerned. Indeed, viewed from a non-economistic perspective, there are grounds for believing sport to be one of the key sites in contemporary societies in this regard.

The simple fact that sport — spectator sport as well as and perhaps more importantly than participant sport — is today a central life interest in the lives of many people suggests that the empirical study and theorising of it ought to occupy a larger, more central place in mainstream ("malestream") sociology than they have done up to now. Some general data from the United Kingdom provide support for this contention. The economists, Rigg and Lewney, for example, estimate that, during the 1980s, £4.37 billion was spent annually in the UK on sports-related goods and services, and that, in that decade, some 376,000 people were employed in sports-related activities, more than in chemicals and artificial fibres (352,000), and energy and water supply (336,000), and considerably more than in motor vehicles (291,000)[8]. Few groups feature more regularly than sportspersons in the advertising of goods and services. Moreover, top-level sport is also heavily sponsored and used by businesses for entertaining. However, in the UK as elsewhere, there is what one might call a "prestige-hierarchy of sports" and within that context, although its image has been regularly besmirched by the occurrence of hooliganism, there can be little doubt that Association football represents the "jewel in the crown". Measured in terms of numbers of clubs, numbers of registered players, spectator attendance, media prominence, revenue, capital expenditure, and even the frequency with which it serves as a topic of conversation, especially among males, it is clearly of great significance socio-economically as well as socio-culturally. Football — and sport more generally — would accordingly seem to be deserving of a much more central status in mainstream sociological theorising and research than it has enjoyed up to now. It is important, however, to note that football stands at the top of a prestige-hierarchy of sports in which *male* versions of particular sports hold sway and accordingly receive the lion's share of the spoils. It is also worthy of note that problems of football hooliganism are fundamentally connected with *male* habituses, values and behaviour.

There are also reasons for believing that sport is more than a mere "hobby", "pastime" or "leisure activity". In fact, one can say that, along with religion and war, sport represents one of the most successful means of collective mobilisation that humans have so far devised. That appears to be the case because of the combination of representational and excitement-generating functions that sport can perform. Sport can even be said to be in certain respects functionally homologous with religion and war That is to say, whilst it clearly cannot pretend to be a context where theological issues can be dealt with, sport can (i) provide a source of meaning in life, (ii) act as a focus of social identifications, and (iii) offer experiences that are analogous to the excitement generated in war and in other "serious" situations like "being in love". It is, as Joseph Maguire has expressed it, a social locus for the generation of "exciting significance"[9]. It is the inherently conflictful, zero-sum character of sport that enables it to be readily adapted to the formation and expression of "in-group/out-group" or, perhaps, better, "we-group" and "they-group" identifications, though, of course, as I shall attempt to establish later, the success of sport in these regards appears to be in large part dependent on the fact that, in its modern forms, the physical dangers that are inherent in any group mobilisation for purposes of conflict have been to a great extent reduced *via* the institutionalisation of personal and social controls. But, of course, in human affairs these things are never permanent. Under specific conditions such developments are liable, on balance, to go in the reverse direction.

Except for people who are professionally involved, sport is, of course, a leisure activity but, if my argument so far has any substance, it appears to be one which is of considerable importance in the identity-formation, particularly of males. Indeed, such is the pressure to participate in sport — from the media, in schools (though, in Britain, this may have declined in recent years), from their age-peers and, of course, in many cases from their parents, especially fathers with whom they identify as role-models — that UK males, virtually independently of social class though not perhaps of religious and ethnic group affiliations to the same degree, are forced to develop an internalised adjustment to it. That appears to be the case whether they conform and follow a sporting route in their leisure and perhaps their occupational lives, whether they deviate and identify with the forms of 'anti-sports' culture that have grown up in British Society, or whether they take a course intermediate between these poles. One thing worthy of note in this connection is the fact that, in many parts of British society, especially in all-male schools, 'deviant' males who, for whatever reasons, opt to follow an 'anti-sports' course are liable to be categorised as 'effeminate', perhaps even as 'homosexual', by their peers. This goes hand in hand with a parallel tendency for sportswomen to be categorised as 'lesbian' or 'butch', an antimony which, in and of itself, is suggestive of the fact that sport poses interesting problems for gender research. Let me begin to explore this a little further. In particular, let me explore whether the theory of 'civilising processes' developed by Norbert Elias can be of explanatory help as far as teasing out some of the connections between sport and gender is concerned.

Aspects of sport and gender in the western civilising process (i)

In her seminal essay, "Discourses on the Gender/Sport Relationship: From Women in Sport to Gender Relations", Susan J. Birrell wrote in 1988 that two British articles published in the 1970s — my own and Kenneth Sheard's "The Rugby Football Club as a Type of Male Preserve"[10] to which I have already referred, and Paul Willis's "Performance and Meaning"[11] — "were apparently so far advanced for American audiences that they lay almost unnoticed for about ten years"[12]. That may have been the case some twenty years ago but, although they have tended to remain "ghettoized" behind the ramparts of the sociology of sport and not been accorded the recognition which is due in the mainstream of the subject, in the United States in the 1980s a creative application by men of "critical feminist perspectives" to the study of sport burst on the scene, producing a body of literature far in advance of most of what is currently available in UK sociology. Among the leading figures in this movement are Donald Sabo, R.W.

Connell, Alan M. Klein and Michael Messner[13]. Writing in 1987, Messner had this to say on the functions of sport in the formation of male-identities:

> How do we begin to understand the intensity of [the] sense of identification that many males get from their status as athletes? First, since men have not at all times and all places related to sports the way they do currently, it is important to examine this reality through a historical prism. In the first two decades of this century, men feared that the closing of the frontier and the changes in the workplace, family, and schools were "feminizing" society. The Boy Scouts of America was founded in 1910 to provide a sphere of life where "true manliness" could be instilled in boys *by men*. The contemporaneous rapid rise in organised sports can be attributed largely to the same phenomenon. As socio-economic and familial changes eroded traditional bases of male identity and privilege, sport became an increasingly important cultural expression of traditional male values — organised sport became a "primary masculinity-validating experience".
>
> In the post-world war II era, the bureaucratisation and rationalisation of work, along with the decline of the family wage and women's gradual movement into the labour force, further undermined the "breadwinner role" as the basis for male identity, resulting in a "defensive insecurity" among men. Both on a persona/existential level for athletes and on a symbolic/ideological level for spectators and fans, sport has become one of the "last bastions" of male power and superiority over — and separation from — the "feminisation" of society. the rise of (gridiron) football as "America's number-one game" is likely the result of the comforting clarity it provides between the polarities of traditional male power, strength and violence and the contemporary fears of social feminisation[14].

The views expressed by Messner here are similar to my own regarding the limitations of approaches to male-identity of authors such as Brittan. Nevertheless, his arguments appear unnecessarily restricted to an American context. After all, organised sports such as cricket and boxing developed and spread in Britain somewhat earlier than they did in the USA. The Boy Scouts Movement also developed in the United Kingdom first. In fact, in England concern about "social feminisation" was expressed at least as early as the writings of Charles Kingsley and appears to have played a part in the development of "Muscular

Christianity". This suggests that a more general social process may have been at work in these regards, part of it involving (possibly two-way) diffusion across the Atlantic, and that, accordingly, a more general, less ethnocentric approach may be needed in order to explain developments of this kind. Ideally such a theory ought to throw light on to an issue which Messner did not touch on in the article from which I have quoted: the sociogenesis and consequences of female entry into sports, a range of activities which, as I have noted, in the still predominantly andrarchal societies of the modern West started out as virtually exclusive male preserves. Let me explore the possibility that Elias's theory of "civilising processes" may provide — not all the answers: figurational socio-logists are careful never to make claims of that kind[15] — at least some clues which may be of help in the construction of such a theory. In order to undertake this task a necessary first step is to respond to some recent critics of Elias's theory. Such a discussion will have to be fairly lengthy because a grasp of the theory of civilising processes is crucial to the argument that I wish to develop.

The theory of "civilising processes" was offered by Elias as a "central theory" in relation to which other work could be organised but no pretence is made by Elias or by sociologists who are convinced of the value of his approach that the theory constitutes a complete or in some sense "fixed and final" theory. Nor, unlike what I take to be the claims made by some "social" (sic!) theorists, was it Elias's pretence that he had "solved" or "resolved" anything or made more than a small but hopefully useful contribution to knowledge. As Elias himself expressed it in 1936:

> This study ... poses and develops a very wide-ranging problem; it does not pretend to solve it. It marks out a field of observation that has hitherto received relatively little attention, and undertakes the first steps towards an explanation. Others must follow.
>
> ... It was not so much my purpose to build a general theory of civilisation in the air, and then afterward to find out whether it agreed with experience; rather, it seemed the primary task to begin by regaining within a limited area the lost perception of the process in question, the peculiar transformation of human behaviour, then to seek a certain understanding of its causes, and finally to gather together such theoretical insights as have been encountered on the way. If I have succeeded in providing a tolerably secure foundation for further reflection and research in this direction, this study has achieved everything it set out to achieve...

...the issues raised by the book have their origin less in scholarly tradition ... than in the experiences in whose shadow we all live, experiences of the crisis and transformation of Western civilisation as it had existed hitherto, and the simple need to understand what this "civilisation" really amounts to. But I have not been guided in this study by the idea that our civilised mode of behaviour is the most advanced of all humanly possible modes of behaviour, nor by the opinion that "civilisation" is the worst form of life and one that is doomed. All that can be seen today is that with gradual civilisation a number of specific civilisational difficulties arise. But it cannot be said that we already understand why we actually torment ourselves in this way. We feel that we have got ourselves, through civilisation, into certain entanglements unknown to less civilised peoples; but we also know that these less civilised peoples are for their part often plagued by difficulties and fears from which we no longer suffer, or at least not to the same degree. Perhaps all this can be seen somewhat more clearly if it is understood how such civilising processes actually take place ... It may be that, through clearer understanding, we shall one day succeed in making accessible to more conscious control these processes which nowadays take place around us not very differently from natural events, and which we confront as medieval man confronted the forces of nature.[16]

I am not sure about other languages but it seems to me that, in English at least, one of the problems which critics have with the theory — apart from reading into it an exaggerated idea of its intended range and scope — may be connected with the word "civilisation", itself. For example, David Harris writes that: "This latter is an unfortunate term since it has undertones of moral evaluation and moral progress ... "[17]. He evidently had not read Elias or the recently published British Sociological Association pamphlet, "Anti-Racist Language: Guidance for Good Practice" (BSA, no date). According to the pamphlet, "civilisation" is a term which "derives from a colonialist perception of the world". It is, we are told, "often associated with Social Darwinist thought and is full of implicit value judgements and ignorance of Third World history". However, the authors of the pamphlet go on explicitly to make an exception in this regard. The work of Norbert Elias, they say, stands outside of and apart from this set of judgmental strictures. "In some cases, such as the work of Norbert Elias", they write, "civilisation takes on a different meaning without racist overtones".

This is a welcome recognition of the reality-congruence of Elias's theory. It runs directly counter to the arguments of a wide variety of critics who have in their different ways asserted that Elias's theory is "evolutionary" and is, above all, massively refuted by twentieth century events such as the "holocaust". It runs directly counter to such arguments because, as the authors of the BSA pamphlet implicitly but nevertheless clearly recognised, one of the principal tasks that Elias sought to accomplish in *Über den Prozess der Zivilisation* was factually to trace the sociogenesis and development of the term, "civilisation", how it came to express the self-image of the most powerful western nations and to acquire in that connection derogatory and racist connotations, not only in relation to "primitive" or "barbaric" non-Western societies but also in relation to "less advanced" societies and outsider groups in the West itself. Interestingly, Elias shows how the First World War was fought by Britain and France against Germany in the name of "civilisation" and how, particularly in the 18th, 19th and early 20th centuries, many Germans were ambivalent about the term and its referents, preferring to express their self-image through the particularistic concept of *Kultur* (culture). It is also interesting to note that, although it is somewhat lacking in the sorts of specifically sociogenetic insights developed by Elias, there are clear parallels between Elias's diagnoses and the analyses of the history of the terms, "civilisation" and "culture" by Raymond Williams in his *Keywords*[18].

From what I have said so far, it should be clear that Elias explicitly recognised the fact that, in popular usage, "civilization", is a value-laden term. By contrast, in his own sociological usage, it, and particularly the related concept of a "civilising process", is intended as a detached, technical term to be used without moral and evaluative undertones. More particularly, Elias used it to refer to the partly shared, partly diverging and potentially reversible sequence of factual long-term changes of society, personality and habitus experienced by the most powerful societies of Western Europe as their social development led, first of all their ruling groups and, later, wider sections of their populations to view themselves as "civilised" and "barbaric". Indeed, in the 18th and 19th centuries and to a diminishing extent in the 20th, these same epithets were commonly used by elite groups in Western Europe as their social development led, first of all their ruling groups and, later, wider sections of their populations to view themselves as "civilised" and "barbaric". Indeed, in the 18th and 19th centuries and to a diminishing extent in the 20th, these same epithets were commonly used by elite groups in Western Europe in the denotation of members of their own "lower orders".

A further way in which Elias sought to distance his theory both from the "evolutionary" theories of the late 19th century and the evaluative connotations of the popular concept of "civilisation" was by means of an explicit denial of the idea that the Western societies of today represent a "high point" or "pinnacle" of civilised behaviour. For example, he speculated that future historians will probably come to see the people of today as forming an extension of the "middle ages" and, in a later work, non-teleologically characterised even the peoples in the present-day world who consider themselves to be most "civilisationally advanced" as "late barbarians". Consistent with this, perhaps the most striking feature of Elias's sociological approach in general was its reality-orientated, anti-ideological character. The sociologist, he argued, ought to be a *Mythenjäger* — a hunter or destroyer of myths. And although he never put it in quite these terms, he recognised clearly not only the exploitative character of modern civilisation but also its **genocidal potential.** Arguing against the perhaps still widespread belief that atrocities such as the Nazi "holocaust" cannot "normally ... take place in the more highly civilised societies of the 20th century", that they are, e.g., the exceptional acts of "irrational", "mentally ill" or "wicked" individuals" such as Hitler, he wrote:

> Explanations such as these shield from people the painful thought that such things could happen again, that such an outbreak of savagery and barbarism might stem directly from tendencies inherent in the structure of modern industrial societies. Just like scientifically conducted mass wars, the high organised and scientifically planned extermination of whole population groups in specially planned extermination of whole population groups in specially constructed death camps and sealed off ghettos by starvation, gassing or shooting do not appear to be entirely out of place in highly technicised mass societies. Instead of taking comfort from the idea that (such events) were exceptional, it might be more fruitful to investigate the conditions in 20th century civilisations, the *social* conditions, which have favoured barbarisms of this kind and which might favour them again in the future. How often ... must such horrors be repeated before we have learnedto understand how and why they happen, and before powerful people are able and willing to apply such knowledge in order to prevent them.[19]

These strictures apply not only to such highly publicised atrocities as the holocaust but also to the less well-known "colonial genocides" perpetrated, among others, by people of British descent in America and Australia. The latter, of course, were genocidal processes closely bound up with the building of the British Empire, i.e. with the development of British world-wide power and hence of British "civilisation" in the 18th and 19th centuries, and it was in the context of this development that the initial development and spread of modern sport took place.

It should by now be clear that, *pace* the authors I cited earlier, Elias's theory is not in any simple sense an "evolutionary" or "progress" theory. Although it does not pretend to offer a complete and final answer, it is attuned to the complexity of long-term processes, strives to capture the shifting balance between "progressive" and "regressive" developments in this regard, pays full attention to the part played by violent struggles and other forms of conflict, and does not posit some ever-continuing, unilinear increase of self-control but rather a movement in Western Europe between the Middle Ages and the early 20th century towards greater evenness and stability of emotional controls. In fact, the figurational perspective with its stress on complex, labile and therefore changing chains or networks of interdependence does not involve thinking of social processes in simple linear terms at all. It is a question rather, of complex "fields" of mutual "influence" or "force" that are generated in the context of complex networks of interdependent human beings with differential embodied and in other ways socially generated power resources.

As I said earlier, "Eliasians" are not committed to any notion of "modern civilisation" as some "perfect" social construct. We are also happy to engage with others in debate but, in my view, that debate will be impoverished to the extent that it is not informed by the results of theory-guided research into these interesting but highly complex issues about which we remain massively ignorant at the moment. Elias once countered the idea, widely accepted in Marxist circles until recently, that Marxism represents the "end of the road of discovery" about human beings and the societies they form by suggesting that it rather represents just "one symptom of a beginning". My view of Elias — which he shared himself — is that, by synthesising elements of the work of Marx with elements of that of Weber, Freud, Comte and others such as Mannheim and Simmel, he managed to push knowledge a little further along the road. Nothing is possible at the present stage other than to make small steps in this way.

Let me, in conclusion to this section, return to the comments on our approach advanced by Richard Gruneau and David Whitson. They are ambivalent towards our work, suggesting that, on the one hand, at its best it is "frequently provocative and intriguing" and, on the other, that it can be "read as a highly sophisticated variant of the theory of modernisation...". They continue:

> More importantly, the implicit assumption that the "civilising process" is characteristic of modern social and cultural order runs the risk of deflecting attention away from the **endemic** conflicts of interest and power struggles that are a continuing part of the production of that order. Some forms of violence simply cannot be explained adequately in terms of their low integration into the abstract apparatuses of control supposedly characteristic of complex, highly differentiated societies.[20]

Elias's theory of civilising processes deals explicitly with the way in which, in Western European contexts, violent "hegemonial" or "elimination struggles" among contenders for the "royal position" led unintentionally over time to the formation of state monopolies over violence and taxation, leading to higher degrees of intra- (N.B. not inter-) state pacification[21]. In its turn, this is held by Elias to have formed an important precondition for the development of modern capitalism in its various forms, types of socio-economic organisation characterised by **highly concrete** forms of control — what could be less "abstract" than a modern army or police force, for example — and in which more or less violent struggles between groups, including ethnic/"racial" and gender groups as well as state agencies and not only corporations and social classes, continue to be of crucial significance in the determination of the unplanned yet structured and determinable dynamics of such societies. Given this, it is difficult to avoid the conclusion that Gruneau and Whitson may have imposed some of their own preconceptions on what Elias wrote.

Although figurational sociologists have examined aspects of the "political economy" of sport, I agree with Gruneau and Whitson when they write that "neither Elias nor Dunning have much to say about the specificity of Western capitalism as a context for theorising about violence in sport"[22]. That is because we would be hesitant to "theorise about" it without carrying out comparative theory-guided empirical research, not only into the differences as well as the similarities that there are between the forms of capitalism, say, in the UK, the USA, Canada, France and Germany, but also into the ways in which these partly different forms interact with variables such as national and sub-national habituses, personality types and traditions, differential "racial"/ethnic compositions, patterns of class conflict, levels of economic development and patterns of gender relations and gender ideology.

I do not agree with Gruneau and Whitson, however, when they equate Elias with Freud, failing to see the specificity and originality of Elias's partly *neo*-Freudian synthesis. Gruneau and Whitson write:

> Elias proceeded from Freudian assumptions (similar to those of catharsis theories) — his foundational idea was that human nature is composed of aggressive drives — but he argues that the civilising process is constituted precisely by the containment and sublimation of aggression within rule-bound and stylised social contexts.[23]

To show, yet again, that this is simply wrong, it is enough to quote something that Elias **actually wrote** on the subject. The *neo*-Freudian and above all **sociological** character of his position emerges clearly in the following passage:

> One false way of posing the problem [of physical violence in social life] is the currently widespread tendency to ascribe social conflicts and the resulting psychological conflicts to people's innate aggressiveness. The idea that people have an aggressive drive to attack others which resembles in its structure other innate drives, such as the sexual drive, is unfounded. People do have an innate potential automatically to shift their whole physical apparatus to a different gear if they feel endangered. The body reacts to the experience of danger by an automatic adjustment which prepares the way for intensive movement of the skeletal muscles, as in combat or flight. Human impulses that correspond to the model of a drive are released physiologically or, as is often said, "from within", relatively independently of the actual situation. The shifting of the body's economy to combat-or-flight readiness is conditioned to a far greater extent by a specific situation, whether present or remembered.
>
> The potential for aggressiveness can be activated by natural and social situations of a certain kind, above all by conflict. In conscious opposition to Lorenz and others, who ascribe an aggression drive to people on the model of the sexual drive, it is not aggressiveness that triggers conflicts but conflicts that trigger aggressiveness. Our habits of thought generate the expectation that everything we seek to explain about

people can be explained in terms of isolated individuals. It is evidently
difficult to adjust our thinking, and, thus, the explanations of how people
are interconnected in groups: that is, by means of social structures.
Conflicts are an aspect of social structures.[24]

Richard Gruneau and David Whitson, of course, think in terms of social
structures, not of isolated individuals. Nevertheless this passage speaks for itself
as far as their erroneous projection of aspects of Freud on to Elias's work is
concerned. Let me return to discussion of the relations between sport, violence
and gender and the Western civilising process.

Aspects of sport and gender in the western civilising process (ii)

Jennifer Hargreaves has perceptively observed that "because the whole history
of modern sports has been based on gender divisions, even radical accounts of
women's sports tend to focus on perceived **differences** between men and
women, rather than on the less obvious **relations** of power between them"[25].
In my view understandably but rather less perceptively, however, she is also
dismissive of the theory of civilising processes as a potential means for shedding
light on this area and even casts doubt on whether such a process can be said to
have occurred, especially as far as women are concerned[26]. However, the theory
of civilising processes and figurational sociology more generally are fundamentally relational and Jennifer Hargreaves has so far failed to respond to my
suggestion that the balance of power between the sexes is polymorphous and
multi-determined and that she tends to remain content with a few one-dimen-
sional, economistic assertions about patriarchy and capitalism in her pioneering
and otherwise highly successful studies of "sporting females". To make the
matter crystal clear, this is intended as a criticism of Jennifer Hargreaves's
reliance for explanation on which I take to be an overly voluntaristic version of
Gramscian Marxism and not, by any stretch of the imagination, as an attack on
the value of her work as a whole.

If Jennifer Hargreaves has failed to see the relevance and "reality-congruence"
of figurational contributions to the understanding of the relations between
patriarchy and the development of modern sport, the same cannot be said about
other contributors to the field. David Whitson, for example, refers to these
aspects of figurational work as "astute" and Todd Crosset acknowledges our
suggestion that "manly rituals associated with sport are related to the power

struggle between the sexes"[27]. And although they find it inconsistent with the theory of civilising processes, Richard Gruneau and David Whitson write similarly in this connection that:

> ... Dunning has suggested in a convincing way some possible effects of sport in the evolution of gender relations. First, he suggests that the power of men in any society is reinforced to the extent that important institutions in that society sanction and indeed celebrate the use of force. Conversely, the power of men is weakened whenever rules against the use of force are exercised to an extent that force becomes widely seen as taboo. Second, he suggests that the power of men is strengthened to the extent that men have their own institutions ("male preserves") that are honoured in the public sphere; and that male power in society is weakened when these institutions are integrated.[28]

I have referred already to Susan J. Birrell's positive reference to my own and Kenneth Sheard's 1973 paper on rugby clubs as a type of "male preserve". She adds in this connection that:

> In a recent revision of that paper, Dunning argues the almost biological necessity for the preservation of such spaces, particularly during times of encroachment by women into traditional male worlds and privileges. Thus the changing relations between the sexes and the ensuing civilising of society lead men to stake out clearly demarcated male turf.[29]

There is, of course, nothing "biologically necessary" about it. Nevertheless, Birrell has grasped here what I take to be some of the connections between civilising processes and the struggle against patriarchy. She, along with several other writers in the field, can also be read as suggesting that the hypotheses offered by figurational sociologists in this regard are well worthy of support from those who make different assumptions. Let me spell out these hypotheses in greater detail:

Although I would not wish to argue that it is entirely unproblematic — despite our persistent avowals to the contrary, for example, use of the term, "civilising process", certainly seems regularly to evoke in many people moral connotations and connotations of "unilinear progress" — it seems to me that the theory of civilising processes has three main advantages with respect to adding to the understanding of problems of sport and gender. More particularly, by looking at such issues in a novel way, it simultaneously provides the beginnings of an explanation of: (i) the significance of sport for males who remain committed to traditional male identities and roles; (ii) the relative empowerment of females to an extent sufficient to allow them to challenge with increasing success for entry into what started out as an exclusive male preserve; and (iii) of the corresponding changes at an ideological and value level regarding what constitutes socially acceptable "feminine" behaviour and in the habituses of females. In order to show how that is the case, it is necessary to spell out some of the core figurational assumptions regarding this area.

The first core assumption of figurational sociologists in relation to issues of gender is the idea that, like all other social relations, the relations between males and females are fundamentally affected by the character and overall structure of the society in which they are lived. The form of the economy and the society's level of economic development are clearly of significance in this regard. So is the position of the society in relation to others and the degree to which its inter-societal relations are warlike or peaceful. Arguably just as crucial, however, is whether a society has a state and, if so, the degree to which the state has managed to establish a secure and effective monopoly of physical force and, correlatively, of taxation. In other words, if Elias's work has any substance, the specific form and character of gender relations and gender identities in a society, together with its specific values and ideologies regarding gender relations, will be in part a function of the particular trajectory of that society's civilising process and the level reached in that connection. The second core assumption is that males and females are radically interdependent because they need each other for reproductive purposes and because any society which did not rank reproduction at least relatively highly in its value-scale would soon die out. Males and females need each other sexually as well, though, of course, variable numbers of each sex develop homo-erotic tendencies. (As an aside, it is worth noting that the degree of tolerance accorded to "gays" can be counted as one mark of a society's level of civilisation). In short, our second core assumption holds that the relations of males and females are characterised by a fundamental interdependence which derives in part from bio-psychological roots and in part from roots that are socio-cultural in character. The third core assumption is that, again like other human interdependencies, the interdependence of males and females is best conceptualised as involving at a fundamental level a "balance of power" or "power-ratio" between them. The term "balance" is not used here in the static sense of "equality" or "equilibrium" but in order to signify and stress the fundamentally dynamic, relational and relative character of power. The fourth core assumption is that, at the heart of the dynamic balance of power between the sexes in any society lies, not only the relative abilities of males and females to control economic, political and ideological resources, but also their relative capacities to use violence and to bestow on or withhold sexual favours from each other.

Connected with this constellation of core assumptions are at least two ostensible facts:

(i) that although there is obviously (a) a degree of overlap between the sexes in this regard, and (b) the size differences of males and females are a function, not simply of biology but also of social processes connected, e.g. with the sexual division of labour and levels of economic development and therefore of the social construction of bodies, males have tended in all known societies up to now to be bigger, physically stronger and faster than females and therefore better equipped as fighters;

(ii) menstruation but, above all, pregnancy and the nursing of infants tend to incapacitate women, among other ways as far as fighting is concerned.

Of course, modern weapons technology has the potential for offsetting and perhaps for removing altogether the in-built fighting advantages of men. Similarly, invention of the tampon has reduced the inconvenience associated with menstruation, modern birth-control techniques have reduced the proportion of their life-course spent by women in pregnancy, and bottle-feeding has made it possible for men to nurse infants. In other words, the power chances derived by men from their strength and capacity as fighters — if I am right, this is one of the principal sources of the origins and development of andrarchy (patriarchy) — tend to vary inversely with scientific and technological development; that is, they tend to be greater when scientific and technological development are low and *vice versa*. However, it is reasonable to suppose — again if Elias's theory has any substance — that the level of state-formation of a society, in particular the degree to which the state is capable of maintaining effective monopoly control over the use of physical force, is likely to be a significant influence on the developing balance of power between the sexes. Let me explore the relevance of these core assumptions for the development of sport.

The first thing worthy of note in this connection is the fact that many sports involve forms of fighting, and both fighting and sport appear to derive in complex ways from the same or similar psychological and socio-cultural roots. This is most obviously the case in combat sports such as boxing, wrestling and fencing which are, quite literally, socially sanctioned forms of fighting. But it also appears to be true of such physical contact sports as soccer, American football and rugby which can be described as competitive "mock battles" between teams. The second thing worthy of note is that, according to Elias, the Western European "civilising process" has involved, on the normative level, an accumulation of controls and taboos, e.g. against males striking females, and, on the level of habitus and personality, a lowering of the "threshold of repugnance" regarding violence and aggression. As a result, to the extent that it has involved males in being deprived of the right to use violence in relation to females, it will have led to the increasing "privatisation" of such violence, to the pushing of it increasingly "behind the scenes", to its confinement mainly to domestic contexts. Correspondingly, although there are complex, primarily class-related differences in this connection which I cannot explore in this paper, it will have led to increased moral opprobrium being aroused by the idea of males striking females and a correspondingly stronger public reaction when the dominant norms in this regard are breached. Perhaps more importantly for present purposes, to the extent that it has involved males in being deprived, not only of the public right to use violence in relation to females but, connected with a deeply internalised belief that it is wrong, of the psychological capacity and desire to do so, such a process will have increased — however marginally — the power of females relative to males. Men, however, will tend to feel their masculinity constrained and threatened, on the one hand by this civilising process *per se* which they experience as "emasculating", and on the other, by the correlatively growing power of women. If Elias's theory is sound, it is this twin development which would appear to lie at the roots of the fears of "feminisation" discussed in recent American writing and which, if I am right, are by no means confined solely to the United States. Taking the argument one step further, in the context of relatively "pacified" and, in that sense, relatively "civilised" societies, sport — along with such occupations as the military and the police — will come to represent an enclave for the legitimate expression of masculine aggression and for the development and expression of traditional masculine habituses involving the use and display of physical prowess and power. It will come, that is to say, to represent a primary vehicle for the "masculinity-validating" experience and to be regarded as a bastion against "feminisation" and "emasculation". However, its status as such will be threatened to the extent that the growing power, and correlatively, self-confidence, assertiveness and independence of women allows them to mount a successful challenge against traditional andrarchal (patriarchal) ideas and institutions and to enter sport themselves.

From the outset, women have had to fight hard in order to secure in the world of sport and, as can be seen, e.g., from the still male-dominated prestige hierarchy of sports and from the correspondingly relatively low exposure of female sports in the mass media, the relatively low rewards which accrue to top-level sportswomen as opposed to those which accrue to men, and the relatively low participation of females in events such as the Olympic Games, their status in this regard remains marginal, if not any longer so seriously insecure. Powerful ideologies questioning their femininity and their sexual orientation, and predicting physical and medical damage, continue to be mobilised against them to this day. Over time, however, in conjunction with the slowly changing balance of power between the sexes — which is, of course, a complex, multi-faceted and not simply linear process — and facilitated by such related developments as the introduction of modern forms of birth control, the related lowering of family size, inventions such as the tampon and modern forms of household technology, increasing numbers of women have succeeded in gaining entry to a greater range of sports. They have presumably been motivated in this connection by such things as: (a) an interest in obtaining the sorts of "mimetic", "sociability" and "motility" satisfactions that can be obtained from sports by men, together with the sorts of gains regarding identity, self-concept, self-assurance and habitus (e.g. greater feelings of security in public spaces and greater ability to defend themselves against a physical attack) which can accrue in that connection; and (ii) a desire for equality with men as a result of frustrations experienced over the constraints and limitations traditionally placed on female rôles.

Women are currently making strides in what are still widely regarded as "non-female appropriate" sports such as soccer, rugby and boxing. Such sports are combat/body contact events which involve a stress on combinations of power, strength, aggressiveness and speed. As such, they come most strongly and directly into contradiction with the still dominant notions of "femininity", ideals widely taken for granted by women and not just by men.

There are, however, one or two anomalies in this connection which deserve to be considered. Hockey is perhaps the prime example. In England, it became established as a game for females in the 1880s and 90s. Writing in the *Badminton Magazine* in 1900, an Edwardian author claimed:

> [For women] ... beauty of face and form is one of the chief essentials, but unlimited indulgence in violent outdoor sports, cricket, bicycling,

> beagling, otter hunting, paper-chasing, and — most odious of all games
> for a woman — hockey, cannot but have an unwomanly effect on a
> young girl's mind, no less than her appearance ... Let young girls ride,
> skate, dance and play lawn tennis and other games in moderation, but let
> them leave field sports and rough outdoor pastimes to those for whom
> they are naturally intended — men.[30]

Such forms of teleological reductionism were common at the time. However, anti-hockey arguments were not put forward just by men. Kathleen E. McCrone cites two females, the first who

> ...asserted that "only the few square, squat, and burly outdoor porter type
> of girls should play ... [the] rough, competitive game of hockey", which
> "with its muddy field, rush and excitement, for the unformed, untrained
> or nervous girl is surely unadulterated lunacy" ...

And the second, a schoolgirl who observed that

> ... hockey made women "mannish" and neglectful of their domestic
> duties and just the "detestable" sort likely to become suffragettes.[31]

McCrone accounts for the apparently anomalous development of hockey as a game for females by suggesting that:

> At public schools hockey was often regarded as effeminate and fit only
> for malingerers, so it never acquired the grandeur or overt masculinity of
> cricket and football. Thus, when women took it up, they were not
> perceived necessarily as trespassing on a sacred male preserve.[32]

This is a powerful argument, consistent with the fact that hockey remained in Britain at least until the 1950s widely regarded in male circles as "effeminate". However, Kathleen McCrone fails to offer direct historical evidence on this score and my suspicion is that such a public school belief may have originated in connection with the emergence of hockey as a game for females. Accordingly, McCrone may have been projecting a more recent value on to the past. Whether that is so or not, however, her reference to the schoolgirl who argued that female hockey players are likely to become suffragettes suggests that a politically conscious element may have been involved in the emergence of hockey as a game for females. More particularly, females who chose to play hockey in the late 19th century were probably fully aware of the then-dominant belief in its masculinising implications and, whether they became suffragettes or not, were probably deliberately setting their staff out against then- contemporary ideals of femininity and female habitus.

The dominant suffragette view, however, seems to have been less radical as far as notions of feminine habitus and identity were concerned. In the context of a society where legitimate violence had been monopolised by the state and in which sport had become one of the principal areas for the legitimate inculcation and expression of relatively unreconstructed masculine values, sport came to form a main target of feminist protest. In the words of historian Brian Dobbs:

> … because sport was such an outpost of male chauvinism and something of a masculine symbol, when the women's suffrage movement had failed with every democratic attempt to get its voice heard, it was sport which had to bear the brunt of the suffragettes" turn to militancy and violence. Throughout 1913, bowling greens, golf clubs, cricket grounds and football grounds had their turf torn up and damaged and their buildings burnt down, all over the country.[33]

Not only did sport come to serve as a target for feminist protest in this way but small but growing numbers of women struggled simultaneously to reduce the idea that sport is legitimately only a male preserve. In this connection, however, in addition to the questioning of their sex and sexual orientations, sportswomen have often had to face problems that are not typically faced by men. It is well known that, despite the move in recent years in the direction of a greater sharing of conjugal roles, married women or women with a stable partner who work outside the home still tend to be expected to perform the lion's share of domestic tasks. Working women athletes with a stable partner or husband and children, however, often experience not a two-way but a severe three-way conflict in this regard. As one of them expressed it in 1981:

> … trying to be a wife and mother, to keep a career and training going and trying to keep an interest in sport causes tremendous conflicts and there is never enough time to go round. There is always the feeling that you are never achieving your optimum in any of the varied roles you are trying to perform. This raises great problems for women about guilt and this is one of society's subtle devices. When a woman is training she feels she should be looking after her children or her husband; if she is marking her essays she ought to be doing her training and so on. So there is a great deal of conflict.[34]

The same sportswoman went on to express criticism of what she described as women's "servicing role" for sport. She said:

> I can remember ... my mother many years ago always washing my brother's rugby strip and even at the age of 10, I was asked to clean his boots, which I resented, even if he was playing in the First XV.[35]

This suggests that a great deal of sport depends on the exploitation of unpaid female labour. Given that, it is not perhaps sociologically surprising that males have tended generally to resist attempts by females to become actively involved in their sporting preserves. It is also arguably the case that the use by males of sporting contexts as sites for the symbolic demeaning and vilification of females has grown as the power of women has increased.

In Britain, the symbolic vilification of women in sports contexts — itself arguably a form of symbolic violence — tends to take place behind closed doors in Rugby Union football and more openly in the Association game ("soccer"). This is largely a consequence of the social class differences of those who play and watch the different football codes, more particularly of the fact that Rugby Union is predominantly a middle-class game whilst soccer and the associated culture are predominantly working class. Since rugby football as a male preserve has been dealt with elsewhere, let me briefly explore this issue by reference to the Association code.

Writing in 1988, journalist Edward Vulliamy offered the following as part of a description of a group of England fans in Stuttgart, where they were attending the European Football Championships. They were, he said:

> ... assembled at the Bierfässle Bar ... in shorts and tee shirts, calculating beer prices, scratching their testicles and singing "Get yer tits out for the lads" whenever a young woman walked by ....

Another standard part of the repertoire of many hooligan and fringe-hooligan groups of English soccer fans when they have travelled away to watch their team is the following refrain: "Leicester (Newcastle, Liverpool, Tottenham, etc.) boys, we are here. Fuck your women and drink your beer". This, of course, signals a predatory intent towards local males but it also symbolises a crude objectification of females and a view of them as the "property" of males. As one can imagine, large numbers of women are deterred from attending football by such displays. They are deterred in less obvious, perhaps less crudely objectifying but no less demeaning ways as well. A prime example is provided by the fact that females are forbidden from entering the boardrooms of many professional clubs, even the female relatives and friends of directors when the latter use the boardroom to entertain guests.

A more blatant example was provided in a TV documentary dealing with women and football in the early 1990s. In it, a Stockport County fan described his technique for preventing a woman who expressed a desire to go from attending football. Here is a paraphrase of what he said: "If she insists on going, by all means take her but take her to the worst part of the ground, somewhere in the open where she's bound to get wet. She won't want to go again in a hurry and things will be as they should be once more. Football is a game for men". This is remarkably similar to what once I heard a former Secretary of the Football Association say at a meeting in 1988. His name was Ted Croker and here, again, is a paraphrase of his words: "Football is a game of hard, physical contact. In fact, it is a form of combat. It is, and must remain, a man's game. Women have no place in it except to cheer on their men, wash and iron their kit, and prepare and serve refreshments." Doreen Massey offers an interesting comment on how many females respond to the male dominance of public space which results from patriarchal values of this kind. She writes:

> On the way into town we would cross the wide shallow valley of the River Mersey, and my memory is of dank, muddy fields spreading away into a cold, misty distance. And all of it—all of these acres of Manchester —was divided up into football pitches and rugby pitches. And on Saturdays the whole vast area would be covered with hundreds of… people, all running round after balls, as far as the eye could see!… I remember all this very sharply. And I remember, too, it striking me very clearly — even then as a puzzled, slightly thoughtful little girl — that all this huge stretch of the Mersey flood plain had been entirely given over to boys.
>
> I did not go to those playing fields — they seemed barred, another world (though today, with more nerve and some consciousness of being a space-invader, I do stand on the football terraces — and love it). But there were other places to which I did go, and yet where I still felt they were not mine, or at least that they were designed to, or had the effect of, firmly letting me know my conventional subordination.[36]

In societies such as modern Britain, it is not only gender but class and race which induce such a sense of exclusion and subordination. In a word, it is not only females who have such feelings but many male members of subordinate, outsider groups as well, though, of course, the female members of such groups tend to be doubly, even trebly disadvantaged. This caveat notwithstanding, Massey's observations of some of the continuing connections between "sport, place and gender" are perceptive regarding the limited degree to which gender equalisation has occurred in modern Britain whether in sport or in other spheres. Let me, by way of conclusion, sum up what I have tried to argue in this paper and tease out what I take some of the major implications to be.

Conclusion

Summing up, what my argument in this paper has been is that modern sport emerged as part of a civilising process and that it is best understood as having come to represent what is, for a majority of males, a principal locus for the inculcation and public expression of traditional standards of masculinity. In short, modern sport emerged as a male preserve, a fact which helps to account for the strength of male resistance to attempts by females to enter it or to develop sporting enclaves of their own. However, another key aspect of the European civilising process has involved a shift in the balance of power between the sexes in a gynarchic (matriarchal) direction.

The civilising transformation I am hypothesising may have had such an effect in at least two ways, the first, connected with the image of ideal masculine and feminine rôles embodied in the form of the andrarchal (patriarchal) nuclear family which became the norm among the expanding middle classes in the second half of the nineteenth century. What I should like to speculate is that, contrary to what is currently a widespread feminist view, this form of family may, in one respect at least, have represented a shift towards the equalisation of power chances between the sexes. That is because it arguably tied more males more firmly into a more egalitarian form of family than had been the case before — diminishing the Victorian rôle of *pater familias*, for example — thus subjecting them to the possibility of a greater and more regular degree of female influence and control. If Edward Shorter is correct, in that context more men would have begun to become more attached to and to identify more with their wives as persons rather than simply as objects for sexual gratification and producing (especially male) offspring[37].

By imposing a complex of internal and external restraints on the expression of aggression by men, for example *via* the code of "gentlemanly" conduct with its simultaneous placing of women "on a pedestal" and the deeming of it as "ungentlemanly" to strike them, this overall civilising transformation may also have been conducive to a degree of equalisation of the power chances of the sexes. It would have been so by restricting the opportunities for men to use one of their principal power advantages relative to women — their generally greater physical strength and superiority as fighters. This, in turn, may have increased the chances for women to engage in unified political action, for example by organising and taking part in demonstrations. If this speculative hypothesis has any substance, such a civilising transformation may have had this effect by reducing the likelihood that demonstrations of nascent female unity, self-confidence, assertiveness and power would be responded to violently by men, especially husbands and fathers in a domestic context. More particularly, to the extent that a non-violent response from men to such political involvements and acts by women could be expected, the fears of women would have been reduced and their confidence correspondingly enhanced to go ahead with the struggle for what increasing numbers of women, supported by a smaller but also growing number of men, were coming to believe were their rights.

In short, it seems reasonable to suppose that the relatively slight but nevertheless significant shift in the balance of power between men and women that first received public expression in the suffragettes movement may have been at least partly a consequence of the "civilising spurt" that accompanied Britain's emergence as an urban-industrial-nation-state. But let me make it crystal clear: to say this is *not* to imply that the state or general public-response to the suffragettes was non-violent. What I am suggesting, rather, is that, although the level of police and public violence against them escalated as the suffragettes themselves felt constrained to adopt violent means, firstly, the levels and types of violence used against them were different from those used against men, and secondly, and for present purposes more importantly, that *one* of the preconditions for the suffragettes movement *may* have been the renunciation of violence towards women on the part of many of the men to whom individual suffragettes were most closely bonded. This hypothesis does not by any means imply a denial of the continuing occurrence of male violence towards females. I have simply sought to suggest: (i) that violence against females has tended to decrease in *public*; (ii) that feelings of outrage regarding breaches of the dominant norms in this regard have tended to increase; and (iii) that, insofar as it continues to occur in societies such as modern Britain, male violence against females *tends* to predominate in the least "incorporated", socio-economically lowest social strata. Indeed, males from these strata are not liable to experience serious feelings of guilt if they behave violently towards females, and women members of such "communities" tend to expect violent behaviour from their men. But let me return to the subject of gender and sport.

Whilst the majority of women have so far tended to accept the hegemonic definition of sport as a predominantly male preserve, this shift in the balance of power between the sexes, whilst not by any stretch of the imagination great, has continued to occur following the initial spadework of the suffragettes — in conjunction with a whole complex of intended and unintended processes — and has clearly been sufficient to make it impossible for males to prevent females from entering this male bastion in growing numbers. The barriers erected against them have been strongest in the contact/combat sports but, in recent years, more and more women have taken up sports such as soccer and even rugby and boxing. Indeed, in the United States this process has gone further than in Britain at least as far as soccer is concerned, with the US women's team winning the Women's World Cup in 1992.

The growing direct involvement of women in sport in and of itself represents an equalising trend. Nevertheless, as we have seen, this growing female involvement in what started as an exclusive male preserve has tended to involve two specific sets of penalties for sportswomen which show that modern sport and modern society still remain predominantly andrarchic. On the one hand, the femininity of sportswomen tends to be compromised in the eyes of others, especially as a result of their participation in contact sports. In some cases, it tends to be compromised in their own eyes, too, a reaction that is typical of "outsider" groups to the extent that they have internalised the "group charisma" of those who are more established, in this case of males. On the other hand, women face numerous obstacles with respect to participation in sport that are not experienced by males. Nevertheless, male sports are at the same time dependent in many ways on "servicing" by women. Such services may, in many cases, be voluntarily given. Nevertheless, to the extent that "servicing" of this kind is based on internalisation of the group charisma of males, and not freely given and fully reciprocated, it can be described quite accurately in *neo*-Marxist terms as the exploitation of unpaid female labour. If I am right, such exploitation, much of it at a taken-for-granted and not fully conscious level, constitutes just one of many continuing sources of opposition to female sports involvement in the "late-barbarian" societies of today.

Notes

1   See especially Eric Dunning, Patrick Murphy and John Williams, *The Roots of Football Hooliganism*, Routledge, 1988.

2   For a fuller explication of this concept see Norbert Elias, *What is Sociology?*, Macmillan, 1978.

3   Susan J. Birrell, "Discourses on the Gender/Sport Relationship: from Women in Sport to Gender Relations, *"Exercise and Sports Sciences Reviews*, Vol. 16, 1988.

4   Part of the personal motivation for writing this paper came when I married my (proto-) feminist second wife who objected to my sports involvement, especially my cricket which, during the summer, kept me away from home for whole week-ends at a time.

5   For example, Ann Oakley, *Sex, Gender and Society*, Gower/Maurice Temple Smith, 1992 and K. Davis, M. Leijenaar and J. Oldersma, *The Gender of Power*, Sage, 1991.

6   Arthur Brittan, *Masculinity and Power*, Blackwell, 1989, p. 77.

7   See Norbert Elias, "The Changing Balance of Power Between the Sexes in the History of Civilisation", *Theory, Culture and Society*, Vol. 4, Nos. 2-3, 1986 "Andrarchy" — which means "male rule" — is preferable to "patriarchy" because, while the latter derives from Latin and Greek roots, the roots of the former are both Greek. It also means "rule by men", whereas "patriarchy" literally means "rule of the father".

8   J. Rigg and R. Lewney, "The Economic Impact and Importance of Sport in the UK", *International Review of the Sociology of Sport*, Vol. 22, No. 3, 1987.

9   Joseph Maguire, "Towards a Sociological Theory of Sport and the Emotions" in Eric Dunning and Chris Rojek (Eds.), *Sport and Leisure in the Civilising Process: Critique and Counter Critique*, Macmillan, 1992.

10 Kenneth Sheard and Eric Dunning, "The Rugby Football Club as a Type of Male Preserve: Some Sociological Notes", *International Review of Sport Sociology*, Vol. 5, 1973.

11 Paul Willis, "Women in Sport in Ideology" in Jennifer Hargreaves (Ed.) *Sport, Culture and Ideology*, Routledge, 1982. "Performance and Meanings: a Sociological View of Women in Sport" was an unpublished paper written in 1975 on which this was based.

12 Birrell, *op. cit.*, p. 481.

13 See especially Michael A. Messner and Donald F. Sabo (Eds.) *Sport, Men and the Gender Order: Critical Feminist Perspectives*, Human Kinetics, Champaign (Illinois), 1990.

14 Michael Messner, "The Life of a Man's Seasons: Male Identity in the Life-Course of the Jock" in M.S. Kimmel (Ed.) *Changing Men*, Sage, 1987.

15 The reason why is that figurational sociologists are acutely aware of the fact that knowledge is developmental, i.e. that all of us are dependent on the "social fund of knowledge" available in particular societies at particular times. As far, specifically, as sociology is concerned, it is our position that sociological knowledge at the moment is far less advanced than that in areas such as physics, chemistry and biology.

16 Norbert Elias, *The Civilising Process: the History of Manners*, Blackwell, 1978, pp. 93-94.

17 David Harris, *From Class Struggles to the Politics of Pleasure: the Effects of Gramscianism on Cultural Studies*, Routledge 1992, p. 162.

18 Raymond Williams, *Keywords: a Vocabulary of Culture and Society*, Fontana, 1976.

19 Norbert Elias, *Studien über die Deutschen: Machtkämpfe und Habitus-entwicklung im 19. und 20. Jahrhundert*, Suhrkamp (Frankfurt), 1989, pp. 395-6, my own translation.

20 Richard Gruneau and David Whitson, *Hockey Night in Canada: Sport, Identities and Cultural Politics*, Garamond (Toronto), 1993, p. 80.

21 Such processes of internal pacification, of course, took place correlatively with an increase in the violence of inter-state wars connected, e.g. with the application of modern science to weapons technology. Inter-state wars act as a brake on domestic civilising processes, sometimes leading to their reversal for greater or lesser periods of time. So, of course, do "civil wars" as the example of former Yugoslavia so graphically shows.

22 Gruneau and Whitson, *op. cit.*, p. 179.

23 *Ibid.*, p. 178.

24 Norbert Elias, "Violence and Civilisation" in John Keane (Ed.), *Civil Society and the State: New European Perspectives*, Verso (London), 1988, pp. 177-78.

25 Jennifer Hargreaves, *Sporting Females: Critical Issues in the History and Sociology of Women's Sports*, Routledge, 1994, p. 8.

26 Jennifer Hargreaves, "Sex, Gender and the Body in Sport: Has there been a Civilising Process?" in Eric Dunning and Chris Rojek *op. cit.* pp. 161-182.

27 David Whitson, "Sport in the Social Construction of Masculinity", Todd Crosset, "Masculinity, Sexuality and the Development of Early Modern Sport", both in Messner and Sabo, *op. cit.*

28 Gruneau and Whitson, *op. cit.*, p. 180.

29 Birrell, *op. cit.*, p. 483.

30 Brian Dobbs, *Edwardians at Play: Sport 1890-1914*, Pelham (London), 1973, p. 177.

31 Kathleen McCrone, *Sport and the Physical Emancipation of English Women, 1870-1914*, Routledge, 1988, p. 135.

32 *Ibid.*, p. 128.

33 Dobbs, *op. cit.*, p. 178.

34 Quoted by Rosemary Payne in "Comment on Margaret Talbot's "Women and sport: Social Aspects" in Bruce Tulloh, M.A. Herbertson and Alan Parkes (Eds.), *Biological Aspects of Sport*, Galton Foundation (Cambridge), 1981, p. 49.

35 *Ibid.*, p. 49.

36 *The Guardian*, 13.6.88.

37 Doreen Massey, *Space, Place and Gender*, Polity (Cambridge) 1994, p. 183.

38 Edward Shorter, *A History of Women's Bodies*, Basic Books (New York), 1982, pp. 294-6.

BIOLOGY, IDEOLOGY AND SPORT

Lincoln Allison

Director of the Warwick Centre for the Study of Sport in Society
at Warwick University

'

The primary objective of this essay is to defend sport in its relation to race. One accusation from which it must be defended is that it has had predominantly negative effects on the interests of black people. Another, logically separate, but causally related, is that modern sport has had a bad effect on race relations. The two charges taken together are summarised by the sub-title of John Hoberman's book on the subject: *How Sport has Damaged Black America and Preserved the Myth of Race*[1]. There is a certain amount of ambiguity in this package of accusation: to what extent is it only about America and only about relations between 'black' people and 'white' (or 'black' people and non-black)?

A secondary objective is to assess what is acceptable and what is not within the range of contemporary assertions about the relationship between race and sporting prowess. By acceptable, I mean logically coherent and compatible with established Darwinian biology and the archaeological evidence about mankind. This naturally generates speculative ideas about the consequences of ideas, acceptable or merely accepted, about race and sport for the practice and ethics of sport itself. Finally, there are some implications for the issues of gender in sport, since the establishment of a coherent doctrine about biological groups has implications for male-female as well as black-white relations.

To some degree, I shall be supporting popular beliefs against contemporary academic orthodoxies. It is a widespread belief outside academic discourse that sport is a natural integrator of peoples. Where victory by fair means is the objective, all are welcome, to be measured by their contribution rather than by their origins or other characteristics. Thus Hoberman is attacking a common American belief that the growing participation of black Americans in major

135

league sport since Jackie Robinson first played baseball in 1945 has been good for American race relations and for the under-privileged races. In Britain, Colin Moynihan, when Minister for Sport, probably spoke for most sports officials when he said, "You get limited and very little racism within sport in this country. That's the beauty of sport"[2]. More radical academics such as Ellis Cashmore[3] and the more critical and intellectual journalists, including Mihir Bose and Simon Barnes, have challenged such optimism, though it may already be apparent that there is a possible confusion between race relations in sport and the effects of sport on race relations in general, insofar as people making statements like Moynihan's about sport are often assumed to be generally optimistic about race relations. Generally, journalists at the tabloid end of the market have supported the more optimistic thesis and have accused sportsmen who complain about racism in sport of whingeing.

If my support for the optimists will be fairly clear, my support for those who believe that race may be a factor in the distribution of sporting prowess will be much more guarded, essentially a sceptical view which calls for a plague in both houses, whilst regarding the extreme form of political correctness which assert the *impossibility* of any racial-biological correlation with sporting prowess as the most foolish doctrine on offer. As it happens, pessimists about race relations tend to be minimisers of the possibility of biological-racial factors having any importance, the combination of beliefs lending itself to a liberal doctrine of race which blames a racist cultural environment for apparent racial characteristics. Logically, it could easily have been the other way round, with believers in biological racial characteristics being the pessimists about race relations. In any case, it is necessary before I discuss sport to outline a doctrine of the concept of race.

The concept of race

It is important in any discussion involving race to stress how extremely ill-formed the concept is. Unlike "nation", the word "race" does not even have a proper etymological history, coming from the Italian *razza*, the origin of which is unknown. The eight meanings which the OED lists for race in this sense are full of generalities and circularities: "the major divisions of humankind" ... "any great division" ... "tribe, nation, etc. regarded as of a distinct ethnic stock". Race in this broad, pre-theoretical sense, has no more meaning than "big group" and races exist insofar as they are perceived. Concepts don't really come any vaguer than that.

The Darwinian, biological concept of race is of a group within a species which shares a common inheritance and therefore common characteristics; it is most usually applied to birds and mammals. However, this is also very vague: races exist insofar as there have been, as a matter of contingency, patterns of breeding exclusivity which have created and maintained common characteristics. It is a defining characteristic of species that two species cannot interbreed in any sustained way. Even so, a lively and interesting debate is possible about how species should be distinguished and how many there are. But this debate is on a different level from that about races. 'Species' is a concept which works for most practical, legal and scientific purposes. 'Races' only exist to a degree, insofar as people just happen to have concentrated inheritable characteristics within a group.

The Victorian and early twentieth century textbooks on racial biology illustrated and discussed a wide variety of racial categories, including 'Anglo-Saxon', 'Teutonic', 'Alpine', 'Celtic', 'Nordic' and so on, all of which are subsumed under the heading 'Caucasian' in modern American (and sometimes British) classifications. The textbooks which explained the characteristics of these categories were still to be found in classroom cupboards in my youth. It was always fatuous to suppose that these supposed races had remained separate enough to have genuinely common characteristics and even in their heyday they were effectively satirised by such writers as Hilaire Belloc:

> Behold, my child, the Nordic Man
> And be as like him as you can

and

> The most degraded of them all
> Mediterranean we call.
> His hair is crisp, and even curls,
> And he is saucy with the girls.[4]

It would be wrong, however, to allow this humorous note to stand alone. As Curtis has argued, the Anglo-Saxon/Celt distinction was in some respects the justifying ideology of British policies towards Ireland and the Scottish High-lands, though one might go on to suggest that Celtic racial consciousness has fed into the darker corners of Irish nationalism and proved far more durable and vicious than the original concept of the Anglo-Saxon[5]. The broad, even huge, 'Caucasian' category is the racial concept for an ideology preoccupied with the difference between black and white, secondarily concerned with the rights and interest of 'Hispanics', 'Native Americans' etc., but no longer politically bothered by the supposed racial differences between "white" people. "Caucasian" is an anomalous and even comical category. I was personally involved with setting up what my Georgian colleagues wanted to call the "Journal of Caucasian Studies" until I explained that this title in English would send some very wrong messages, particularly to an American audience. We eventually called it the *Journal of Caucasian Regional Studies*. 'Caucasian' comes to mean 'white' because of an entirely false theory that the "white" race evolved in the Caucasus. The paradox is that contemporary Caucasians are called 'black' by the Russians (because of their black hair and swarthy skins) and are often the victims of racial harassment within Russia.

In short, much of what has been said about race is untenable: not only, as a matter of biology, can reproduction break down racial boundaries, but, as a matter of history, it usually has. The textbooks on racial biology did not usually tell us much about hybrids, about the Malaccans, the Cape Coloureds, the Anglo-Indians, the Burgers of Sri Lanka, the Laskers and so on. Even more importantly, they told us nothing about the complete melting pots of Tunis, Istanbul, Moscow, Vienna and London, let alone New York or Los Angeles. "Not known" is the response which I have always adopted to racial categories on forms; other prefer 'human". Current biological orthodoxy has it that the amount we have in common as a species dwarfs what divides us as races. Current anthropological and archaeological arguments (popularised by such writers as Stringer and McKie and Leakey and Lewin) suggest the overwhelming probability of a common (African) origin for mankind[6].

So far, so politically correct. But a thoroughgoing racial scepticism of the sort I have just tried to outline does not necessarily put one on the radical, or even liberal wing of contemporary debate. It is perfectly possible, within my sceptical assumptions, that there do exist genetic groups which correlate black skin and certain characteristics translatable into athletic ability, just as there *may* also exist bad tempered red-haired groups or groups whose biological characteristics cause a *lack* of athletic ability. We do know that the tiny elite of professional sport shows marked genetic clusters: this is true in football and cricket and even more so among racing jockeys. But there is no serious suggestion that any of these groupings are more or less human than people of more ordinary sporting ability. Egalitarian political theory has not and does not need to stipulate that human beings have identical characteristics before they can have equal rights or equal utilitarian consideration. For that matter, if a different species existed on the planet, perhaps from extra-terrestrial origins, which were wholly different in shape, size and colour, but which possessed the capacity to feel and the capacities to think and communicate with us, we should properly consider them as essentially human, considering their interests and engaging them in debate. It is highly likely that at any given sport they would be vastly inferior to us or vastly superior. Thus racial scepticism is not committed to saying that there are no correlations between racial characteristics and that any apparent correlations must have environmental origins, because it regards such correlations as trivial. To an outsider, it is positively bizarre that the usual premise of the American debate is that if Afro-Americans are racially more athletic than their compatriots, they must also be less intelligent.

I have argued elsewhere that we ought to stipulate a distinction between racism and racialism[7]. Racism consists of a tendency to make racial distinctions, to discriminate on racial grounds. Racialism consists of doctrines of racial difference and of the importance of racial distinctions in the understanding of human affairs. Racism exists in many forms, including paradoxical forms like 'affirmative action' and 'positive discrimination' which are designed to counteract other forms of racism. Racialism now hardly exists; it is not ideologically respectable to suggest that race, *per se*, is an important determinant of human affairs, and those who do so are pilloried.

I have argued that racialism was an important factor in western societies for about a century, from the 1850s to 1945. Before then, although people were perfectly capable of being beastly to each other and of dismissing each other as 'savages' or 'barbarians', and 'white' men were particularly capable of beastliness and contempt to others in the course of developing their commercial empires, all of this was done in an ideologically disorganised way. It was only in the 1850s that the racial doctrines of Ronald Knox and the Comte de Gobineau were articulated and Darwin's theory of evolution finally published. This coincided with the Indian Mutiny and the subsequent formalisation of the British Empire, but also with the Civil War and the emancipation of slaves and the subsequent establishment of segregation in the United States. Racialism became the ideology which justified discrimination and exploitation in an age in which ideas of equality and democracy were otherwise rising to the fore. There was, particularly, a change in patterns of sexual and social behaviour in the British

Empire. Before the 1850s 'mixing' with local people had been common in many parts; after that segregation became the norm in most places and inter-marriage taboo. It was only in the 1880s that racial biology became an integral part of prevailing ideas.

Biology was the supreme, dominant, fashionable science of the period. Thus, in many ways, the attitudes of many writers before 1850 may seem to us less dated that those of the second half of the century. For example, the Reverend Sydney Smith, founder of the Edinburgh Review, commented in 1820:

> A great deal has been said of the original difference between men and women … this, we confess, appears to us very fanciful. That there is a difference in the understanding of the men and women we every day meet with, everybody we suppose, must perceive: but there is none surely which may not be accounted for by the difference of circumstances in which they have been placed…. As long as boys and girls run about in the dirt and trundle hoops together, they are both precisely alike.[8]

Whereas in 1889 Sir Patrick Geddes, as a 'pure' biologist, long before his re-invention of himself as a theorist of town planning and on the other side of the nature/nurture debate in some respects, could comment loftily that, "What was decided among the prehistoric Protozoa cannot be annulled by Act of parliament"[9].Both writers spoke for their times. They were commenting on issues of gender rather than race (Geddes had female suffrage in mind), but 1820, like us, understands 'environment' and 'social constructs' whereas 1889 sees biology as transcendent. (There is an interesting debate about the extent to which Charles Darwin was himself responsible for the social doctrines generated by his wildly successful theories. The answer appears to be that he was innocent insofar as the theories in *The Origin of Species* do not logically imply 'Social Darwinism', but that Darwin was actually, and, perhaps, illogically, "guilty" of Social Darwinism.)

It is important to stipulate at this stage that, however vague the concept of race is, it is concerned with *biological* differences. In doing so I have to acknowledge that large areas of contemporary moral and academic concern talk about race in the contexts of "race relations" and "racial hatred" in an even vaguer way, so that almost any difference of identity between groups, including national, regional and religious differences (though not normally differences of class) can be subsumed under the heading of "race". Thus Serbs and Croats are different races and it is possible to talk about "cultural racism". For example, many explanations of the dramatic under-representation of players of Asian origin in English professional football cite a variety of *cultural* stereotypes and obstacles, but tend to subsume these can be treated as forms of racism in its now extended sense[10].

However, there are a number of powerful reasons for confining my treatment of "race" to the narrower biological sense. Historically, the importance of the concept of race was precisely that it attributed explanatory importance in human affairs to "nature" rather than "nurture". Ethically, it is entirely different to blame or persecute someone for a characteristic which they cannot change as opposed to one about which they have some choice: thus the anti-Jewish sentiments of Feuerbach, for example, are quite different from later German anti-semitism. While I would wish to support crusades against ethnic intolerance and religious or cultural hatred, I think to subsume these phenomena under the category of racism weakens the moral force of the criticism of racism as well as making a concept less clear than it might be. In any case, I am principally concerned here with arguments put by Hoberman and these are very clearly about a remaining legacy of biological racism.

This legacy is the theory of black athletic superiority, of the 'natural' ability of Afro-Caribbeans and Afro-Americans at short distance running and other "explosive" activities. It is this belief which has Professor Helmut Digel, president of the German Athletics Federation, pondering the possibly non-existent future of German athletics with the thought that "No young person is going to train for the title of 'the world's fastest white man'"[11] and Sir Roger Bannister speculating similarly about the "obviousness" of black superiority[12]. The *Daily Express* pointed out in 1997 that Haris Papadias, a white Greek, was the only non-black man to win a major sprinting championship (the 1997 indoor 60 metres world title) in seventeen years and that the twenty four men to run the 100 metres in under ten seconds were all black[13]. 'Race in sport' may be about many things, but this is the big one.

In its sophisticated version it is not about 'black' people as such, but about the descendants and diaspora of a relatively small West African genetic pool, possibly honed by the artificial selection of slavery, who are naturally dominant in the explosive sports: a kind of Afro-Diaspora master race. Racial biology may have been disgraced (in most of the world) since 1945, but genetics has actually expanded its explanatory empire. The ideology, the political correctness, of contemporary post-imperialist commercialism suggests that theories of racial difference are unacceptable. So the struggle between biology and humanism continues. Into it I now want to inject a fairly simple, even naïve, dimension of optimism.

The good side of sport

I was brought up in a normally racist English racial environment. Most of my male relatives had served as soldiers or sailors in the second world war and several of them were career merchant mariners. Thus they had moved about the British Empire and assumed a kind of racial arrogance; "we" were better than "others" and they needed our leadership and guidance. This was not, however, a hostile racism; rather it was patronising, assuming that the other races of the British Empire had some very good points and were basically on our side. It was deeply ambiguous about whether the child-like status of certain other races was permanent or temporary. Anything which might be described as racial hatred was addressed to the Japanese, the Germans and to a lesser extent other Western Europeans and not to Africans, Indians or Jews. If such racism had intellectual progenitors or ideologues, they were Gobineau (who opposed slavery and anti-semitism) or imperialist intellectuals like Milner; they were certainly not Houston Stuart Chamberlain, Wagner or Hitler, with their assumptions of a natural enmity between races and a struggle for racial supremacy.

I have so far been talking about my family. Our neighbours in Colne, Lancashire, were proportionately far less experienced in matters of Empire and other races and their opinions on these subjects did not have a high profile. So far as I can tell, for what it is worth, their opinions were very similar. There is some literary evidence of a lack of racial hostility and even of a sense of human brotherhood in mid-century North Lancashire. This was reported by Learie Constantine, who played for Nelson as a cricket professional in the 1930s and formalised his relationship with the town in his noble title (Baron Constantine of Nelson and Trinidad) and by his friend C.L.R. James[14]. A similar story of friendliness and an absence of racial enmity is told by the playwright Jack Rosenthal, who was evacuated to Colne, which he compares very favourably to Manchester in these respects. However, this innocent xenophilia was fairly fragile: when large-scale immigration came to this part of Lancashire the open detestation of 'Pakis' became common. I shared most of the attitudes of those around me including a fairly liberal attitude to overtly 'racial' issues as we saw them through the media, emanating from South Africa and the southern states of the USA.

Now consider the entry into Lancashire of one Clive Hubert Lloyd, born in 1944 in Georgetown, Guyana. Lloyd first came to the county as cricket professional for Haslingden, but made his debut for Lancashire under the rules of qualification in 1968. At this point, I must confess my prejudices: I have rarely, if ever, willed another human being to success as I willed Lloyd, especially in the 1972 Gillette Cup Final. There was a quality about this large, bespectacled left-hander which suggested a latent power combined with thoughtfulness and fragility. In that 1972 innings he played and missed at the ball for half an hour as the required run rate mounted. Finally he unleashed a drive of such perfectly timed cracking power that it qualified for the Caribbean epithet of the "bandit shot" ("Don' nobody move": there wasn't time to move). A small man from Oldham, a complete stranger, sitting next to me, literally trembling with tension and anticipation, tugged at my sleeve and said, "now, we'll see some stuff". And so we did: Lloyd's 126 won the match and left many thousands of us in a state of euphoria. Here was "black power" demonstrated at the highest possible level of human activity (to a true cricket fan) demonstrating temperament, technique and calculation. And he did it all for *us*. Racialism was no longer tenable; if there was anything which black people lacked, or which distinguished them from us as we wished to be, it could not possibly be anything which mattered. That some Lancashire fans called Lloyd "Supercoon" was overtly "racist", but their attitudes, in my experience, were deeply respectful.

Lloyd does feature in Hoberman's book, but not by name. He was later to be the captain of the West Indies cricket team which was to become the most successful of all time, a success based on the use of four fast bowlers. Hoberman focuses on one dimension of this experience, the English frustration, in defeat, at its inability to cope with the remorseless athleticism of an all 'pace' attack, attributable by some to an unspecified racial superiority[15]. A dimension which he does not mention is the admiration many cricket fans felt for Lloyd's leadership, his ability to form disparate elements into a team combined with his polite ruthlessness.

Lloyd was not a pioneer: he stepped behind a long line of black West Indian cricketers who had played for clubs in Lancashire. This line stretches back to Constantine and includes Frank Worrell and Garfield Sobers (both Radcliffe), Conrad Hunte and Clyde Walcott (Enfield), Everton Weekes (Bacup) and George Headley (Haslingden). In many cases close friendships were created between black and white teammates which have lasted into subsequent generations. Bacup and Barbados could be symbiotic.

It was not so easy for the first two black players to play for Burnley Football Club, John Francis and Roger Eli, who were employed by the club in the dark days of the 1980s when Burnley seemed permanently marooned in the Fourth Division of the Football League. They played in front of a crowd which had, before their arrival, taunted black players with ape noises and banana references as much as any. Neither was exactly a superman: Francis had considerable pace when fully fit, but both were essentially jobbing pros who had been passed around the clubs and spent a high proportion of their careers trying to shake off injuries. But they were triers, honest and loyal to a bad team when some of the white players seemed to be going through the motions. I well remember comments like, "Give it to Johnny; 'e's t'only one who knows what 'e's doing" and "Come on, Roger lad, you're show 'em. You're t'only one wi' any guts". Eli, on a famous occasion when all the club's strikers were injured, was drafted in as centre forward and scored a hat trick. Francis scored vital solo goals in play-offs. Their names came to be chanted and sung more often than any others; the ape noises and banana references all but died out. It did help, of course, that they were both prominent in the event which turned an important corner for Burnley Football Club, the winning of the Fourth Division Championship in 1991-92[16].

In my view, race relations have improved enormously in Britain, and the likes of Clive Lloyd, Roger Eli and Johnny Francis have played their part. Nothing could more completely establish your credentials as a person to a true sporting audience than a demonstration of true sporting values. Of course, racism still exists and probably always will, not least because it is progressively redefined as a broader vice. Many people would disagree with, even abhor, my optimism, both about British race relations and the part played by sport in them, but we must be careful in dealing with their judgement because there are many researchers, journalists and so on who have a vested interest in the ubiquity and problematical nature of racism. That is their justifying ideology.

The case against sport

The central thrust of the case made by Hoberman and others to the effect that black sporting success has increased racism against black people is that it classifies them in terms of "physicality". They are "physically gifted...wonderful natural athletes...superb physical specimens". Indeed Hoberman is able to demonstrate quite convincingly that white racist ideology has sought more or less any port in a storm in its attempts to categorise black people as physically different.

From the end of the Civil War until the end of the nineteenth century this difference was usually couched in terms of inferiority and degeneracy and there appears to have been genuine white American concern about the decline of the "negro race" outside of the paternal care of slavery. From the end of the century, however, the quest for difference has shifted to forms of limited, physical superiority which are assumed or asserted to complement a mental inferiority. Since 1945, with the steady growth of black participation and success in athletics, boxing and most major league sports, these assertions have become more important.

There has been a considerable variety of explanations of the athletic abilities of the West African slave Diaspora. They have been said to have slower and faster constitutional metabolisms, more 'fast twitch' muscle fibre, a denser bone structure, relatively longer and more flexible spines, thicker skins, longer achilles tendons and several more. While we can observe a kind of ideological desperation in the search for the key to black success, it must also be remarked that none of these has been satisfactorily proved, *nor disproved*, and that some combination of them may well turn out to have real explanatory power. Certainly, "environmental" arguments of the sort that black people are only better at sprinting because it was the only activity they could afford (the whole white race was presumably feeding its polo ponies or playing golf?) seems equally ideologically motivated and considerably less plausible. If the spiritual equality of mankind rests on its physical equality, it rests on a fragile foundation indeed.

The consequences of the ideological assertion of black 'physicality' are several, all bad for the interests of black people. They are thereby assumed to be more stupid. This is, one must assert, *not* a valid inference, but it seems to come naturally within American culture and to be backed by some version of the "middle passage" theory which lost the sports commentator Jimmy ("the Greek") Schneider his job in 1988[17]. In other words, the experience of transportation and slavery has honed the qualities of the black race by making survival much tougher and selectivity more effective. It does, of course, seem equally plausible to argue that the Darwinian effects of the "middle passage" would be to produce a race which was superior in every way and this version has been propagated by some black writers, but Jimmy the Greek's assertion that blacks were bred for thigh rather than brains is the more common version. Hoberman makes no acknowledgement of allegations that some plantation owners deliberately restricted the breeding opportunities of 'clever' slaves; such allegations reflect badly on both races[18].

'Physicality' easily spills over into brutality and criminality and Hoberman is able to demonstrate a long history of white fears of black toughness, sexuality and menace. Black men in the United States are, after all, sixteen times more likely than white men to become professional basketball players, but they are also seven times more likely to spend time in gaol. Some black figures combine the athletic, the brutal and the criminal: Hoberman comments that "What the public career of Mike Tyson has cost black Americans is incalculable in the literal sense of the term, but it is reasonable to assume that his well-publicised brutalities in and out of the ring have helped to preserve pseudo-evolutionary fantasies about black ferocity that are still of commercial value to fight promoters and their business partners in the media"[19].

Black 'physicality' also undermines the worth of black sporting achievements. In a powerful essay on Gary Sobers, C.L.R. James argued that the dismissal of his cricketing success as the expression of "wonderful natural ability" ignored two related dimensions of what Sobers was about: his devotion to developing the techniques of the game was not 'natural', but artifice and dedication and behind it was a racial consciousness which wanted to show white men, however legally and politely, who was best[20].

But the worst consequences for black people consist in the internalisation of the images of physicality. The 'animal' style of 'cool' (previously of 'cats') suggest that for many black youths the choice is basketball, rap or crime. And, as has often been pointed out, there isn't much paid basketball to go round: this is the implication of the film *Hoop Dreams* and of a study chaired by Arthur Ashe in 1979 who suggested three million young black men at any one time competing for nine hundred places in professional sport[21]. Perhaps one might extend 's arguments to suggest that the real problem is not that whites classify blacks as 'physical' beings, but that blacks accept this classification. If black people defined themselves as intellectuals, white prejudice would no longer prevent them from achieving the elusively 'normal' levels of social mobility. Instead the self-definition involves low intellectual self-esteem personified *in extremis* by the "self-loathing ... self mutilating" (Hoberman's description) basketball player, Dennis Rodman.

The extent of the contradiction

My story is about England; Hoberman's about the United States. It is true that there are people who have given a similar sort of account of race and sport to

Hoberman's about Britain, but not at the scholarly level which he has attempted. There are cultural differences not only between "white" Englishmen and Americans, but also between Afro-Americans and Afro-Caribbeans. In any case, the whole issue of 'race' is conceived differently in the two societies. In the U.K., "race relations" are conceived as complex questions within a "multi-cultural society". Paradoxically, in the US, much more genuinely a multi-cultural society, race relations are preponderantly conceived in terms of black and white. The Afro-American "minority" in the USA is huge: more than forty million people, the size of a large European nation. In Britain, the Afro-Caribbean minority is dwarfed even by other, Asian, minorities who have a reputation in many respects for being *less* "physical" (less tough, less athletic, less sexy) than the whites. These proportions and images must surely make a difference.

But I want to suggest that what is most important in understanding the differences is the separateness of sporting culture. Most major American sports have evolved from English origins, but in a highly un-English context where commercialism and professionalism achieved early and complete victories. American sport really is about *citius, altius, fortius*: to continue the Latin motif it is *quod erat demonstrandum* to most American sports fans to show that the highly localised phenomenon of American Football is played at a high standard to illustrate examples of players who weigh 300 pounds and can run the hundred metres in eleven seconds. Increasingly, therefore, American sport has become something of a freak show, a place of specialism and spectacle, where it is assumed that the public do not want to see a hitter throw or a thrower hit if they fall below the very highest standards at the secondary activity.

By contrast, English sport is about character in that the virtues which are most admired are 'guts', 'bottle', 'class', etc. demonstrated in the abilities to be cool in a crisis, to be resolute and loyal. We are still, surely a culture which admires the capacity to cope with Sir Henry Newbolt's definitive crisis of "ten to make and the last man in" over mere physical prowess. It was precisely the Newboltian virtues which my two black Burnley players demonstrated: commitment and courage when the going got tough. Clive Lloyd, too, showed a cool intelligence under fire: in cricket, great batting like his is ultimately about discipline and judgement — and a good eye and a strong physique are not enough.

Hoberman's references to Britain, scattered throughout the book, but also in a concentrated section in the middle, contain some interesting arguments, but they fail to appreciate fully the cultural differences[22]. If the perception of black

West Indian cricketers were dominated by the enormous "natural" power of Joel Garner and Curtly Ambrose, then perhaps white England would look upon black athleticism as white America does. But these are minor figures compared with the bespectacled Lloyd and the averagely sized Sir Garfield Sobers who were both captains and middle-order batsmen, the precise roles reserved for gentlemen of high intelligence in the traditional, class-bound world of English cricket. Equally, Hoberman pays much attention to Ron Noades' famous comments (in August 1991) about the need for "hard" white men footballers to complement "artistic" black ones in English football in winter, but fails to appreciate the significance of the overwhelming scorn and indignation with which his remarks were greeted[23].

Indeed, I am inclined to think that most contemporary English football fans can recognise that the 29% of black players in the game actually duplicate the abilities and *personae* of the white players. There is the footballer as articulate officer and gentleman (Gary Lineker and Trevor Brooking, white; Garth Crooks and John Barnes, black); the clumsy, hard, dumb centre-back (Tony Adams, white; Carlton Palmer, black), the English specialty of the ball-winning midfielder (David Batty, white; Paul Ince, black), the brilliant misfit (Paul Gascoyne, white; Ian Wright, black), the "good old-fashioned" centre-forward (Mark Hughes, white; Cyrille Regis, black). The list goes on: I am not claiming that such perceptions totally exclude racial stereotyping, but they are increasingly offering an alternative picture of the world. Stereotyping, of course, still exists and I must report an incident which occurred in our [University of Warwick] Staff Cricket Club in the early 1990s. It was late on a dark-clouded afternoon and we were fielding. The conventions governing play on such occasions are that fast bowlers are not used, otherwise the batting side can "appeal against the light" and play stops. As a fresh bowler, the captain selected the only black man in our side, a scholarly young man of no outstanding athletic ability whose bowling was considerably slower than that of the (white) player he was replacing. However, as he began to measure out his run-up the opposition captain protested that we could not possibly use such a bowler in the prevailing conditions. For, as everybody knows, all black men are ferocious fast bowlers .... ,

It is also surely true that black English sportsmen present themselves to the white public in quite different ways to their American counterparts. There is much less of the Mohammed Ali arrogance or deliberately black street style. Rather, from the likes of Frank Bruno, Daley Thompson and Linford Christie we have seen the English virtues of patriotism, humour and self-deprecation which make them seem part of us. Perhaps the Afro-Caribbean is far more secure in his identity than the Afro-American or considerably more distant from cultural memories of slavery and lynching. Maybe, also, our class system complicates and blurs questions of race. When the American sociologist Edward Banfield typified the "lower class" in the United States as possessing a time-horizon tending towards zero, an excessive concern with physical prowess and an inability to resist the temptations of immediate gratification, most of his audience would envisage that class as predominantly black[24]. Whereas if you typified a group of children in England as ignorant and anti-intellectual and possessed by fantasies of playing for Manchester United rather than by any orientation towards academic work or personal enterprise, an English educationalist would envisage children at least as likely to be white as black. When there was a bitter legal battle between two formerly great all-round cricketers, Ian Botham and Imran Khan, in the English courts in 1996 and the court found in favour of Imran, it was widely commented that, faced with a dispute between an upper class Asian and a working class Englishman, any judge's loyalty would go with class rather than race. English responses to race are in important and complex ways very different to those in America and we should be rigorously sceptical of any "they too"ism on the part of Americans. Hoberman is at least a little guilty in this respect.

Conclusion

I have been seeking to defend common sense and common optimism about the effect of sport on race relations; it is a case of the ordinary obvious defended against academic subtlety backed by vested interests. In this respect I have been keen to emphasise that the history of ideas about race relations is very much a history of ideology in the sense of doctrines devised and defended for their political consequences rather than for their scientific and logical coherence. It is a neat historical irony that a pluralistic, multi-racial, "politically correct" society naturally creates broadening definitions of race and racism (so that it becomes difficult, if not impossible, to establish one's innocence of the crime, as it once was of witchcraft) because this is so closely parallel to the insistence of white racial scientists in the century of racialism that there must be some significant physical differences between races.

Often, broader definitions of racism face people with logical dichotomies in which choosing either prong of the fork leads to racism. You are damned if you say "they" are different (stereotyping, false racial science) and damned if you say they are the same (cultural imperialism, failure to acknowledge ethnic diversity). Hoberman quite rightly attacks that kind of "political correctness" in its medical form, suggesting that there is a reluctance to allow that different races may have different propensities to the same illness (breast cancer is the particular example) and concluding that "it is black patients who will eventually pay for the kind of political correctness that puts the study of racial physiology beyond the pale"[25]. In any case, I must insist that there is no significant ethical theory which treats being able to jump higher, run faster or throw further — or for that matter being fatter, taller or heavier — as having any bearing on human worth or moral responsibility. There are specific theories, quoted by Hoberman, to the effect that more athletic means more stupid, but they are feeble, dated efforts and their duplication in American popular culture does not render them worthy of serious consideration. In Britain we draw on a different tradition of *mens sana in corpore sano* in which it is half-expected that England's best batsman will be able to write fluently in four languages and be solicited for the throne of Albania. For that matter, I am inclined to assume that Clive Lloyd would make an excellent president of Guyana or Lancashire.

I based my case for the beneficial effects of sport on the classic Weberian combination of introspection and observation. While accepting several forms of cultural difference, must not some of this apply to the United States? Even though sport there is more specialised and physical and black people have notoriously been cast in the most physical roles, must not there be some white people who have come to look more favourably on blacks because of the activities of Jackie Robinson and his successors? Many black American professional sportsmen present themselves on television as charming, modest and articulate to a far greater degree than do (white) English professional footballers; this must surely help counteract the image of Mike Tyson. The effects of black sporting success on American race relations must be a matter of degree and Hoberman's book a perfectly proper scholarly polemic which tells one side of the story, but not the whole story.

Whether it is due to nature or nurture, increasing black domination of certain sports is bound to affect the commercial value of those sports. In contemporary athletics it appears to be having a negative effect, but it is hard to distinguish, in explaining the dramatic decline of the sport in the 1990s, the importance of that factor against the consequences of an image tarnished by drugs, greed and corruption. Basketball seems to have suffered much less: the NBA has become "global" during a period of black domination and has successfully cultivated worldwide identification with black heroes. Boxing presents the paradoxical combination of an image tarnished by schism, crime and brutality with a buoyant market in the television rights for the highest level of the heavyweight division. It is as if, as Hoberman hints, that many people want to see the spectacle of brutal, black 'King Kong' figures battering one another, the effect being the opposite of watching Clive Lloyd bat.

Logically, we ought perhaps to introduce racial athletic events, as we have events based on gender in most sports and on size in some, such as boxing and rowing. I do not think there is any chance, I am pleased to say, that we will ever do so. Rationally, this should be because we are incapable of defining race. But emotively, we will be more constrained by the echoes of earlier societies' attempts to define it, by the Nazi ethnometers and the administration of *apartheid*. In this context it is odd to remark that we do accept a separation of competition based on the biology of gender (with appropriate and squalid mechanisms for testing categories) and there are even those who want equal rewards in professional sport for the category in which performance is lower. Might the "white" men's 100 metres be as highly paid as the "black" even though it is of a lower standard?

Finally, a note of reservation rather than conclusion. I have expressed optimism about "race relations". But we must always set against any optimism the knowledge that human capacity for hatred of the "other" is large and often hidden beneath cultural layers. I well remember the enthusiasm of the comments of many western journalists on the tolerant multi-culturalism of a city chosen to host the Winter Olympics. That was Sarajevo in 1984.

Notes

1 John Hoberman, *Darwin's Athletes, How Sport has Damaged Black America and Preserved the Myth of Race*, Houghton Mifflin, New York, 1997.

2 Quoted in Simon Barnes, "Racist myths that refuse to go away", *The Times*, Wednesday May 2nd, 1990, p. 46.

3 See Ernest Cashmore (sic), *Making Sense of Sport*, London, Routledge, 1990.

4   Hilaire Belloc, "The Three Races", *Selected Cautionary Verses*, Penguin
    (Puffin Books), London 1964 pp. 169-171.

5   P. Curtis, *Anglo-Saxons and Celts: a study of anti-Irish prejudice in
    Victorian England*, University of Connecticut, Bridgeport, 1968.

6   Chris Stringer and Robin McKie, *African Exodus*, Cape, London, 1996 and
    Richard Leakey and Roger Lewin *The Sixth Extinction: Biodiversity and Its
    Survival*, Weidenfeld, London, 1996.

7   Lincoln Allison, "Race and Politics", in Iain McLean (Ed.), *Concise Oxford
    Dictionary of Politics*, OUP, 1996, pp. 418-420.

8   Quoted in "The Enfranchisement of Women" jointly published with John
    Stuart Mill, "The Subjection of Women", introduced by Kate Soper, Virago,
    London, 1983, p. 15.

9   Patrick Geddes and J. Arthur Thomson, *The Evolution of Sex*, Scott,
    London, 1889, p. 267.

10 See Jas Bains with aj Patel, *Asians Can't Play Football*, report to the
    Football Association, 1996.

11 Quoted in Hoberman, op. cit., p. 134.

12 Ibid., pp. 143-144.

13 Richard Lewis, "Why Black Athletes Have Run Away with Sprint Gold",
    The Express Sport, July 30th 1997, pp. 8-9.

14 I was fortunate to meet James through the agency of Tony Gould, then
    literary editor of *New Society*, in the early 1980s.

15 Hoberman, op. cit., pp. 128-129.

16 Eli had played for Leeds United, Wolverhampton Wanderers, Cambridge
    United, Crewe Alexandra, York City, Bury and Northwich Victoria before
    arriving at Burnley in 1989, aged 24. Francis had played non-league football
    for Emley, followed by spells with Halifax Town and Sheffield United
    before he arrived at Burnley, also in 1989, aged 26. Ray Simpson's account
    of post-war Burnley players, *The Clarets Collection* (self-published,
    Burnley, 1996) refers to Eli as a "folk hero" (p. 94). The fanzine *Kicker
    Conspiracy*, Vol. 2, No. 2, October 1997 had a picture of Chris Waddle, the
    Burnley player-manager on the cover, contemplating nine league games
    without a win and wondering, "I wonder what Roger Eli's doing now?".

17 See, "Of *Mandingo* and Jimmy the 'Greek'", *Time*, February 1st, 1988.

18 I am grateful to my colleague John Halliday for drawing to my attention the
    existence of unpublished research on this point.

[19] Hoberman, op. cit., p. 209.

[20] C.L.R. James, "Garfield Sobers" in Anna Grimshaw (Ed.), *The C.L.R. James Reader*, Blackwell, 1992, pp. 379-389. Originally written in 1969.

[21] Quoted in Hoberman, op. cit., p. 46.

[22] Ibid., pp. 122-129.

[23] Ibid., pp. 126-127.

[24] See Edward Banfield, *The Unheavenly City, the nature and future of our urban crisis*, Little Brown, 1968.

[25] Hoberman, op. cit., p. 225.

THE STATE OF PLAY:
SPORT, CAPITAL AND HAPPINESS

Fred Inglis

Professor of Cultural Studies
at the University of Sheffield

The marvellously spectacular end of the Cold War announced more vividly than anything else could have done the sheer impracticability of continuing to use Marxism as a lens through which to behold the modern world. The human sciences, dominated since 1968 by the application of Marxism in the political economies of liberal consumerism as a way of *seeing negation* and throwing white into sharp, black relief, were struck in large part myopic, able only to see in very close-up, losing the power of long sight altogether.

The symptoms had been there for a long time, of course[1]. It had become more and more a matter of queasiness to invoke the redemptive power of the organised working class as the historical agent capable of bringing about social transformation. Those misgivings had been tided over by the demands of method. Freedom, the great simple of Enlightenment thought, which offered to link critical reason and significant action in the exhilarating moment of emancipation, fell in half. Without the promise of happiness held out by turning social criticism into practical action, principled opposition became impossible; it was now, as they say, merely academic.

For the hired mouths of old corruption this is just fine. It has been one of the more intellectually revolting sights of recent years to see the dance of the word-processors celebrating the end of the evil empire and the final victory of liberal consumerism. The end of history, by God, first baptised in the waters of Babylon as the end of ideology, has delivered the people into the imminent shopping malls, theme parks, and leisure wear of the future, if a little postponed in Angola, Herzegovina, or the salt marshes of Iraq.

In these grisly circumstances, the existence of a university centre to study sport looks as though it can only do one of two things. First, it can give itself over

155

to its subject in the accents of managerialism. It can treat what is obviously there
— sport as a hugely substantial element in the vast structure of the cultural and
leisure industries — and recommend the means of its management according to
the familiar protocols of efficiency and productivity (defined together as cost-
effectiveness), hierarchical divisions of labour (orders coming down the line and
report coming up: the systematisation of obedience known as accountability),
and the organisation of both production and consumption against specifically
targeted outcomes with the key indices of class and status (what Robin Murray
has called the Benetton economy).

On the other hand, such a centre may simplify both bureaucracy and intellectual life by choosing an agenda of issues and items more or less cognate with its
title, and going through them in any old order and with no particular regard for
theory or practice. This is, however, a *university* and we have our obligations in
honour of the Many and the One, or as one may more familiarly put it, duties to
balance as best we may the empirical claims of local knowledge and the
rationalist's call to grand theory, a balancing act which I take to be the key
performance of the acrobat of Cultural Studies.

That same performer, like any scientist of the human, is given poise, stability
and lightness by what I shall call the integrity of his or her metaphysics. (This
integrity is close to what Collingwood called "absolute presuppositions"). Such
integrity derives in the greatest thinkers and artists from the essential tension
between actual contingency, its hard facts and temporal delights, and abominable
eternity. Philip Larkin puts it wonderfully:

> And once you have walked the length of your mind, what
> You command is clear as a lading-list,
> Anything else must not, for you, be thought
> To exist.
>
> And what's the profit? Only that, in time,
> We half-identify the blind impress
> All our behavings bear, may trace it home,
> But to confess.
>
> On that green evening when our death begins,
> Just what it was, is hardly satisfying,
> Since it applied only to one man once,
> And that one dying.

Thus both thinker and artist, as they should be, on behalf of ordinary man and woman. The point of working at these matters in a university is certainly, with Walter Benjamin, "to find our image of happiness", but to find it "indissolubly bound up with the image of redemption". And he goes on, "…like every generation that preceded us, we have been endowed with a *weak* messianic power"[2].

Well the Messiah in Stalinism turned out to be a Caliban, and nobody, *nobody* could mistake the life either of the devout consumer or the good manager for the state of redemption. No doubt the class struggle struggles on, striving to be resolved, or reconciled, but neither that nor the inanities of choice as commended by the desperate incompetents of our very own government can do anything for the integrity of our metaphysics. In the new epoch, now the battle of the titans of ideology is at last over, the new metaphysics is located in the crises of humankind in its relation to nature.

Political economy tells us, in the master's voice, that:

In itself the sum of money may only be defined as capital if it is employed, spent, with the aim of increasing it, if it is spent expressly in order to increase it. In the case of the sum of value or money this phenomenon is its destiny, its inner law, its tendency, while to the capitalist, i.e. the owner of the sum of money, in whose hands it shall acquire its function, it appears as intention, purpose.[3]

Political economists further advise us that the leading edges of this process at the present time are to be found in the giant structures and their interconnections of the weapons industry, the tourist business, hard drugs, and telecommunications[4]. The mutual play of civil war, heroin, camcordering and soap in the sitting room is what most threatens all forms of life on the planet. Not world annihilation now, but a little local nuclear unpleasantness in the Horn of Africa perhaps: the clearing of the Orinoco for the easier passage of Thompson's launch to visit the Yanomani; the shipment of deathly cargoes of powder to sustain the life-in-death of the starving Colombians or Afghans who grew the raw stuff, and the endless circulation of the brainwashing suds of *Twin Peaks* dubbed into as many languages as the novels of Enid Blyton; *these* are the forces and modes of production which starve and kill and poison whole ecologies and the ways of life which go with them, whether of the turtle, the lotus fruit, or the toothless 30-year-old woman dried up by many pregnancies. The promise of abundance brought by intelligent industrialisations, foreseen in *The Wealth of Nations* and *News from Nowhere* alike[5], is exploded by a licentious rush of consumption, destroying development here, absurdly and trivially over-producing there, everywhere intensifying gross asymmetries of life and death.

It is not likely that these monstrous distortions can be put right either in the names of humanity or of nature without colossal catastrophe. But in spite of this apocalyptic beginning, my preoccupation is with the small enticing details of everyday life, consciousness and symbolisation rather than with eschatology. The trouble is — as it is the *point* of devising a subject such as Cultural Studies to explain — those details and the local knowledge they issue as are precisely what makes worlds and ends-of-worlds happen.

• • •

I shall simply define Cultural Studies as the study of values, where value means a concentration in action or artefact or human significance or preciousness. Certain traces of historical activity, particularly in the handled forms of experience classified as culture, and within culture the vital and vitalising sub-class of *art*, become fiercely charged-up in tight little nodes of significance. Such nodes rest in the texts which are their vehicles, travelling through time. New values emerge from the great shifts of cognition and emotion which inaugurate epochs, and embed themselves in such narratives of the day as they may discover and within which they may live. New and old jostle each other and fragments break off and blend in the temporarily dominant narratives, those which carry the no less temporarily victorious nodes of value.

Putting things in this highly metaphoric way represents an effort to turn to rather more dynamic account of Raymond Williams's rather sketchy remarks about the play of values within epochal "structures of feeling" (his well-known term of art), and values as separable into the *orders* of dominance, emergence, and residuality[6]. I have set this modestly Hegelian heuristic in the larger field of force of competitive cultural practice and, for our immediate purposes, that corner of the field where sporting lives find stories worth telling about themselves, worth living and dying for.

For if new epochs are announced by new modes of feeling and thinking, I shall not be caught-out saying so as an innocent old idealist. Those modes of feeling *also* correspond to the form of the new means of production.

There is no primacy in all this. The doctrinaire fight between idealism and materialism was not resolved but dissolved years ago by Quine[7] and Wittgenstein. With Quine, let us say that all inquiry is intrinsically holistic, working not down the items of an agenda but within a *set* of propositions. Each proposition is no more than an element in a system, and as such is always corrigible (or indeed abandonable — as constantly happens not just to scientific explanations but scientific *facts*). So much for analytic truths. But, relatedly, synthetic truths cannot be *proved* tautologically because no definition nor synonym can be shown to be a perfect translation of the first term. Translation or synonymity is too slippery a criterion with which to fix perfect synthetic propositions. Thus an end to materialism *tout court*.

This is all a bit sharpshooting. But these postmodern days method must precede commitment. I shall return methodically to values by saying that residuality and emergency fight it out in the narratives of practice, according to which not only is sense made by each of us of experience, but action itself—including the key actions of production and the final instance of profit—is rendered efficacious. Thus in the new epoch, residual and emergent values struggle to make the new narrative, each mingling with the other in images of the good life.

These images prefigure ideals in which the epoch seeks — in Walter Benjamin's words — "not only to transfigure but also to transcend the immaturity of the social product and the deficiencies of the social order of production". We may say in a more homely idiom that culture is a competition to win the day for the story which best imagines a good life and good society out of the bits and pieces of present historical experience.

This is to put things optimistically. More bloodily, we have to recognise that the fight to win the day for a story is indeed a matter of life and death, but that every story lays its claim to break with what is out-dated in the most immediate past. Benjamin goes on:

> In the dream in which every epoch sees in images the epoch which is to succeed it, the latter appears coupled with elements of prehistory — *that is to say of a classless society* ... [emphasis added [8]

The benevolence of this needs to be stained with the malignance of what Raymond Williams elsewhere dubs "Plan X"[9] and its architects, the irresponsible wielders of power whose object is always "temporary competitive advantage within a permanent and inevitable danger", a danger he saw that same power elite as happily working-up by way of keeping labour under and organised dissent as ineffectual and widely derided as possible.

> For this is percentage politics, and within its tough terms there is absolute contempt for those who believe that the present and the future can be

managed in any other way, and especially for those who try to fudge or
quality the problems or who refuse the necessary costs.

The locus of cultural struggle is the narratives of the day, as emergent
ruthlessness battles with residual communality. This is the old story, of the duel
between good and evil, that I wish to tell of contemporary sport.

•••

First, metaphysics; second, ontology.

The metaphysical point of sport is that it presages and embodies the active,
expressive, and beautiful life of men and women contained within a benign and
munificent nature. Once upon a time such a vision spoke truthfully through the
great frescoes of Renaissance Christianity and the ideal cities which were their
frames and spaces. A few centuries later, the hospitable poetry of Wordsworth
and Keats, the busy sociability of the paintings of Constable and Turner marked
the last moment, for a very long season at least, at which the great artist could
capture the hope of a new epoch for common rights and mutuality and use it to
put human beings back down in a loved and natural home.

> And in the frosty season, when the sun
> Was set, and, visible for many a mile,
> The cottage windows through the twilight blazed,
> I heeded not the summons; happy time
> It was indeed for all of us; for me
> It was time of rapture! Clear and loud
> The village-clock tolled six — I wheeled about
> Proud and exulting like an untired horse
> That cares not for his home. All shod with steel
> We hissed along the polished ice in games
> Confederate, imitative of the chase
> And woodland pleasures, the resounding horn,
> The pack loud-chiming, and the hunted hare.
> So through the darkness and the cold we flew,
> And not a voice was idle: with the din
> Smitten, the precipices rang aloud;
> The leafless trees not unnoticed while the stars
> Eastward, were sparkling clear, and in the west
> The orange sky of evening died away.[10]

This is the loveliest and most moving statement I know about the metaphysics of games, and their absolute, necessary meaning as holding humankind and nature in a single imagery and a field of force.

Both field and image held, as, first, industrial capitalism in its hemispheric imperium of England, Europe, and North America organised, legalised, and bureaucratised games into sport. A little later, it did the same the world over. Of course, from the first the football fields were situated in the heart of the new industry, and housed in its vernacular. The huge stands were made to *look* like factories, the huge, civic crowds were identical with the men going through factory gates, the figures produced by the game — goals, points, numbers of spectators — were analysed like industrial statistics. Nonetheless the industrial architecture enclosed the little sacred plot of the field — at Ayresome and Roker Park where I learned my own love of football, the only patch of green grass for miles, the uniform the players wore — that unexpected mixture of the nursery and the holiday, with the small but touching touch of the quotidian called up by the goalkeeper's flat cap — was a deliberate, colourful negation of working clothes.

By the same token, the great cricket fields enclosed the field like a holy grove. As befitted the summer game, they made room for a few trees; the terraces were more gradually raked so that the summer sun could warm the joints stiffened and made knobbly by hard labour. The players wore the leisure clothes of the leisure class which codified the game, and the key building — unlike soccer, whose offices were hidden under the girders and masonry of the stadium like warehouse or shipbuilding stations — the country pavilions were, in Scarborough, Tonbridge and Manchester, seaside Queen Anne affairs, with little runs of white fencing along the front, and fretted barge-boarding along the roof. They quoted holiday resorts and country house weekends quite explicitly in their rhetoric.

Finally, the last of the first mass spectator sports systematically re-invested in the 19th century, was horse-racing, and that too took a very substantial strip of green real estate on the outskirts of some of the biggest industrial cities in England (it was only transplanted to Celtic Ireland, not Wales, nor — or not properly — Scotland). But its real co-ordinates were at Epsom and Ascot, two points of a calculus whose ellipse was the revealingly named Home Counties, and its grandstands, enclosures, gambling industry and display were tokens of a sport unusually dominated by the emblematic summits of the old ruling class. The monarchy shook hands with cricketers and gave cups to footballers; but it *owned* bloodstock. In racing, the co-operation of the classes was assured by the presence of status and old corruption. In football and cricket and in such endearing siblings as bowls, tennis, hockey and even mountaineering or golf, first British and then world class and race divisions and oppositions were transcended in the celebration of a natural enclave in which all that was produced was beauty, happiness and victory.

To talk about happiness I need a hand from that unhappy man, Walter Benjamin, once again. If each epoch dreams its utopia, a good society in which the best form of a prehistoric past is perfected upon the unknowable form of the future, and if this *is* popular culture, then sport dreams of a garden in which the free, productive effort of equal men and women issues in efficacious action and the happiness of victory unresented by the losers. In this utopia, the struggle of the game represents that labour of love and love of labour in which nature gives us her motherly sustenance without herself being depleted. We win, and neither she nor you mind. We embrace, afterwards, as equals. To be a good sport is to be virtuous.

This is indeed the residuality of the value of sport. It is its meaning as a criticism (as a negation) of the victory of consumer capitalism which has, for the time being no countervailing mode of opposition. (Socialism no longer offers to humanise the forces of production, and cause reason to coincide with happiness.) Sport like art, holds out — in Stendhal's great phrase — *La promesse de bonheur*. It does so as a consequence of its metaphysics, and of what metaphysics must do for being. Of necessity, like any other story-telling cultural practice, it does so as part of the unstoppably recursive operation of consciousness upon experience, in which reason, the sense-and-story-making faculty of mind, loops back on itself and reclaims the myths of the past, merely because there is nowhere else to find a plot to use.

Such recursiveness is no doubt the mode of emancipation, but emancipation, as we have learned from *The Dialectic of Enlightenment*, does not guarantee either freedom, reason or happiness. As Adorno and Horkheimer write there in their strange re-reading of *The Odyssey*, "It is homesickness that gives rise to the adventures through which subjectivity escapes from the prehistoric world". The self, forever called to by the lost homeland, makes itself an identity on the journey home. Returning home, as all children of all ages know, is at once a restoration and an estrangement.

Sport was conceived as a dream of coming home and being happy. For once, the journey and its adventures end by returning us to blissful reunion with nature. Benjamin writes of fairy tales that "the liberating magic which the fairy tale has at its disposal does not bring nature into play in the mythical way, but points to its complicity with liberated man"[11]. In the fairy tale, that is, nature is not mythicised as Pan or Proserpine, the clear blue light of reason and the dark value of myth are not dramatised as being forever *at odds*. Rather, as in Ruskin's *King of the Golden River*, or Joan Aiken's *Necklace of Raindrops*, nature, whether as wind, rain, doe or fruit tree, lends a loving hand or obtrudes with a timely, cunning obstacle. Thus also in such works of art as *The Magic Flute* or *The Caucasian Chalk Circle*; thus also in the sports which have made us happiest and within the sport, the individual games in which we have done our best and been, for that sunny afternoon in April or August, the best there.

It is the proper childishness *and* childlikeness in sport which restore us to nature and, we feel, to our true nature; as Dickens remarked in a similar context, it is a close and accurate observation of life which is remarkable in those people who typically "retain a certain freshness, and gentleness, and capacity of being pleased, which are also an inheritance they have preserved from childhood"[12]. One of the happiest consequences of a love of sport is precisely that close observation of the life-in-action which sport *is*, and which (we may hope) is a form of attentiveness learned in play and subsequently brought to bear upon the game of art.

It is a familiar thing to notice the closeness of sport to aesthetics as well as the arts, especially where play, like art, devotes itself to the purposive and excited exploration of other versions of life but with the deadlier consequences of such exploration taken away. Certainly people fall off mountains or have their brains dulled by boxing, but both sports try to balance a reasonable safety (padded gloves, prohibited areas of the body, crampons, belaying) against the violence and danger which are their meaning and value. When the climber battles up and across the overhang or the cricketer makes the scuffed turf turn the ball with a magical impossibility through seventy-five degrees and catch the edge of the bat just so, nature itself has shown her complicity and, it seems, broken natural laws to please us.

Perfect happiness is a matter of a sweet fit between sudden eventuality and the frame of the action which realises it; between accident and achievement. Perfect happiness is only possible in a place which, for that moment, perfectly fits the experience. The beach. The field. The garden. The Coast. The bedroom. It is, if we are lucky, the most familiar as well as one of the most loved of anonymous experiences to find a place in which one is perfectly at home, and happy (not merely contented) as well. It is my contention that, at their best, sports conduce to this experience and do so, so to speak, from both ends. That is, we can love sporting accomplishment like one loves artistry because it seems good in itself, once you know enough about it to speak its language and move with its rhythms. Once this is the case, there is no need to give reasons for admiring Glenn Gould or Garfield Sobers so lovingly; it would be quite supererogatory. Instead one would try to describe how they did what they did so wonderfully. At the same time, a sport is good because it is such that we love it. It has both intrinsic and attributable force.

It is its combination of aesthetic power, its deep psychological familiarity, its physical expenditure (and compassable end), together with its topographical grace which makes a sport matter as it does. If one of these fails, because of age or accident, the sport fails for us. If all work together, the sport tells a tale like the fairy story, of the complicity of a free woman, man or child with nature.

John Berger, writing once of a field he particularly liked[13], concluded that he liked the field so much because seeing it exactly fitted the time in and of his life which he had, waiting beside it at some level-crossing gates, to devote to looking at it and the small events — dog, bird, wind in the willowherbs, the slanting lines of rain — which it neatly contained. "The visible extension of the field in space displaces awareness of your own lived time". He looks at it and likes it for *what it is* and then, "suddenly an experience of disinterested observation opens at its centre and gives birth to a happiness which is instantly recognisable as your own".

So it is watching the player you most support (there must be this giving of support) bring off as magnificently as he or she may the actions called for by the moment of the match: Tom Watson's final drive at the 18th at Carnoustie; Sebastion Coe's victorious finish in Moscow; or to bring the point home both personally and actively, a try I once scored in the final of a coarse rugby seven-a-side final at Iffley Road. As for you, you will all have your own such anthology of such moments when feeling and action discovered the form which opens at its heart into happiness.

• • •

It is a risky, and, it may be, shy-making thing to speak in these terms. That was my *adagio*. What follows is much darker. In making it so, I am most anxious not to lapse into routinely middle-aged threnodies on the end of sporting civilisation as we know it, and the usual deturpation of values and the inexcusably younger people who defile them. As I have noted before[14] the people who write about sports do so on the whole either because they're no good at playing any of them, or more often, because they are now too old to do so. And yet I believe that the consumer totalitarianism which now pervades and saturates being, threatens with obliteration the residual values of play, its art-like good-for-nothingness, its spontaneity and joyfulness, its healthful restoration of the adult to her and his original childishness, its glowing image of the happy harmony of human being and the natural world. These strong presences live in our cultural practice and the narratives which give them form and intelligibility and, as I have said, travel through time. From time to time text meets context, or story meets opportunity, in such a way that the nodes release their charges of value into the culture. They show themselves to an audience of receivers with the right transistors switched on.

My fear is that fewer and fewer people have acquired the psychic and emotional circuitry which will enable them to see the ghost. Experience, itself, as Adorno said longest and said first, is wearing too thin to charge up the emotional receptors.

That this is so — or seems so to me — is not alone the result of the invasion of capitalism into the special realm of sport. Capitalism began to turn leisure into the spectacular display of status over a century ago, as T.J. Clark[15] has shown us so completely; the Impressionists invented the original imagery of advertising power long before cheap colour photography and the accompanying reproductive technology brought us the weekend supplement. "The spectacle", Debord[16] put it in his most famously Pascalian aphorism, "is *capital* to such a degree of accumulation that it becomes an image", and Manet couldn't foresee a fraction of it.

But we do not have a model to analyse what is happening to that wide important margin of cultural life which occupies the space between the civic polity (such as it is) and private life, strictly so called. I mean by this the realm of leisure, I suppose, as well as the neighbouring but not always assimilable area of hard-won and hard paid-for (*and* steadily diminishing) 'free time'; but I also mean the realm of life in which profit is specifically *not* at stake, the transactions of which are as free as possible from the ignoble taint of a *reward*, and in which the pleasures of free creativity and production whether collective or individual, have no cash value at all.

It is indicative that the definition has at first to be couched in negatives. What is more, no such public realm could exist without somebody being paid. (Artists are paid for their pictures.) The point might be more doctrinally put by saying that this is a realm untouched by commodity fetishism; where a painting is a painting, a game is a game, and the promise of happiness is kept both unexpectedly and as an occasion of beautiful familiarity.

Well, this realm is in the grip of the hellhounds. Sport, holidays, nature, sex, food, wine, even the inevitably creative life of ordinary gossip and friendliness, are all invaded and pervaded by the deadly torque of capital upon technology, by the routinisation and bureaucratisation of all social assembly (the modern state cannot bear a crowd) and by the exiguity and attenuation wrought upon experience itself by what I have to call, in a mouthfilling phrase, the spectacularisation of both culture and history.

This quadrilateral of forces drives contemporary sport, and drains away its residual values, injecting from above the emergent values of fully achieved consumerism, currently called postmodern. Capital: technology: routinisation: spectacle; I shall take each in turn for its effects, and the interlocking of each in the first, fully totalitarian culture.

The original threat of totalitarianism was of course held to be either Stalinist or Fascist and not at all our home grown liberalisms. Those mechanised and military states grew spontaneously enough from the relations of production of the day. Smokestack industries and the lines of Ford's mass production made for mass and collective policies. The other side of an admirable solidarity and the united force of labour is the delirium of Nuremberg, street corner crowds listening to Goebbels' radio propaganda, and the sheer credulity as well as complicity of the Soviet people up to the tyrant's death in 1953.

What has happened with our own more vegetable totalitarianism may be headed, in an off-the-peg slogan, the systematisation of fragmentariness. Capital, forever seeking and saturating new markets, moved massively into leisure time once the reconstruction of Europe was complete and the productive structures of the Cold War thoroughly grounded by, say, 1955. On the way it scooped up the realms of play, art, and of sociable freedoms, transmuting these into a highly differentiated but fully regulated management system. Blocked in the rich societies by saturation in the early markets of heavy industrialisation — coal, steel, chemicals — capital turned aside to sweep into and occupy the space and time won from its former depredations and transformed into freedom. Planned obsolescence and innovation, the accurate targeting of taste, the generation of hitherto unknown desires and the fixing of these as needs — all this mechanism was bent to capture the homely, at time makeshift culture of sociable freedom and playtime.

Technology at once follows and anticipates the surges of capital. Radio and telephone preceded world war by a long time, but it was the first war which really made electrical communication systems into world industries, and the second which made those industries electronic. Television was quickly sub-servient to capital — television, we may say, brought down the Berlin Wall by driving those who watched the screen from the wrong side mad with envy. Television spoke the language of capital*ism* in every household: it created consumer totalitarianism by *separating* the masses into a massive but entirely individuated audience. Of necessity, this new totalitarianism must speak of freedom not obedience, of choice not the Party; but its multiple voices utter the single message of consumerism.

Technology doesn't stop with television of course. Its televised presence exactly complements its physical prowess, very obviously in sport. It seems likely that expressive culture depends for its success upon happy accident. Games exemplify this. Chess, cricket, or golf are such *unlikely* combinations of place, object and rule — as unlikely as the pianoforte. The joys to which they give rise depend on an articulation of physicality, symbolism, topography and friendship. Chess turned out to be pretty well immutable as well as infinite from an early stage, no doubt because of its propinquity to numbers. Open air games have proved resilient but not immortal. Capital-driven technology, working merely upon substance and surface has almost destroyed the point of, for instance, car-racing, sailing, golf and mountaineering. There are movements in all these sports — the 'gaffer' races under sail, the Austin-Healey racing rallies, the single climbers with no oxygen following the footprints of Odell, Mallory and Irving, the five-club golfers — to repudiate the domination of technology and recover the risk, spontaneity and approximation of instrument to art which the sport captured at its happiest moment.

Such resistance is hopeless, hopeless on the larger scale. For capital and technology work together as technique. The third force at work in my all-enclosing quadrilateral model of totalitarian consumerism is technicism, or the routinisation of all experience, and the transfiguration of experience into production. Aristotle, you will remember, distinguished between *poesis* (roughly, making or creation) and *praxis* (roughly, purposive action) joining both with *tekné*, which we might translate as the skilful use of craft. In each case, activity was inseparable from its own 'character' — no doubt a symptom of its pre-technological nature. For the technicist, however, all making is instrumental; action for the technicist can only be described in relation to a product, or more broadly, to bringing about a state of affairs (contemporary management has no difficulty with defining thought, art, and education as all, indifferently, products and objects of management). Making indeed loses all character; it becomes a sequence of techniques and it is the realisation of *that* that renders practitioners substitutable and experience irrelevant. Teaching technique is exactly intended to eliminate character, judgement, tradition, experience — all the great names in the conservative lexicon. And as we have learned, training in technique eradicates the idea of apprenticeship and the indentured study of attentive application.

In sport, to take one simple instance, this has meant the ruin of professional football. Capital has ensured, for reasons we shall come to under the heading of spectacularisation, that the rewards of victory are stupendous. Routines of play subtending strict divisions of labour have, as far as possible, removed both chance and genius from the game, and replaced them with work rates. Endless, dull possession is what will pay off. Highly routine techniques, adorned with the preposterous jargon of the commentators, are devised to ensure possession and enough of a lead to win.

The routinising of technique must lead to simplification. But simplification is never simple, any more than competitive capitalism merely competes. Capitalism takes on local colour; at times it would rather kill than win. So the simplifications of technique in, say, international cricket and rugby have borrowed enough of the horrible new chauvinisms to bring a new murderousness to rough old games. Very fast bowling deliberately aimed to wound the body, the brutal disregard of bodily sanctities shown on the international rugby field are pure examples of technicism fired by 'Plan X': that is, by absolute commitment to the edge of advantage, whatever the dangers.

At this point, technicism crosses not into ideology, always a more settled and complacent concept than can live easily with radical risk, but into terror, which has its special pleasures and politics. I doubt, however, if consumerism can afford to tolerate its pressure, while at the same time, I also doubt that present politics can control its own terrors, either. The last angle on my model is spectacularity, "the accumulation of capital to an image", in Debord's phrase; the dioramas of parade, in mind.

Television, it is a truism to say, has done more than anything to turn experience into spectacle. What this means is that significant action has been almost completely struck out of the citizen's life. Democracy is either out of the question or has been *put* out of it as unfeasible by old power: the best we can hope for is *responsible* government. People watch and they learn (there is a deep contradiction here) about what is going on. But they cannot act. The only political action they can take, apart from a largely symbolic four year vote, is to turn out in the streets to demonstrate and bear witness to their own helplessness. The protest march protests against unitary powerlessness in the name of private lives; the moment it goes public and a window is broken or a razor wire fence cut, the state stops it.

In the spectacular society, the star has been appointed to perform our significant actions for us. The star is the crux of that institutionalisation of envy which we call glamour. The emergent meaning of sport in the larger redefinition of the culture is glamour. Sort has, with popular music, become the vehicle of glamour, and sporting stars the essential bearers of the imagery whose dazzling silhouettes are represented as the irresistible enviability of the ads. This is painfully evident in the narcissistic fatuity of the stars' very own self-expression. *Their* individual feelings, poor wretches, are bent by routine towards the tiny range of mass gesture; punching the air, sinking to the knees or that frenzied crazy running with outstretched arms of the goal scorer — each of them an utterly fake, dreadfully sincere acting out of the role of the star even unto crocodile tears.

Stars are emanations of pure charisma. Charisma, much disputed in the literature, at the least connotes propinquity to the centres of serious power. Nowadays, its numinous aura is conferred by enormous success (typically of the girl next door, the ordinary young man in the street), by the symbolic meaning of the individual's employment or style of life, by high spectacularity allied to remoteness of activity (the stadiums, the palace, the screen), and by appeal to a generality of otherwise inexpressible emotions.

This is the social problem — with a downward intonation — of all popular culture in general, as well as sport in particular. Sport is required to contain and express too much. Significant action being difficult, membership gone and democracy non-existent, sport remains a human arena — for all it is a vehicle for fantasy, it *does* actually take place — for connecting a tumult of personal feeling to public endeavour. The trouble is that personal feeling and personal experience are presently incommensurate. Too much of the first and not enough of the second. This is true of both star and spectator, especially where the star is detached from any geographical loyalty or tradition of class by stardom itself. Hence the fan at fever pitch, queer as a clockwork orange and ready to kill for West Ham even though he comes from Bradford.

This is an outline of a new psychology of jingoism, grounded not in any army and a distant war, but in a football team, a beautiful German or Argentinian tennis player, a gigantic black baseball pitcher or fast bowler.

Stardom distantiates and magnifies the dominant images of liberal capitalism, so that they appear both hugely familiar and quite untouchable. In the star personality itself this is certain to produce an ultimate version of the narcissism so general in the culture. The star understands herself as the object of other people's gaze. Typically, there must be a displacement in her identity to correspond with this: there is herself-as-watched-by-the-spectators and herself-as-capable-of-autonomy. The two will coincide as fulfilment when her desires and the spectators' desires converge to fuse in a single action. She makes the winning serve on the Centre Court; she scores 9.9 for her pirouette on the Olympic ice rink.

The lens which focuses and holds steady this tension of distance and familiarity is television and its partner the long distance telephoto news camera. That tension provides the form for the apotheosis of the spectacle. The spectacle of sport, whether live or screened (an increasingly difficult distinction to make) betokens a society unable to tell the difference between using and continuing, between lust and boredom. The playback and the sports video anthology take the depth out of history and the treasure from memory. The star, having no place to rest his or her head, breaks the link between game and home. The spectacle replaces lived experience with the imagery of glamour. Its power is the contemporary version of the timeless attribute of all power to actualise itself in public show[17]. Its present-day version emphasises our distance from it and our mutual irresponsibility. We cannot affect it; it has no affection for us.

• • •

The strain between the knowledgeability of most individuals today and their helplessness is the most radical historical contradiction of the new epoch. All the experience of the last epoch teaches that the authoritarian state of modern capitalism is mightily settled and secure. It offers too much; it even offers, in its debased way, some glimpse of happiness. Even Adorno acknowledged that.

But it is a monster. Somewhere in that great modern fable *The Book of Laughter and Forgetting* Kundera makes his artist-heroine say fiercely, "My enemy is kitsch, not communism". Kitsch he defines as "a folding screen set up to curtain off death". Let us say more broadly it is the propaganda weapon which denies the joke, and in consumer totalitarianism denies the joke not by crushing it but by ignoring it. Jokes are helpless and hurtless. Kitsch is of course totalitarian: "In the realm of totalitarian kitsch all answers are given in advance and preclude any questions". Kitsch occludes laughter and diffuses meaning.

The ghastly studio fun of *A Question of Sport*, its punctually grisly instructions as to laughter and joviality take one measure of the contemporary joylessness of that important corner of the conversation of culture which discusses sport. Spectacularity and the deracinated stars who make up the pictures combine to dispel the weight of memory, the thickness of experience, the facts of continuity. A fearful lightness of being causes everyone to float up and away from the actuality of things, the life-heaviness of old history. We have to beware most of all of our own monster children who are so light in being they have become murderously forgetful.

Sport has, for a century and more, rooted men first and women later to the solid earth of mud and grass. All-weather technology has broken that tie. Sport embodied unspoken refusals of profit and glamorous wealth. Capital has swamped and drowned those refusals. It made possible audacity, flair, dash, ridiculousness. Routine has put a stop to all that. It pictured a democracy of players even when the players were gentlemen, which recognised great gifts and great artists but gathered them into a common culture of sociable, experience, reminiscent judgement. The figures of stardom on the ground of the spectacle have broken down these honoured names until they are a bare trace, a faint residue in the culture.

This is not a waste land; it is a *Blade Runner* city. Pessimism of both intellect and imagination has everything to work from. The optimistic will, however, find little solace in sport.

Notes

1   I am developing a case about the end of Marxism which I first put in my *Popular Culture and Political Power*, Harvester, 1988.

2   Walter Benjamin, *Illuminations*, Jonathan Cape 1972, p. 256.

3 Penguin Library Karl Marx Edition, *Capital*, Vol. 1, p. 976.

4 The contention about the 'leading edge' of capitalism at the present time in part by Nicholas Garnham in his *Capitalism and Communication*, Sage Books, 1990.

5 Hume is a strikingly early qualifier of Smith with his notion of national economy being best advised to place itself judiciously on the 'product cycle' see J.G.A. Pocock, *Virtue, Commerce and History*, Cambridge University Press, 1988, Part III, Chapter 11:2.

6 Williams' theorisation of this is set out in his *Marxism and Literature*, Oxford University Press, 1977.

7 W.V.O. Rhine, 'Two Dogmas of Empiricism' in his *From a Logical Point of View*, Harvard University Press, 1961.

8 In Walter Benjamin, *The Lyric Poet in the Era of High Capitalism*, New Left Books, 1974, p. 159.

9 Raymond Williams, *Towards 2000*, Chatto and Windus, 1983, p. 245.

10 William Wordsworth, 'On the Influence of Natural Objects' *Collected Poems*, H. de Selincour (Ed.), Oxford University Press 1931.

11 Walter Benjamin, 'The Storyteller', in *Illumination*, Jonathan Cape, 1970.

12 Charles Dickens, *David Copperfield*, Penguin English Library, 1974, p. 71.

13 In his 'The Field', *About Looking*, Writers and Readers Collective, 1979.

14 See the last chapter of my *Popular Culture and Political Power*, Harvester, 1988.

15 T.J. Clark, *The Painting of Modern Life*, Thomas and Hudson, 1985.

16 Guy Debord *The Society of the Spectacle*, Red and Black Press, 1983.

17 Compare Clifford Geertz's *Negara: the theatre state in 19th Century Bali*, Princeton University Press, 1985.

SPORT IN THE CINEMA

Roger Philpott

Introduction

From Harold Abrahams breaking the tape to win Olympic gold in *Chariots of Fire*, to Michael Caine huffing and puffing his way through the football action in *Escape To Victory*, sports films have ranged from the occasionally sublime to the, all too often, completely ridiculous. A general perception of sports films as contrived and unconvincing, and so not to be taken seriously, is certainly borne out by the almost complete lack of research into the genre. This study, which is consequently exploratory in nature, redresses the balance, by illustrating the importance of sports films in reflecting, maintaining and challenging dominant Western values.

The films I consider here (drawn largely from a list by Gill[1]) are mainly American. The relative proportion of American films in this selection reflects the country's huge influence over Western culture. The films themselves show how the hopes and dreams of America are inextricably linked to sport, most notably through the baseball myth. The origins of this myth, and how the films reflect its influence on personal, political, professional and national values, form a major part of this discussion. This study also considers the origins and influence of British sporting culture. The analysis, using *Chariots of Fire* as a pivotal reference, reflects especially on the often strained relationship between amateurism and professionalism. In relation to this I highlight definitional problems associated with the two concepts, as well as an inherent ambiguity within the philosophy of amateurism in regard to how seriously sport should be taken.

Using the archetypes of the British amateur and the American professional as a basis, this study produces a general comparison between the value systems of the two nations: unsurprisingly, the films reflect values which are culturally specific. I have also illustrated how they question both America's embrace of professionalism and Britain's desire to 'play the game'.

In regard to structure, this study looks at the values portrayed in sports films in relation to personal identity, national identity, politics, tradition, professionalism and nostalgia. While all the sections are distinct, their inter-connectedness highlights not only how enmeshed sport and its values have become within society, but also that the much maligned genre of sports films has an interest and importance which until now has not been acknowledged.

Personal identity

After his fight with Apollo Creed, Rocky Balboa triumphantly declares, "I'm somebody, not a bum". Through the use of physical rather than intellectual skills, sport has provided him with his only realistic opportunity of creating an identity and enhancing his status within society. This ability to emerge from a harsh environment, which is also demonstrated by Jake La Motta in *Raging Bull* and Frank Machin in *This Sporting Life*, while evoking notions of survival of the fittest, also reflects the belief in Western Society that anybody can be successful so long as they try hard enough.

In fact it could be argued that the sporting cinema overstates the case, as the attraction of stories about overcoming the odds has produced an apparently disproportionate number of underdogs who win. This is tempered to a degree, however, in films such as *Rocky*, for although after fighting Apollo Creed, Rocky announces, "I'm a winner, not a loser", he in fact has only drawn the contest. This points, therefore, to a broader view of success for the underdog which is concerned with exceeding expectations and not just about winning.

Seemingly, though, it is not enough for our sporting heroes just to be good at what they do, for there "has always been a tendency of all branches of the media to set up sportsmen and sportswomen, not simply as mini gods, but as moral exemplars, especially for the young"[2]. The sporting cinema is no exception in this regard, but in its search for good narratives, it reflects on some morally dubious sportsmen as well.

Of the 'good guys', Isiah Thomas returns to his old school in *Hoop Dreams* to encourage the latest crop of aspiring basketball players, thus displaying loyalty to his roots and a desire to 'put something back in'. Although Rocky Balboa is drawn to the periphery of crime by his lack of status and his capacity for physical threat, he displays a simple generous morality by doing the right thing and encouraging them to do the same.

The heroes of *Chariots of Fire*, Harold Abrahams and Eric Liddell, are not typical cinematic sporting heroes as they are running for idealistic reasons: Abrahams for the purpose of acquiring the identity of a true Englishman and Liddell to affirm his Christian beliefs. Abrahams believes he has to win the 100 metres gold medal at the Olympics in order to acquire his new identity. Indeed, he says to Aubrey Montague that he has got "ten seconds to justify my existence". Abraham's heroism is contained, therefore, in achieving his goal through single-minded determination. The fact that he also wins the hand of Sybil, with whom the gallant Montague is also in love, suggests that the sporting hero is a winner in life as well. Liddell's heroism is also about single-minded determination, but in his case it relates to his refusal to compromise his beliefs, rather than to his quest for a gold medal. But for the intervention of Lord Lindsay, his Sabattarianism would have prevented him from running at all. Although Liddell sees running, and thus his victory in the Olympic 400 metres, as a glorification of God, on a more material level, winning the gold medal also suggests that people will be rewarded for staying true to their beliefs.

The moral dubiousness of sporting heroes such as Jake La Motta, Frank Machin and Ty Cobb can be viewed as an expression of contradictory values within society: they are lauded for their aggressive behaviour in the sporting arena, but for displaying similar 'attributes' in wider society they find themselves ostracised by the people who matter to them. There is a clear message here that sporting heroes should behave in a certain way, as ultimately all three characters end up friendless, embittered and impotent.

In *Eight Men Out,* an ailing Ty Cobb still has notions of personal redemption, illustrated by his starting to recite the Lord's Prayer while coughing up blood, although he quickly realises he is beyond help. However unfulfilled in that film, the theme of personal redemption is nevertheless a popular one in the sporting cinema, frequently played out around the fall and rise of an ex sportsman who, being down on his luck, gets a coaching job and turns a team of no-hopers into winners. In *A League Of Their Own*, Jimmy Dugan is an alcoholic ex baseball player who, in his own view, has sunk so low that he has to coach a women's team. Through some cajoling by the women, however, he realises there is a job worth doing and that he is capable of doing it. As his own pride is gradually restored, so the team becomes increasingly successful.

However, the film emphasises that success does not come easily, either in sport or in life, for in response to Dottie's question about why playing the game is so hard, Dugan says that if it was not hard, everybody would do it. A more startling example of sporting redemption, however, occurs in *Field of Dreams*, as not only do the Chicago White Sox players, who were banned after throwing the 1919 World Series, get to play ball again, but their 'resurrection' allows Ray Kinsella to play catch again with his dead father. This 'eases the pain' caused by Ray's refusal to do likewise when his dad was alive, a refusal born out of his father's adoption of the supposedly crooked Shoeless Joe Jackson as his baseball hero.

It is very apparent from this section on identity in the sporting cinema that the overwhelmingly dominant identity is male. While sport itself, which "embodies male values and its practices express male identity"[3], has made strides towards greater sexual equality, this has not been reflected in most sports films, where the main characters still tend to be male. In only a few of the films do the female characters play anything other than long-suffering partners to the male protagonists. Even in *A League Of Their Own*, the story about women's wartime baseball is somewhat subverted by the strength of the Jimmy Dugan character and by stressing that the League would not have been set up if the men were not away fighting. It is only the characters of Dorothy in *Gregory's Girl* and Amanda in *The Bad News Bears* who get to take their places on the sporting field on merit. It is in the former film that sport as a male preserve is more seriously challenged, though this is done as part of a wider comedic look at gender roles, which was reflective of a time that produced Britain's first woman Prime Minister.

National identity

It seems that the further the discussion about identity moves away from the personal, the less straightforward it becomes. This is due to the fact that "multiculturalism is embedded in virtually all states [and] any claims that people have to a single culture or a single identity becomes almost impossible to maintain"[4].

Over the centuries, various factors have been important in establishing national identity, such as language, religion and natural boundaries, but in recent European history political settlements have been the most influential factor. In this regard it has been argued that "identities are not 'natural', nor are they fixed. Rather, identities are socially constructed and are subject to change across time and place"[5].

With so many disparate identities in multicultural societies such as England and North America, it is not surprising that sport in its role as a universal symbol has been used effectively to produce a sense of nationhood. However, the notion that sport allows "different groups ... to represent, maintain and challenge identities"[6] can be questioned, as the values associated with cricket and baseball, which came to define the national identities of England and North America respectively, are still dominant. It would seem, therefore, that the sense of unity and belonging that sport inspires, far from fostering a broader national identity, tends to incorporate outsiders within the dominant cultural identity.

An example of the confusion that can arise from the complexities of national identity occurs in *The Bad News Bears*. Struggling to reconcile the traditional image of baseball with notions of multi-culturalism and sexual equality, one of the boys is prompted by Amanda's appointment as pitcher to say in a slightly aggrieved tone, "We've got Jews, spics, niggers and now a girl!". Similar confusion also arises in *Rocky* where it is evident that Apollo Creed does not feel truly American. For when thinking of offering the world title fight to Rocky, he says that it was an Italian who discovered America, so what better than to put one over on one of his descendants. The fact that the fight is in Philadelphia, the historical home of American independence on the first day of the country's bicentennial year, seems to add to Creed's sense of wanting to reject or re-write his country's origins. While apparently seeking to disown his national identity, however, the way he organises the fight and then enters the ring dressed as Uncle Sam is, culturally, very American.

In *Chariots of Fire*, although the athletics team is representing Great Britain, there is no doubt that the dominant identity being portrayed is English. This is illustrated when reminders of old enmities with France surface, as Lord Cadogan rejects out of hand the notion of asking the French administrators to change the day of Liddell's 100 metres heat by saying, "We can't go cap in hand to the Frogs". To my mind, however, the emphasis on Englishness in the film detracts from a wider examination of national identity, for other than notions of Sabbatarianism, Liddell's Scottishness is not explored. Similarly, we are left in the dark as to what Abraham's Jewish heritage means to him, other than to make him feel excluded from the English Establishment.

One symbol of national identity which is very evident in the American films is the 'star spangled banner'. This suggests that whatever level sport is played in America, whether it be the world heavyweight championship in *Rocky* or Little

League baseball in *The Bad News Bears*, the participants are in effect representing their country and all its ideals. It is to baseball and *Eight Men Out* and *Field
of Dreams*, however, that we can look for the strongest possible connections
between sport and national identity. These connections also illustrate how myth
and invented tradition can be used to forge a country's history and consequently
create a largely false identity which is then difficult to live up to.

Many of the original settlers in America believed that they were on a journey
to a new promised land, away from a tired and corrupt Europe. Their beliefs led
to the development of a civil religion which was "concerned that America be a
society as perfectly in accord with the will of God as men can make it"[7].
Consequently, certain beliefs, symbols and rituals within American society came
to be considered sacred. As baseball spread across America after the Civil
War and became increasingly popular, its devotees found it difficult to accept that
their national sport was based on the English game of rounders. American pride
and patriotism required that baseball be a native game and so the Mills Commission of 1908, which was set up to examine the origins of the game, established
that baseball had been invented by General Abner Doubleday at Cooperstown
in 1839.

The Commission's findings not only made baseball American but, by placing
its origins in a rural setting, further mythologised a game which was first played
by New York businessmen in the 1840s. These rural roots gave the game an aura
of purity which was in keeping with the new Eden the settlers wanted to create.
(This is invariably expressed in baseball films through the imagery of open fields
and fluffy white clouds drifting across clear blue skies.) As baseball became
intrinsically tied to the American values of "innocence, the land ...[as well as]
equality under the rules"[8], it produced a heady mix of nature and morality.
Consequently the game's rituals took on the air of the sacred, turning baseball
into a pseudo religion and resulting in the deification of its heroes. Despite
baseball having declined slightly in popularity recently, its influence on
American beliefs remains. This is illustrated in *Bull Durham*, when Annie Savoy
declares that "the only church that truly feeds the soul is the church of baseball".

In the early twentieth century, the game was so linked in with the nation's
morality that "the belief that baseball was honest and upright constituted an
article of secular faith in America"[9]. The throwing of the 1919 World Series by
the Chicago White Sox therefore shattered the myth of innocence for baseball,
and thus by implication for America as well. The promised land had turned out
to be just as corrupt as the one the settlers had left behind.

Whereas at the time of the scandal, the fault was laid firmly at the feet of the players, both *Eight Men Out* and *Field of Dreams* attempt to redress the balance. In the former, the players are portrayed by and large as honest, hard working professionals, exploited by the game's powerbrokers, whereas in the latter they are the complete innocents of the baseball myth. Within this latter portrayal is the implication that, despite all the corruption, baseball, like America, remains pure and innocent at heart. Seemingly one of the effects of maintaining this myth is the perpetuation of an immature society, afraid of growing up because of the corruption of the adult world. At least in *Bull Durham*, some sort of balance is struck, as baseball goes beyond the myth into more mature and experienced identities, through the eventual union of Annie Savoy and Crash Davis.

Politics

The universal nature of sport, its associated values and intrinsic characteristics have led to its being used politically for everything from image creation to supporting a genocidal doctrine. Ronald Reagan, through his association as an actor with the character of George Gipp in *Knute Rockne, All American*, was able to portray himself as an honest, sacrificial person. This enabled him in the eyes of many Americans to be distanced from some of the corrupt practices of his administration. (Indeed, as Charles Wheeler said, his presidency, informed by his acting career, was "a triumph of appearance over reality"[10].)

In regard to the interaction of sport, politics and image, it is interesting to examine the apparently conflicting values portrayed in *Field of Dreams*. On the surface, the film appears to espouse the merits of the liberal values of the 1960s as, firstly, Ray Kinsella obeys a voice and ploughs up much needed farmland to build a baseball pitch and, secondly, his wife, Annie, produces a forthright defence of liberal author Terence Mann at a school meeting. These displays of idealism struck a chord in America, where the film was seen as an antidote to Reaganism.

However, the theme of men and women working together for a better world (which is the framework used in 'Shoeless Joe', the novel on which the film is based) becomes subverted, as a patriarchally based political message emerges. Ray Kinsella expresses regret that it was his student radicalism which led to him dismissing his father's hero and consequently to committing the ultimate crime of refusing to play catch with his dad. Ray's student days are also ridiculed, for when attempting to bring Terence Mann into his dream, he calls at the author's apartment, to be greeted with, "O my God! You're from the sixties".

This desire to "re-do the past and to disavow the 1960s break with parental values"[11] has been described as political fundamentalism, a resurgence of the conformist values of the Eisenhower era. However, despite calls for a return to family values, it is clear from the film that, with Annie Kinsella's character playing an increasingly secondary role, the only dreams to be recognised are those of the father. The ultimate symbol of the patriarchy was, of course, Ronald Reagan. However, it is *Eight Men Out*, rather than *Field of Dreams*, which questions the image, for it shows the father as a corrupt figure who "controls the game in as many ways as possible, but denies his culpability"[12].

Despite Margaret Thatcher having no connection with sport, this did not stop her from trying to use it to enhance her image. In this country, sport had traditionally occupied a private, leisure time realm, from which it managed its own affairs with minimal political interference. As sport became increasingly global, however, its populist nature and position outside of mainstream government policy led to it being perceived as a high profile, inexpensive, 'soft option' for making political gestures.

An example of this was Thatcher's call to British athletes to boycott the 1980 Olympic Games in Moscow. This was portrayed as a show of solidarity towards our American allies, who were not sending a team to the Games as a protest against the Soviet Union's invasion of Afghanistan. Her primary motivation in pursuing this course of action, however, was that it gave her an opportunity early in her premiership to present herself on the world stage as a strong leader.

On reflection, this exercise in image creation contradicted a central tenet of her New Right political vision, that of creating an environment free of government interference and red tape, so that individuals can make the most of their abilities. This contradiction can be illustrated through a reading of *Chariots of Fire*, for whereas Thatcher was highly embarrassed by British athletes rejecting her call for a boycott, the defiance of Abrahams and Liddell "implicitly endorses the Thatcherite ethos of a nation based on a meritocracy of the ambitious, the diligent and the gifted"[13].

Another politician who realised to his cost that there are no certain outcomes in regard to sport was Adolf Hitler. As an advocate of the ideology of the kind of pure and noble German race which emanated from the recreation of the national image by nineteenth century intellectuals, Hitler sought to use the 1936

Berlin Olympics to demonstrate Germany's physical and cultural suitability for pre-eminence in modern times. This is illustrated in the propaganda of *Olympiad*, which emphasises a link between 1930s Germany and its adopted classical Greek origins. To confer credibility on notions of supremacy, however, you need to be seen to be dominant. Not only did Germany's finest blond-haired, blue-eyed athletes get beaten but they were dominated by Jesse Owens, whose racial origins were in complete contrast to those of his Aryan opponents. Regardless of where Leni Riefenstahl's political allegiances truly lay, much of her treatment of the games emphasises a kind of transcendent beauty which she finds in sport and thus suggests a view of sport which is above and beyond politics..

Even though this link between Germany and Ancient Greece was invented, the connection between sport and nationalism, especially apparent at Berlin, did have its origins in the ancient games. The qualities required by the participants of speed, agility, accuracy and strength were prerequisites for military success and explains why "Sparta at the high point of its military power was able to dominate the Ancient Olympics"[14]. Despite this connection between sport and (readiness for) war, it is also apparent, most notably at the height of the Cold War between America and the Soviet Union, that sport can act as a war substitute.

In regard to the films, this concept is played out, most notably, later in the *Rocky* series, where symbolically he fights a Russian for world supremacy. These sequels generated a sense of national unity in the face of an external threat, a factor which was missing in the original film, as it raised the internal issue of white versus black America.

This issue also links back to the Berlin Olympics, for while the focus was on the Nazis' supremacist theories, in American sport at the time, exclusionist racism was the norm. It has been argued that in order to establish what a nation's values are, an examination of its sports and pastimes is necessary, and in this regard "at play, Americans felt themselves at liberty to indulge in prejudices that economic necessity sometimes moderated in other situations"[15]. Although Owens did achieve a degree of acceptance as an athlete, the predominant attitude was that here was a negro who happened to be representing America.

The racism in America's sporting history is hardly acknowledged by either *Field of Dreams* or *Eight Men Out*. The former suggests that by refusing to allow only Ty Cobb to play on Ray Kinsella's field, just a few players were racist. However, while there is no doubting Cobb's racism (at least as shown in his biopic), the reality was that, as with the corruption which came to light in 1919, racism was also institutionalised. What is not acknowledged at all in *Field of Dreams*, and only merits one line of dialogue in *Eight Men Out*, is the existence of black players and the black leagues. By not addressing issues of racism and the parallel history of black baseball, the films can be accused of promoting the cultural hegemony of white America.

Where power resides in America is graphically illustrated in *Hoop Dreams*. The film shows William Gates and Arthur Agee living in socially deprived black areas, which promise little other than a bleak future. While this situation encourages many young men like them towards the riches of professional sport, relatively few make it through a system riddled with discrimination. The apparently laudable system of collegiate sport, which provides aspiring professionals with an education, can easily count against those from socially deprived areas. Also, in regard to the education system, it is revealing that the first person of real influence William and Arthur meet, the coach of the High School basketball team, is white.

From the concept of stacking, which puts white players in key positions, especially in American football, to there being few black coaches and owners of sports franchises, it is clear that, as in Britain, power is jealously guarded by the dominant white culture.

Traditional views

In the discussions I have had about sports films, *Chariots of Fire* has invariably been mentioned. Although this could be put down to the fact that there are few good sports films, I believe that the film captured the public's imagination because its portrayal of traditional values "unashamedly put one in touch with sentiments [such as patriotism] that had so long lain publicly unexpressed"[16].

This link between sport and traditional values goes back to the birth of modern sports in early Victorian times. With the more popular leisure pursuits of the time being associated with violence and gambling, the educated middle classes felt that this behaviour was unbecoming of the civilised society which was supposedly emerging.

It was public school headmasters who played a major role in promoting change, for in an attempt to quell the riotous behaviour of their pupils they introduced the discipline of organised sport, along with the civilising values of fairness and gentlemanliness. The upper classes, impressed by the controlling effect sport had on their unruly offspring and concerned by the potential destabilising effect of increasing working class leisure time due to the Industrial Revolution, encouraged the wider population to play sport.

The 'Muscular Christians' were also very influential in this process. Typified by Eric Liddell, they believed in a link between physicality and spirituality, and that there was something "innately good and godly about brute strength and power, so long as it is devoted to noble purposes"[17].

With the playing of sports being encouraged by such influential groups, the values of fair play and sportsmanship consequently came to represent Anglo Saxon values in the third quarter of the nineteenth century. The subsequent growth of the British Empire, which was staffed largely by ex public schoolboys, meant that the sporting culture and its values became influential all over the world.

The personification of Victorian sporting values was the amateur, who, by playing major sport as a pastime, reflected the Victorian belief in the separation of work from leisure. More importantly, however, the amateur ethos comprised a complete moral code of conduct.

The link between sport and morality is illustrated in *Chariots of Fire*, when the Master of Trinity, in expressing concern to Harold Abrahams about his pursuit of success, says:

"Here in Cambridge we've always been proud of our athletic prowess. We believe, we've always believed, that our games are indispensable in helping to complete the education of an Englishman. They create character, they foster courage, honesty and leadership, but most of all an unassailable spirit of loyalty, comradeship and mutual responsibility".

What this emphasises is the belief that the way of the amateur was the only way to provide satisfactory results. It can also be seen, however, as questioning modern day attitudes within sport and suggesting that there would be benefits from re-introducing the amateur code. Indeed, it has been argued that "the true joy and meaning of the thing [i.e. sport] is lost if it becomes a sole occupation generating a commodity to be bought and sold"[18].

Although Abrahams does not receive payment for running, it is his adoption of a professional attitude (including the employment of Sam Mussabini as his coach) which offends the college masters. What lies behind this offence is that, in his determined pursuit of the 100 metres gold medal, Abrahams contravenes the ideal of the effortless amateur. In challenging the ideal, Abrahams says to the masters, "You yearn for victory just as I do, but achieved with the apparent effortlessness of gods". The implication of hypocrisy, which is confirmed later when the masters bask in the reflected glory of Abrahams' success, highlights an ambiguity within the amateur code, in that you are encouraged to do your best, but trying too hard is distasteful.

The code's lack of clarity does not stop there, however, for we are told about the cultural importance of games, but also that sport is not to be taken seriously. While sport might not be the most important aspect of life, I believe that because of the link between sporting and cultural values, not taking our sporting efforts more seriously has, under the guise of 'it's only a game', produced a society which is more comfortable with coming second than winning.

Interestingly, it is an American film, *The Bad News Bears*, which best illustrates this point when the Bears coach, Morris Buttermaker, says "it's only a game", not as a way of encouraging the team to relax, but as a way of covering up a lack of pride in his own performance. Not taking sport seriously, therefore, comes to mean that you are not taking youself seriously and you end up as a loser. Surprisingly, after turning the team's performance around with a highly professional approach, Buttermaker then re-adopts the amateur philosophy, albeit in a much more positive form. Consequently, the Bears are seen to have a good experience as a result of doing their best, and by losing the farcical final, they also emerge with a healthy attitude towards winning.

Professional values

Because amateur sporting values had become an intrinsic part of English culture, professionalism within sport was perceived by the Establishment as a threat to a way of life. It was thought that paying players would undermine social values, with 'fair play' being replaced by corruption, and doing your best giving way to an emphasis on winning. Fears about a spread of gambling and corruption were often influenced by the 'perception' that, before the Victorians began to codify sport, matches were often set up for the purpose of upper class wagers. By advocating that sport remain amateur, they were, in effect, denying working class people the chance to make a better living, while they relied on inherited wealth or well paid jobs.

That professional sport can improve a person's material status is clearly shown in *This Sporting Life*. Here Frank Machin takes his physical strength from the coal mine to the rugby pitch and, as a result, can buy the cars and coats, and can eat at the restaurants previously out of his reach. Also, in *Eight Men Out*,

Shoeless Joe Jackson is shown to be illiterate, but baseball enables him to make a living he would have struggled to achieve outside of sport. What emerges in both films, however, is that the greater material rewards from a life in sport do not necessarily equate with having greater control over one's destiny. Indeed in *This Sporting Life*, Machin is seen as nothing more than a plaything which his employer, Weaver, could discard at any time.

However, despite the influence that the money men had within sport in this country, it was amateur regulatory bodies such as the Football Association which remained in control. With deep regrets, however, they did acknowledge that sport could not be entirely amateur, and so what evolved was "a system that resisted commercialism and professionalism, but realistically sought compromise and containment rather than outright rejection"[19]. In the United States, however, the absence of a traditional class structure, coupled with a belief in the rights of the individual, led to the amateur sporting ethos giving way to professionalism by the late nineteenth century.

Concerns that the Victorians had about professional sport becoming excessively oriented towards winning find their embodiment within the competitive ideology of the American Dream with the notion that "the United States is a land of boundless opportunity in which upward social and economic mobility and success are regularly achieved by the ambitious and hardworking, regardless of their social origins"[20], it is no surprise that, through underdogs such as Rocky Balboa, sport became and remains a powerful symbol of the dream.

Although one's chance of sporting success can be restricted by factors such as discrimination, the competitive ideology within the dream remains undiminished. By giving the message that if you have not achieved success yet, you need to try harder, the ideology provides people with "a continuing source of hope"[21], however unrealistic this may be. This quest for success has, for example, led adults into children's sport and to running the 'little leagues', with the result that these leagues have become a highly structured and professional in nature. *The Bad News Bears* provides a wonderful satirical view on the subject of unrealised adult ambition, most notably in the behaviour of Ray Turner, manager of the Yankees, who rationalises his own competitiveness by saying that it is how the boys themselves want it to be.

Morris Buttermaker, coach to the Bears, initially considers the children's emotional well being, but once the team's form improves, his desire to be a winning coach takes over. He bribes Amanda to pitch for the team and boasts how he taught her to use 'spitballs'. He also uses Amanda to entice the talented

Kelly to the team and then orders him to hog the ball in a crucial game in order to keep the winning run going. Ultimately, the championship game becomes a contest between Turner and Buttermaker, as they destructively push their teams towards victory. Although Buttermaker finally realises what his team needs, and the importance of their not winning is shown, the film's final shot of the American flag flying over the stadium has been interpreted as an "allegory about U.S. aggression and its hatred of losers"[22].However, while the scene of the trophy presented to the Yankees reflects America's desire for winners, the fact that Turner alienates both his son and his wife with his bullying tactics, brings into question the 'win at all costs' professional approach.

In fact it is surprising that, despite America's wholehearted embrace of professional sport, the films portray a generally negative view of professionalism. Seemingly central to the pursuit of victory is the notion that if something underhand improves your chances of winning, and you can get away with it, then do it. In *Slapshot*, Reggie Dunlop winds up the opposition goalminder by saying he knows that his wife is a lesbian. Also in *Bull Durham*, Crash Davis uses all his experience to teach 'Nuke' Laloosh the tricks he will need to succeed in Major League baseball.

Ironically, it is *Chariots of Fire* that presents professionalism in its most positive light, in the form of Harold Abrahams. Although technically an amateur, he adopts a professional approach, seeing victory as a reflection of excellence and the fulfilment of potential. Before his race against Liddell in the Scotland v England international, rather than returning his opponent's offer of "Good luck", Abrahams declares "May the best man win". Within this is an implication that by adopting a professional approach, the best possible performance is produced. This point is further emphasised when, in response to questioning by the Master of Trinity about his employment of the professional coach Sam Mussabini, Abrahams replies "What else would he be, he's the best".

On reflection, it seems that, especially in regard to America, the Victorians' prediction that professional sport would produce an over-emphasis on winning has come true. That professionals would be vulnerable to corrupt commercial interests has also been borne out. As portrayed in *Eight Men Out*, the 1919 White Sox scandal showed how gambling organisations were able to control baseball, once the players felt unfairly treated by their employer. Of course, what emerged subsequently was that the scandal was "a culmination of corruption and attempts at corruption that reached back nearly twenty years"[23], and while it was the players who were accused, the fact that many rival presidents enjoyed gambling on their team did little to discourage the spread of corruption within the sport.

The control of professional sport by outside interests is also depicted in *Raging Bull*, where the notion that the best man wins comes a poor second to what the Mafia wants. Despite being the outstanding contender, Jake La Motta has to throw a fight of the Mafia's choosing in order to signify his acceptance of their control. Only after painfully swallowing his pride and losing a contest to an inferior boxer is he allowed to fight for the world title.

Nostalgia

Nostalgia can be defined in terms of "the remembrance of the past that is imbued with positive feelings..."[24]. However, these feelings may also be "tinged with melancholy and sadness, because the positive feelings are mixed with negative feelings, or because the pleasures are perceived as in a past that cannot be relived in the present"[25]. An important function that nostalgia performs is to invoke memories from which a confirmatory sense of identity can be drawn. How true these recollections are, however, is open to doubt, due to the selective nature of memory. Indeed, it has been argued that "the past is not preserved, but is reconstructed on the basis of the present...and in accord...with the predominant thoughts of society"[26].

The popularity of sport and its general characteristics of collectivity and youth provide great potential for nostalgia. This is especially evident in America, where because the main sports of baseball, basketball and football are very physical team games and are linked into the collegiate system, they tend to be played by young men. With the sporting culture changing with age to individual sports such as tennis and golf, the stronger memories, which are usually collective, tend, therefore, to be 'young' memories. From this it is evident that an important part of sporting nostalgia is the rekindling of the energy and vitality of youth.

Through the establishment of halls of fame and museums to celebrate the great players, coaches and teams, sporting nostalgia has also taken on an important role in American society, for "by eliciting nostalgic feelings associated with the acceptable behaviour of the honoured athletes, sport assumes a social control function"[27].

As the media cover sport in such depth, they also have great potential for triggering positive nostalgic reflections. This is especially so in regard to film, for in the dramatisation of events, cinematic licence has often been used to create happy endings. This rose tinted view of the past, as portrayed in *Field of Dreams*, invariably favours traditional values and so emphasises the inherently conservative nature of nostalgia.

It is the medium of photography which is used in both *Slapshot* and *Hoop Dreams* for nostalgic effect. In the former, it elicits feelings of a time when sport was clean (that is, without the dirty tricks) and in the latter, when it was simply fun. What both examples can be seen as expressing, therefore, is a dissatisfaction with the 'win at all costs' professional attitude.

In *A League Of Their Own*, the nostalgia invoked by the reunion of the Rockford Peaches has less to do with rekindling a love of baseball than with reflecting on the opportunity presented to the women through the upheaval of war. Contained within this is a message about making the most of your chances, as well as an endorsement for being part of a team, especially in difficult times.

The theme of upheaval is also present in the nostalgia surrounding *Chariots of Fire* for, at the time, Britain's declining economic status, combined with the influence of the European Community and an increasingly multi-cultural society, led to traditional notions of national identity being upset. It is no coincidence, therefore, that the 1980s saw a spate of costume dramas (such as *Chariots of Fire*) which reminded and reassured us of our past, when we not only ruled the world, but also won at sport.

In regard to baseball, spring training is potentially a time of great nostalgia, for as the game is re-born after the winter break, all the optimism of youth comes flooding back. This is not a time for the big city teams, but for resurrecting the rural myth, as large crowds at small venues rekindle "memories of the way it used to be in a kinder, gentler society ... when baseball wasn't exploding scoreboards and multi-purpose stadia"[28].

While *Eight Men Out* and *Cobb*, with their portrayals of corruption, cheating and violence, destroy the myth of baseball as part of a kinder, gentler America, *Field of Dreams* attempts to re-establish its validity. The game's urban origins are ignored and rural nostalgia is invoked as the myth finds an ideal home in the farmlands of Iowa. The redemptive aspect of the myth then takes over, as Terence Mann says to Ray Kinsella, "This field, this game, is part of our past. It reminds us of all that once was good and could be again". Clearly, there is a plea here for a second chance, as the film "wishes aloud that America could return to the innocent days of white baseball, when there were no stains on American honour, no scandals, no dirty tricks, no surprises"[29].

Conclusions

From my examination of the values portrayed in sports films, I have drawn out the following conclusions:

Firstly, while values associated with sport and sports films have a role to play in maintaining dominant western ideology, the films also present anti-Establishment messages, which is a role sport itself rarely performs. In regard to sporting role models, the films show the moral sportsmen as ultimately happy and fulfilled, while the more dubious characters end up as sad, broken figures. By providing behavioural role models and giving a strong message that people do not prosper through violence, the films can be seen as performing a social control function which helps maintain the dominant ideology. The patriarchal element of this ideology is reflected by the absence of women in the main roles of the films, producing the message that sport, like society, is male dominated. The cinema's wholehearted embrace of the underdog can also be viewed as culturally supportive. For although the underdog does win in sport, the instances occur at a disproportionate rate in the cinema, so providing the encouragement to work harder and exceed expectations, while giving the slightly unrealistic message that everyone can work their way to the top.

In the text, I mentioned how British athletes ignored calls for them not to go to the Moscow Olympics. While this was a rare anti-Establishment sporting gesture, there are a number of such examples in the films. Abrahams, Liddell and Jonathan E. (in *Rollerball*) all defy the powers that be; the emphasis on winning and the means used to achieve it are negatively portrayed in a number of American films; while both *Eight Men Out* and *Slapshot* (with its Watergate-style dirty tricks) reflect and imply corruption within the political system. It would seem, therefore, that sports films as part of the arts in general have a role in exposing the limitations and excesses of society, as well as in supporting the dominant ideology.

Secondly, it would seem that the emphasis placed on winning is the biggest difference portrayed in the films between the cultures of Britain and America. Despite sport having become increasingly professional in Britain, especially at the top level, a sense remains that the amateur ethos still underpins our sporting world. This is illustrated in *Chariots of Fire* by Abrahams' argument for the adoption of a more professional approach, an argument which was as relevant when the film was released in the early 1980s, as it was in the 1920s when the film was set.

With America being a young and ambitious country without a well-established class structure, status has depended much more on what you do, rather than who you are. Consequently, as shown in films such as *The Bad News Bears*, winning has become all important both in sport and wider society. This situation has led to probably the most marked technical difference between our sporting cultures, for in their desire to produce winners, Americans rejected the notion of the honourable draw and introduced overtime in order to get positive results.

Thirdly, to my mind, the popularity of sports films in America comes out of a need for Americans to be consistently reminded that the vision of a glorious future envisaged by the original settlers is still alive. With the baseball myth representing all that America could and should be, sport has become a potent symbol for the country, as illustrated by the presence of the 'star spangled banner' and the singing of the national anthem in most of the films. However, with the above-mentioned emphasis on winning, the pressure to succeed has been immense. This has often led to personal disillusionment which, combined with the corruption within American society, has led people back to the myth of the pure, unsullied America, full of hope for the future, which sports films can provide.

Notes

1   A. Gill, "Sport on Film", *Total Sport*, 1996, No. 5, pp. 82-8.
2   N. Sinyard, "Sporting Screen", *Films and Filming*, March 1982.
3   J. Maguire "Patriot Games? English Identity, Nostalgia and Media Coverage of Sporting Disasters", *Warwick Centre for the Study of Sport in Society Working Papers*, Vol. 3, 1994, p. 94.
4   G. Jarvie, "Sport, Nationalism and Cultural Identity" in L. Allison (Ed.), *The Changing Politics of Sport*, Manchester University Press, 1993, p. 72.
5   Maguire, op. cit., p. 89.
6   Ibid., pp. 90-91.
7   R. Bellah, *Beyond Belief*, Harper & Row, 1970, p. 186.
8   F. Ardolino, "Ceremonies of Innocence and Experience in *Bull Durham, Field of Dreams* and *Eight Men Out*" *Journal of Popular Film and Television*, Vol. 18, No. 2, 1990, p. 45.

9 H. Seymour, *Baseball, the Golden Age*, Oxford University Press, 1971, p. 274.

10 In *Wheeler on America*, first broadcast on BBC2, 24.3.96.

11 Ardolino, op. cit., p. 47.

12 Ibid., p. 45.

13 J. Quart, "The Religion of the Market" in L. Friedman (Ed.), *British Cinema and Thatcherism*, University College, London Press, 1993, pp. 25-26.

14 J. Sugden "Sport and Nationalism in the Modern World", *Warwick Centre for the Study of Sport in Society Working Papers*, Vol. 3, 1994, p. 30.

15 A. Gattmann, *A Whole New Ball Game — An Interpretation of American Sports*, University of North Carolina Press, 1988, p. 122.

16 A. Walker, *National Heroes — British Cinema in the 1970s and 1980s*, Harrap (London), 1986, p. 179.

17 K. Sandiford, *Cricket and the Victorians*, Scolar (Aldershot), 1994, p. 35.

18 L. Allison, "If the Price is Right", *New Statesman and Society*, 17.11.95.

19 Ibid., p. 25.

20 H. Nixon, *Sport and the American Dream*, Leisure Press (New York), 1984, p. 10.

21 Ibid., p. 17.

22 Sinyard, op. cit., p. 18.

23 Seymour, op. cit., p. 292.

24 E. Snyder, "The Sociology of Nostalgia: Sports Halls of Fame and Museums in America", *Sociology of Sport*, Vol. 8, 1991, p. 228.

25 Ibid., p. 229.

26 M. Halbwachs, *On Collective Memory*, University of Chicago Press, 1992, p. 40.

27 Snyder, op. cit., p. 232.

28 A. Spander in the *Daily Telegraph*, 18.3.96, p. 57.

29 H. Jacobsen, "Shot in the Dark: Born Again Baseball", *Film Comment*, May/June 1981, pp. 78-79.

Filmography

[*Film (*Year). Director: Main Producer.]

A League of Their Own (1992). Penny Marshall: Columbia Pictures.

Bull Durham (1988). Ron Shelton: Mount Co. & North State Films.

Chariots of Fire (1981). Hugh Hudson: Enigma Productions.

Cobb (1994). Ron Shelton: Warner Brothers.

Eight Men Out (1988). John Sayles: Sanford-Pillsbury Productions.

Escape to Victory (1981). John Huston: The Victory Company.

Field of Dreams (1989). Phil Alden Robinson: Gordon Co. Productions.

Gregory's Girl (1980). Bill Forsyth: Lake Film Productions.

Hoop Dreams (1994). Steve James: Feature Film Company.

Knute Rockne, All American (1940). Lloyd Bacon: Warner.

Olympiad (1938). Leni Riefenstahl: Olympia Films.

Raging Bull (1980). Martin Scorcese: United Artists.

Rocky (1976). John Avildsen: United Artists.

Rollerball (1975). Norman Jewison: Algonquin Films.

Slapshot (1977). George Roy Hill: Universal Pictures.

The Bad News Bears (1976). Michael Ritchie: Paramount.

This Sporting Life (1963). Lindsay Anderson: Independent Artists.

Index

South African Non-Racial Olympic
 Committee (SANROC *68*
South African Rugby Board *69*
South African Rugby Union *69*
South Korea *85*
Soviet Army *62*
Soviet Union *62, 77, 87, 91, 101,
 102, 180*
Spain *88*
Sport and Leisure in Social Thought 54
Sport and the British 54
Sport: Raising the Game 97
Sporting Females 13
Sports Council *96, 97, 100*
Sportsmedical Service (SMD) *36*
Sportsmen's Party *59*
St. Bernards *20*
Stalin *62*
Steinbach, Klaus *33*
Stevenson, C.L. *70*
Strutt, Joseph *12*
Study Group in the History of Physical
 Education *10*
Sugden, John *16*
Surrey CCC *20*
Sutcliffe, Herbert *18*
Swiss National Olympic Committee *35*
Sydney *140*
Syria *88*

T

Taylor, A.J.P. *17*
Taylor Report *17*
Taylor, Rogan *16*
Tester, Keith *58*
Thailand *62, 63, 65, 66, 67*
Thatcher, Margaret *60, 97, 98, 180*
Third Lanark Rifle Volunteers *20*
This Sporting Life 174, 184
Thomas, Keith *12*

Thompson, Daley *148*
Thompson, E. P. *13, 21*
Three Sides of the Mersey 16
Tom Brown's Schooldays 96
Tour de France *33, 34*
Trafalgar [Battle of] *88*
Transvaal Rugby Football Union *69*
Tranter, Neil *11, 16*
Trevelyan, G.M. *21*
Ty Cobb *175*
Tyson, Mike *146, 150*

U

Union Jack *96*
United Kingdom *9, 53, 93, 107, 110*
United Nations *84*
United States *1, 10, 20, 33, 41, 42,
 60, 90, 91, 93, 109, 110, 116,
 122, 130, 139, 142, 146, 147,
 149, 150*
Urry, John *57, 58*

V

Vale of Leven *20*
Vamplew, Wray *22, 61*
Vertinsky, Patricia *13*
Vulliamy, Edward *126*

W

Wagg, Stephen *15*
Wagner, Richard *142*
Walcott, Clyde *143*
Wales *16, 85, 95, 161*
Walker, Graham *16*
Wallerstein, I. *84*
Walvin, James *22*
Ward, Andrew *16*
Warwick Centre for the Study of Sport
 in Society *5*
Waterloo *101*
Weber, Max *9, 115*